Great Breads

GREAT Breads

Home-Baked Favorites from Europe, the British Isles & North America

MARTHA ROSE SHULMAN

PHOTOGRAPHY BY
STEVEN MARK NEEDHAM

CHAPTERS PUBLISHING LTD., SHELBURNE, VERMONT 05482

Published by
Chapters Publishing Ltd.
2031 Shelburne Road
Shelburne, Vermont 05482

Library of Congress Cataloging-in-Publication Data
Shulman, Martha Rose.
    Great Breads : home-baked favorites from Europe, the British Isles and North America / by Martha Rose Shulman ; photography by Steven Mark Needham.
        p.   cm.
    Includes bibliographical references (p.) and index.
    ISBN 1-881527-61-1 : $29.95 — ISBN 1-881527-62-X (pbk.) : $19.95
    1. Bread. 2. Bread—Europe. 3. Bread—British Isles. 4. Bread—North America.
    I. Title.
    TX769.S427 1995
    641.8'15—dc20   94-43744
                                                     10 9 8 7 6 5 4 3 2

Trade distribution by
Firefly Books Ltd.
250 Sparks Avenue
Willowdale, Ontario
Canada M2H 2S4

Printed and bound in Canada by Metropole Litho, Inc.
St. Bruno de Montarville, Quebec

The following recipes, in slightly different form, appeared in *Martha Rose Shulman's Feasts & Fêtes*, by Martha Rose Shulman (Chapters Publishing, 1992): Whole Wheat Sourdough Country Bread; Mixed Grain Bread; Cornmeal and Millet Bread; Sicilian Bread; Fougasse; Cumin and Cornmeal Bread; Pesto Bread; Texas Cornbread.

The following recipes, in slightly different form, appeared in *Mediterranean Light*, by Martha Rose Shulman (Bantam Books, New York, 1989): Sourdough Italian Country Loaf; Whole Wheat-Sesame Breadsticks; Rosemary and Thyme Bread, Sesame Bread Rings; Whole Wheat Focaccia with Herbs; Whole Wheat Pita Bread; Sardinian Flatbread; Bruschette with Tomato Topping; Crostini; Italian Bread Salad; Syrian Salad with Crisp Pitas; Chicken and Pita Casserole.

Cover photograph: Rosemary and Thyme Bread, page 140

Designed by Susan McClellan and Eugenie Seidenberg Delaney

for Bill, again, with love

Contents

Introduction

THIS IS A BOOK ABOUT one of my greatest passions: bread. Of all cooking activities, bread-making is the most thrilling. Over the years, I've made thousands of loaves, and I never tire of the process. I love the physicality of breadmaking—the way the dough feels and changes and, of course, how it smells as it bakes. Every time I witness flour and water miraculously turn into our most basic food, I feel wonder.

My fascination with bread grew during the 12 years I lived in Paris, when I was lucky enough to be half a block away from Paris's most famous bakery, Poîlane, a small storefront on the rue du Cherche-Midi. When friends came through, I would always take them to see what I considered one of Paris's greatest tourist attractions—the baker at work downstairs in the vaulted, low-ceilinged cellar, once a four-teenth-century abbey. The baker, wearing only boxer shorts and sandals, worked one of three eight-hour shifts, mixing up the dough in a huge mixer, shaping 40 five-pound loaves at a time, slashing the loaves and sliding them, on long-handled paddles, into a huge stone wood-fired oven. Lionel Poîlane, the owner, got to know me well and always greeted my friends and me with warm rustic apple tarts, another specialty of the Poîlane bakery.

I was so enthusiastic about Lionel Poîlane's bread that I went to work at his brother Max's bakery, where the same type of bread is made. Every day for several weeks, I would ride the bus to work a four-hour shift with a nice baker (also clad in boxer shorts), who showed me how to handle the sticky dough, shape the loaves and slide them into the oven. I would come home glowing through the flour, which covered me from head to toe.

I learned how to make baguettes and the other yeasted pastries we associate with France—croissants and brioches—at a week-long bread course at the École de Gastronomie Française Ritz-Escoffier in Paris. It was aston-ishing to watch Bernard Burban, the master baker who taught the course, work with dough. No matter how sticky the dough or how satu-rated with butter, it never stuck to his large hands. He manipulated it briskly, pushing it away from him and pulling it off the table as he kneaded, often with just one hand. He tried to teach us to do the same, admonishing us if we added too much flour to the table, but the dough always stuck to our hands anyway. Nonetheless, the bread, brioches and croissants that we baked and took home were always heavenly.

WHENEVER I TRAVEL, I seek out bakers the way tourists seek out monuments and museums. Bread and bakeries are always foremost in my mind when I visit the countries of the Mediterranean, where this food is such an important staple—the main source of calo-ries in many countries. In Bologna, my days are spent scouring the city to sample breads, bread-sticks and focacce; my Italian friends are always amused when I come home with bags of tempting breads, rather than postcards of Renaissance paintings. In Florence, I try to taste every kind of pizza I see. I love the bracelet-like sesame breads sold from poles or strings all over Athens and often make a meal of them, with feta cheese and tomatoes. I have spent hours watching bakers in Egypt make flatbreads outdoors in stone ovens. One of the high points of a recent trip to Morocco was when a young girl invited me to accompany her to the communal ovens with her tray of ready-to-bake dough. I was astonished when, an hour or two later, all of the loaves ended up back on their proper trays, freshly baked, in time for lunch.

Even in England, where I went to live not for the food but for love, I found a wealth of breads. During the 18 months that I lived in London, I sought out tea breads and scones to enjoy with afternoon teas, pored over books about traditional English breads and tried my hand at making scones, rich spicy breads and marvelous yeasted pancakes in the tiny oven in my apartment.

ALTHOUGH I'VE ALWAYS LIVED near great bakeries, most of the bread that I eat comes out of my own oven. I have to admit, I have a preference for my own bread. I love the whole-grain earthiness of the sourdough country loaves and mixed grain breads that are our staples at home. When I entertain—and that is often—I take great pride in the fact that the bread is homemade and that I have chosen it to go with the menu. If I am serving a Provençal dinner, I will make French country bread, a ladder-shaped, Provençal *fougasse* (page 92) or a country bread packed with olives (page 124). My Italian menus may feature a bread flavored with pesto (page 142) or with rosemary and thyme (page 140) or an Italian sourdough country bread (page 110). Mexican and South-

western food beg for cornmeal, so I whip up some of my rich-tasting Texas cornbread or serve one of the many yeast breads in this collection that also contains cornmeal. People notice when you serve homemade bread and remember it, especially in a place like Paris or Berkeley, where it's easy to go out and buy good bread. They almost always ask, "Did you make this?" and I'm happy to be able to answer, "Yes."

WHEN I GIVE A BIG PARTY, I often bake a selection of breads, especially black breads and herb breads because they go well with other foods I serve—cheeses and savory dips and spreads—and they slice up nicely. A couple of slender baguettes go a long way and look lovely in a basket. Blinis are another item I love to include. These small yeasted pancakes make an elegant addition to any buffet. I make the Russian-style buckwheat blinis (page 243) to serve with smoked salmon and caviar, and cornmeal blinis to show off salsas and other Mexican toppings. A selection of different kinds of focacce (page 192), with fresh herbs, olives or sun-dried tomatoes, cut up into small squares and arranged on a platter, are also terrific for parties.

When I don't have time for yeast-raised bread or when my Irish husband has a craving for Irish soda bread, I make quick breads. Soda breads, savory muffins, pancakes or scones can fulfill the need for fresh bread as well as a long-risen country loaf. When I lived in France, my French friends loved the novelty of some of these cake-like breads, such as the cornmeal muffins (page 231) or cheese-filled muffins (page 230).

Sweet breads, both quick and yeasted, are another important part of my bread repertoire. My friends now expect their Christmas gifts to be edible; my favorite gift breads are the French Spice Bread (page 215), which only gets better with time, and the beautiful braided challah with fruit (page 158). In addition to making good gifts, these breads—and muffins and scones—really hit the spot with late-afternoon tea, a ritual in our house. A thin slice of fruit-filled tea bread or a warm whole wheat scone filled with currants (page 223) is always a treat. And, of course, they make terrific after-school snacks for children.

Stale bread never gets thrown out at my house. At the very least, I make garlic croutons with country bread to add to my salads and soups. People all over the Mediterranean basin are ingenious when it comes to turning stale bread into something tasty. In Spain, they use it to thicken soups, and they rub slices of it with garlic, olive oil and tomato for lunch. Italians make soups and salads with stale bread and also use it for delicious *bruschette*—thick slices of lightly toasted bread topped with savory ingredients like thick tomato sauce, sautéed peppers or mushrooms (page 250). In the Middle East, stale pita bread goes into salads and into delicious casseroles called *fatta* (page 256). The French use their dry brioche for *pain perdu* (French toast, page 260), and Americans and the English make marvelous bread puddings.

Although making bread is fundamentally simple, it remains a mysterious and exciting process, even to the most experienced baker. Each dough feels and behaves somewhat differently from another, and even the experience of making a particular kind of bread is never quite the same from one time to the next. This is because dough is a living thing involving live yeasts multiplying within a framework of flour and water. Until the dough reaches a certain temperature in a hot oven and becomes bread, it will continue to be alive and subject to variables—ingredients, temperature, moisture, the way it is handled.

In my 22 years of baking, I have learned that there are probably as many different rules about making bread as there are bakers. All seem to work, as long as certain principles are observed. This is a book designed to give you the confidence to make bread at home and methods for working with it. It's a very personal "how-to" book, with the recipes for my favorites, the ones I bake each week or serve to guests.

My goal is to take the worry out of breadmaking and provide you with recipes for truly extraordinary breads. So roll up your sleeves, take off your rings and begin.

Ingredients

I KNOW A PROFESSIONAL BAKER whose bread business has made him a rich man. "Why shouldn't it?" he once said. "I need only three ingredients—flour, water and salt—for what I make, and one of them is free." The simplicity of the ingredients is one of the things that makes baking my own bread so appealing to me.

Since so few ingredients go into bread, their quality must be good. I buy my flours and grains in bulk at health food stores. I get the best price this way, and I'm sure to find stone-ground organic flours there. These are the best flours and grains for the breads in this book. The flours have lost no nutrients in the milling process, and no chemical pesticides have been used on the grains. I shop in stores where the turnover is high so that I can be sure that the grains and flours have not been sitting around too long, which could cause their oils to become rancid.

It's worth getting acquainted with your local health food store when you embark on breadmaking. You can find everything you will need there, from flours and grains to yeast, honey and molasses to oils and sea salt.

Storing Grains and Flours

GRAINS AND WHOLE-GRAIN FLOURS should be stored in airtight containers in a cool place. Grain contains a certain amount of fat, which can go rancid if they are not kept cool. The refrigerator is the ideal place, but few of us have the space in the refrigerator: a cool, unlit cabinet is a good second choice. Nuts and seeds, on the other hand, should always be stored in the refrigerator or freezer, as they have a high fat content and need to stay cold to avoid rancidity.

Wheat Flours

WITHOUT WHEAT FLOUR, bread will not rise properly. Breads can be made from other grains, but wheat is essential for yeast-risen bread.

Wheat flour is milled from whole wheat berries—small, hard, brown grain kernels that resemble brown rice. The hard, fibrous outer shell of the kernel, called the bran, adds bulk and fiber to the flour and comprises 13 to 17 percent of the weight of the wheat berry. The embryo, or sprouting section of wheat, is the germ. It is the most flavorful part of the wheat berry, comprising 2 to 3 percent of its weight.

Full of nutrients, it contains good-quality protein, unsaturated fats, vitamins and minerals. The rest of the wheat kernel is the endosperm, which is made up of starch and protein. The protein component is the gluten. When dough is kneaded, long strands of gluten form; they stretch and expand in the presence of fermenting yeast, and the dough rises. It is the endosperm that remains when the bran and germ are refined or sifted away. Modern white flour contains only this part of the grain. It is processed in high-speed roller mills—fast-turning steel cylinders that crush the grains—and all but the endosperm is sifted out.

Stone-ground 100 percent whole wheat flour is flour from which nothing has been removed and to which nothing has been added. It tastes sweet and nutty. The wheat has been crushed between large, flat, slow-moving stones, and the germ and bran remain. The process has changed very little since ancient times. If the bag does not specify that the flour has been stone-ground, then it has probably been roller-milled and had the bran and germ added back to it. This kind of flour will be about 95 percent whole wheat, and it won't have the same sweet flavor or coarse texture of the stone-ground. Whole wheat flour makes denser, tackier doughs than white flour because it absorbs less water.

Whole wheat flours vary in texture from mill to mill. Some are quite coarse, others finer. I prefer the fine-milled flours, as they yield lighter, finer-textured breads. Shop around, if you can, to find the fine ones; if the only ones you can find are coarse, you might want to substitute one-quarter to one-half whole wheat pastry flour in some of the recipes (where this is appropriate, I suggest it).

You can test the coarseness of flours by taking up a handful and rolling it between your thumb and forefinger. If you feel little cracked-wheat grains, the flour is quite coarse. The bran and germ will be apparent in finer flour, but the light beige flour will feel soft.

Whole wheat pastry flour: Made from soft wheat, this flour is more finely milled than whole wheat flour. Consequently, bread made from whole wheat pastry flour is lighter, with a finer crumb. However, it has less protein than whole wheat flour milled from hard wheat and so is less suitable for yeast-risen breads. I use whole wheat pastry flour in combination with unbleached white flour in many of the sweet quick breads in this book when I want the flavor of whole wheat flour but not the bulk.

Unbleached white flour: This is white flour that has been bleached by a natural aging process, not by chemicals. (Many manufacturers bleach flour to get it out on the market as soon as possible.) Most white flour is milled in high-speed steel roller-mills. The grain is ripped open rather than crushed, and the germ and bran are sifted out, leaving 70 to 73 percent of the grain—the endosperm, or starch and protein. The small, hard granules that remain are then pulverized into fine, white flour. If the flour is unbleached, it has a slightly off-white color, instead of the snow-white color of bleached flour. Bread made from unbleached white flour has a richer flavor than bread made from bleached flour.

Stone-ground unbleached flour is also available at some health food stores. It has a creamy color and is sweeter than roller-milled flour. Stone-ground unbleached flour is achieved by milling the grain in a stone mill and extracting or sieving off the bran. Residues of germ remain, resulting in a superior-tasting flour.

White-flour doughs are much softer and more elastic—sometimes they're like sticky taffy—than whole wheat, rye or other whole-grain doughs.

Semolina flour: Semolina is the coarse, golden flour ground from the endosperm of durum wheat, the hardest wheat variety. The best commercial pastas are made with semolina flour; it absorbs much less water than other flours. For breadmaking, semolina flour should always be used in combination with wheat flour. The doughs made with semolina are stiff and elastic. One of my favorite breads, from Sicily, is made with this lovely yellow flour (page 90). If you can't find it, grind up coarse semolina in a blender with some unbleached white flour. Sometimes fairly finely ground semolina is packaged and sold in supermarkets, and this can often be substituted for semolina flour. Be sure it's finely ground.

Do not use gluten flour and self-rising flour in the recipes in this book. Gluten flour is a highly refined flour in which much of the starch has been removed so that it is 50 percent protein. It gives a rising boost to breads, but loaves made with it dry out quickly. Self-rising flour contains baking powder and salt.

Other Flours, Grains and Meals

Barley flour and barley flakes: Like rye, barley has a low gluten content, so it must be mixed with whole wheat or white flour to achieve a good loaf. But it has a delicious tangy flavor and makes marvelous earthy breads. Barley flour is used for Barley Flour Crêpes (page 246). Barley flakes, like oat flakes and rye flakes, make a nutritious and tasty addition to Mixed Grain Bread (page 50).

Bulgur and cracked wheat: For cracked wheat, the wheat berry is crushed into small pieces rather than ground. Bulgur is cracked wheat that has been parboiled and dried. They make good additions to whole-grain breads, adding good texture and sweet flavor.

Buckwheat flour: Buckwheat flour has a very strong, distinctive flavor—earthy and rather fruity. I add it in small quantities to some breads, and it is essential for blinis, Russian yeast-raised pancakes (page 243).

Cornmeal: Ground from hard corn kernels, cornmeal has a grainy texture, a sweet taste and a lovely golden color. Polenta can be substituted as long as it isn't too coarse. Stone-ground yellow cornmeal, or medium to fine polenta, combined with wheat flour makes delicious grainy-textured breads. Use cornmeal for dusting baking stones and sheets.

Millet, millet meal and millet flakes: Millet is a sweet, tasty grain that looks like tiny yellow beads. It can be ground to a coarse meal that adds texture, yellow color and flavor to breads. The flakes are lighter than oat, rye or barley flakes but have the same chewy texture.

Oatmeal, rolled oats, oat flakes and oat bran: Oats have a sweet cereal flavor that, together with their chewy texture, makes them a lovely addition to breads. Oatmeal, rolled oats and oat flakes can be used interchangeably as additions to breads and muffins.

Oat bran is a high-fiber bran which differs from wheat bran in that it is soluble, whereas wheat bran is not. Some people find it easier to digest than wheat bran, and research has shown that this kind of fiber helps lower blood cholesterol and helps control blood-sugar levels in diabetics.

Rye flour: This flour is milled from whole rye berries, which resemble wheat berries. Like wheat flour, it is best when stone-ground. It has a rich, earthy flavor and a grainy texture, and it is excellent in sourdough breads. Rye flour has a lower gluten content than wheat flour and must be used in combination with it. Doughs made from rye flour are quite sticky and often unwieldy, but a proper balance of rye and wheat will result in good elasticity.

Rye flakes are rolled or flaked rye berries and resemble oatmeal or oat flakes. I use them in some of my mixed grain breads.

Sesame seeds: These tiny, nutty-tasting seeds are used in Italian, Middle Eastern and Greek breads and as a topping for many whole wheat and mixed grain breads.

Soy flour: Milled from soybeans, soy flour has a very high protein content as well as a high fat content. It can be added in small quantities to breads to increase their protein value.

Raising Agents, Sweeteners, Oils and Salt

Yeast: The yeast called for in the recipes in this book is active dry yeast, the type most widely used in this country. It is easy to find in supermarkets and health food stores. It comes in the form of small, salt-like granules, packaged in ¼-ounce envelopes (2½ teaspoons) or 4-ounce glass jars (more economical and neater than envelopes). You can often find yeast sold in bulk in health food stores—by far the cheapest way to buy it if you bake often.

What is the secret to these hard, dry little granules that come to life when they are dissolved in warm water? When we buy the yeast, it is dormant. But it's far from dead. All it needs is a bit of warmth, moisture and sugar to bring it back to life. It is amazing to think that a teaspoon of these lifeless granules can become the power behind a huge loaf of country bread.

When yeast is activated in warm water and flour is introduced, the yeast feeds on the starches in the flour and metabolizes them, releasing carbon dioxide and alcohol in the process. This is called fermentation. The long strands of gluten that are created when dough is kneaded stretch as the yeast releases these by-products, causing the dough to rise.

Yeast should always be stored in the refrigerator or freezer to keep it alive for the longest possible time. Jars and envelopes come with expiration dates printed on them; check the date before you buy the yeast. But even after the date has passed, the yeast may still be viable. Just dissolve it in a little water with a pinch of sugar and wait for 5 to 10 minutes to see whether it bubbles. If it does, it is still alive. You do not have to bring yeast to room temperature before using it for bread.

Yeast remains dormant at temperatures under 50 degrees F and dies at temperatures over 120 degrees.

Baking powder and baking soda: These fast-acting substances are used to raise quick, moist doughs and batters, in which gluten has not been developed. Baking soda reacts with acids in the dough and/or with acids in baking powder, releasing bubbles, which cause the dough to rise.

Baking powder, which contains baking soda and an acid such as tartaric acid, creates two gaseous reactions, one when the dough is mixed and another when it is exposed to high heat (which is why it is called "double-acting baking powder"). Breads raised with baking powder and baking soda should be handled as little as possible for the lightest results.

Honey: Small amounts of sweetener give yeast a boost. I usually use a mild-flavored, light-colored honey, such as clover. If you use strong honey, such as buckwheat or orange-blossom, even in small amounts of a tablespoon or two, the flavor can be overpowering.

Malt extract: Malt extract is a thick, viscous syrup, usually made from malted barley, that is added in very small amounts to some bread doughs to aid the yeast and give the bread a golden crust.

Blackstrap molasses: This gives a dark color and distinctive flavor to black breads, rye breads and some mixed grain breads and muffins.

Butter and oils: I generally use mild-tasting oils like sunflower, canola or safflower. Olive oil or walnut oil contributes a distinctive flavor. When melted butter is called for, always use unsalted, to avoid adding more salt than you intend to the dough.

Salt: Salt is important for the flavor of the bread and also helps regulate the action of the yeast. I use sea salt, which has the best flavor.

Equipment

DESPITE THE AVAILABILITY of lots of attractive and useful gear, breadmaking does not require much in the way of equipment. I have baked bread in the most primitive, rented kitchens in Yugoslavia, Italy and southern France, where I had little more than a wooden spoon and a big wash basin for mixing up the dough. I've improvised measuring cups with tea cups, measuring spoons with kitchen spoons, and I've baked bread in a tart pan. Handling the dough properly and getting to know what it should feel like does not require special utensils—quite the opposite is true. In breadmaking, experience is more important than equipment.

A reliable oven, gas or electric, is the most useful piece of equipment you can have. It does not have to be a professional oven, a convection oven or a bread oven. Some of the ovens I've baked in have been tiny—just big enough for a large, round loaf—and some have not even been reliable, but I've been able to ascertain how they cooked so that I could make the necessary adjustments. Get to know your oven.

Most of the following items necessary for breadmaking will be in a working kitchen already.

Measuring spoons: It's convenient to have two sets, one for liquids and one for dry ingredients so that you don't have to keep washing and drying them as you go.

Measuring cups for liquids: A 4-cup Pyrex or clear plastic measuring cup with a spout.

Dry measuring cups: These should be the nested type, either metal or plastic, for each main unit of measure (¼ cup, ⅓ cup, ½ cup, 1 cup). Do not use liquid measures for measuring solids because they will not be accurate. This is especially important for quick breads, which require precise measurements.

Kitchen scale: Because most home cooks aren't accustomed to using scales in the kitchen, I have used cup measures in the recipes in this book. However, I actually prefer weighing rather than measuring. The reason is that the scale is an easier, more accurate way to measure the amount of flour that should go into a bread. When you use a scale, you don't have to worry about how you scoop the flour; all you do is pour the flour into the bowl of the scale. If you want to experiment with scales, refer to the table on page 265 for flour weights and measures. If you do purchase a kitchen scale, be sure to buy one that has a bowl (2-quart) rather than a box that sits on the weighing mechanism. It will be easier to work with.

Electric spice mill: For grinding spices and small amounts of grain (like millet), a coffee grinder is perfect. Don't use the same mill for both coffee and spices, or your coffee will take on off flavors.

Large whisk: Used for beating in flour.

Large wooden spoon: Used for stirring in ingredients.

Mixing bowls: Stainless-steel, earthenware, glass, plastic or ceramic can be used. Earthenware bowls are probably the best for maintaining temperature, but I have used everything from a plastic tub to an enamel washbasin with equally good results. If using a metal bowl, be careful not to place it too near a heat source, such as a pilot light, as the metal can heat up too much and ruin the dough. The bowl should hold at least 3 quarts, preferably more. You should have more than one bowl for the quick breads, for which you must mix liquid and dry ingredients separately.

Pastry scraper: A scraper is essential for turning and kneading many breads, since many doughs are sticky. The blade may be made of stainless steel with a wooden handle or of plastic with a curved edge, which I prefer. The plastic scraper is useful for scraping dough out of the bowl and for scraping the work surface during kneading, but it's not as effective as the metal type for cutting the dough.

Heavy-duty electric mixer with a dough hook: If you make bread regularly, you will want to invest in either a KitchenAid or a Rival heavy-duty mixer. A mixer with a dough hook makes a real difference when you are kneading sticky doughs, like sourdoughs. It does the work for you and saves you the job of cleaning doughy hands and the work surface. That said, you should learn the feel of dough before you begin to use a machine for kneading. And even if you do use an electric mixer, finish the kneading by hand to make sure the dough has the right feel.

Banneton: A traditional French banneton is a round, slant-sided, flat-bottomed, wicker basket that is usually lined with muslin. Free-form loaves are set, rounded side down, in the baskets to rise. When the bread is ready to be baked, the dough is reversed onto a baking pan or a hot baking stone.

You flour the muslin heavily before putting in the dough so that the dough doesn't stick over a long rising period, and the resulting bread will have a rustic-looking, floury surface. Sometimes the baskets are not lined with muslin but only heavily floured, and the floury surface of the bread takes on the pattern of the basket. Bannetons can be purchased at some good cookware stores.

But you don't really have to go to the expense of buying a real French banneton. They are easy to improvise by lining a bowl or a basket with a clean dish towel or muslin (I have even used a pillowcase) and dusting the material with flour. The advantage to using a banneton or towel-lined bowl for free-form loaves is that the dough keeps its shape as it rises and doesn't spread out. When you reverse a banneton-risen loaf onto a hot baking stone or a baking sheet and put it directly into a hot oven, you get a beautiful, round country loaf.

Plastic wrap: Cover the bowl with plastic while the dough is rising to create a constant, warm, gaseous atmosphere, much like an incubator. I usually put a towel over the plastic to ensure that no air will creep through any gaps.

Nonstick baking sheets: I use these for some breads, pizzas and focacce. They should be at least 15 inches long and 12 inches wide.

Nonstick loaf pans: These facilitate removing loaves from the pans. I use two sizes, 8½ x 4½ x 2½ inches and 9 x 5 x 3 inches, and both work very well. Earthenware and Pyrex loaf pans can be used for baking breads, but I prefer metal pans because they conduct heat better and the loaves are less likely to stick to them, whether or not they are nonstick. I oil my non-stick pans lightly just to be sure.

Oven thermometer: Having one of these is the only way to ensure that your oven is baking at the temperature you require.

Baking stone or tiles: Baking tiles distribute the heat evenly in your oven, transforming it into something approximating a stone oven. The tiles absorb the moisture of the dough and give the breads a harder, thicker crust. Tiles are about 5 inches square, and you must put together at least four in the oven. Because tiles have a tendency to move apart when the dough is turned out onto them, a round baking stone, 14 to 15 inches in diameter and ¼ to ½ inch thick, is more convenient. I like to use one even when I'm baking the bread in pans or on baking sheets. Baking stones can be found in kitchenware shops and some hardware stores. They are often called pizza stones.

Shallow pan and/or water-spray bottle: A little steam in the hot oven helps to ensure a hard crust and can be accomplished in two ways: by placing a pan on the floor of the oven or by spraying during baking. I usually spray the loaf and the oven immediately before and after putting the loaf in and repeat the spraying two or three times during the first 10 minutes of baking. Spray bottles are easy to find in hardware stores, drugstores and supermarkets.

How to Make Yeast Breads

TRICKY AS BREADMAKING may seem to the beginner, only a few things are essential for success. Yeast-raised bread requires, in its simplest form, six basic steps: activating the yeast and mixing up the dough; kneading; shaping the dough into a ball and setting it to rise in a covered bowl; deflating the dough (sometimes by punching it down, sometimes merely by turning it out onto the work surface); shaping it and setting it to rise again; and baking.

For the bread to be good, the basic ingredients have to be of good quality: the flour not too old and preferably stone-ground, the yeast active, the water fresh-tasting, without the harsh flavor of chlorine and minerals. The liquids and solids must not be too hot, or they'll kill the yeast; nor should they be too cold, or the action of the yeast will be slowed. The dough must be properly mixed and effectively kneaded to develop its gluten, the element responsible for the dough's elasticity. The dough must have enough time to rise and develop its full flavor and potential, and the loaves must be properly shaped and baked.

Handling dough can at first seem awkward and mysterious, and it's difficult to describe such a tactile experience in words. But I'm going to give it a try.

If you are going to make bread, you are going to have to put up with doughy, sticky hands. One phrase comes up again and again in bread recipes and lies at the root of many failed attempts at breadmaking. It is: "Knead until smooth, silky and elastic." Elastic and pliable is a better description. In my experience, dough is hardly ever smooth and silky, and if it does achieve that quality, it doesn't last for long. (It must be elastic, because elasticity is what you develop in the dough when you knead.)

IF THE DOUGH IS NOT STICKY, chances are you've added too much flour. More often than not, my doughs reach the smooth and silky stage after sufficient kneading, but they quickly become tacky again. If I were to keep adding flour when kneading, just because the surface was a bit sticky, I would end up with an overly heavy loaf. If the dough is especially sticky, these recipes will say so; don't keep adding unnecessary flour. With coarse whole wheat flours and especially with rye flour, which contains no gluten, the dough is always sticky and hard to handle, both at the kneading and shaping stage.

Remember that well-kneaded, elastic dough will rise, no matter how sticky it is. When you begin to mix the dough, it will be a formless, sticky mass that can be manipulated easily only with the aid of a dough scraper. Some bakers are adept at manipulating the dough briskly, whereas novice bakers have more difficulty. No matter: The finished breads will be almost indistinguishable from one another.

Before you begin, remove your rings, keep a cloth or a plastic bag by the phone so that if it rings during kneading you don't get dough all over it and have on hand a special sponge with a rough side for rubbing dough off your hands and the work surface. Moisten your hands with water when you shape the loaves to make the shaping easier. Dough will not stick to wet hands.

Measuring Flour

IN THE RECIPES FOR YEAST BREADS, you will find a range of flour, whereas with quick breads, the flour measurements are precise. This is because the amount of flour used in yeast breads can vary: Flour in one bag may have absorbed more moisture and be heavier than flour in another bag. The coarseness of the grain from one flour to the next may vary, which has an effect on the amount of moisture the flour will absorb. The weather conditions on the day you bake can alter the texture of the dough, so that you need to add more or less flour to get a sufficiently elastic, workable dough.

It is much easier to add flour to a wet dough than to add water to a stiff dough. Dough absorbs water with great difficulty, whereas flour absorbs moisture readily. That's why, when I make bread, I stir flour into water, rather than vice versa. Always begin with the lesser amount of flour called for, and use your sense of touch to determine how much more flour to add, remembering that the less flour added, the better texture your bread will have. If you begin with a conservative amount of flour, you won't risk producing a dough that will result in a leaden loaf. As you become more experienced at kneading, you will begin to have a sense of the way dough should feel, and precise flour measurements will become less crucial. Successful breadmaking is, above all, a question of touch.

How to measure flour: Whether you are using exact measurements for quick breads or a range for yeast breads, it's important that you measure the flour correctly. The actual amount—i.e., the weight—of flour varies in a cup, depending on how you have filled the cup. If you don't fill the cup correctly, you could add too much flour to your dough and end up with heavy bread. To get the most accurate measure of flour in a cup, always stir the flour before you fill the cup; if you simply scoop the cup into the flour bin or bag, you can get 1 to 2 ounces more flour per cup than if you stir the flour first. After stirring the flour, swiftly dip the cup into it, or spoon the flour into the cup; spoon or dip the flour higher than the top of the cup, and then run a butter knife or spatula between the edge of the cup and the mounded flour to scrape off the excess.

Basic Breadmaking Technique, Step by Step

Before You Begin

Your work surface should be the size of a large cutting board, at least 14 inches square and preferably larger. Ideally, it should be lower than a cutting surface—about waist or midriff level—so you can put more of your weight into kneading, as you lean into the dough. When I began making bread, I used to wear platform shoes and stand on a box to be high enough above my ordinary kitchen countertop. A large plastic, wooden or marble board on a kitchen table works well. A countertop will do, but you may have to stand on your toes while you knead.

Make sure your flour and other ingredients, except the yeast, are at room temperature or warm, or they will slow up the yeast action. The yeast is the exception because you will be warming it in lukewarm water. Before you get started, you may want to put on a record or a tape or turn on the radio. There is a rhythm to kneading, and music helps you achieve it.

Mixing the Dough

The first thing you need to do when you mix up a yeast dough is dissolve the yeast in the liquid, usually lukewarm water. Lukewarm is warm but not hot, anywhere from 95 to 105 degrees F. I usually test it by dipping my fingers into it. If the water is hot, it will kill the yeast. Yeast takes just a few minutes to dissolve in lukewarm water and longer in milk.

Many recipes have you dissolve the yeast in a small bowl and add this mixture to a larger bowl when you mix the dough. This is unnec-

essary, resulting in one more bowl to wash, and in addition, a little bit of the yeast is lost when you transfer it to the other bowl. Begin with a mixing bowl that is about three times (or at least twice) the volume of the dough because the dough will nearly double in size during the first rising, which is done in the same bowl.

If a sweetener is called for, such as sugar, honey or molasses, add it along with the yeast. The yeast feeds on the sweetener. Mix the yeast and liquid together with a whisk or a wooden spoon, and add the sweetener; wait for 5 to 10 minutes, or until the liquid is creamy-looking. You will see the yeast moving like little clouds in the water.

Now stir in the oil or melted unsalted butter, if either is called for in the recipe. Good French bread can be made with nothing more than flour, water, salt and yeast. But bread with oil added will last longer, freeze well and have a slightly moister texture. Some of the recipes in this book call for oil, some do not. Feel free to experiment with leaving it out or adding it wherever you wish.

Salt is added with the flour. It should be mixed with the flour in a separate bowl and not, as many recipes instruct, added to the yeast mixture before the flour is added. Salt has a traumatic effect on yeast when it comes into direct contact with it, slowing down its action. When properly added—mixed with the flour first—salt allows the dough to rise in a more controlled way than when it is not present, and it imparts flavor as well.

Add the flour mixture to the yeast mixture by large spoonfuls or by cups, folding it in after each addition. To fold, scoop the wooden spoon under the dough, working from the middle of the bowl, slide it to the opposite side of the bowl and turn the batter over itself. Gently flick your wrist as you bring the spoon up the side of the bowl, and end with the spoon in the middle of the bowl, pointing down. Each time you add flour and fold, turn the bowl a quarter turn. Folding in this manner is the neatest, easiest way to incorporate the dry ingredients into the liquids and get the dough to a state where you can turn it out of the bowl.

By the time you've added about three-quarters of the flour, the dough will be sticky and formless, but cohesive enough so that you can scrape it out onto the work surface. Do this as soon as possible, lightly flouring the surface first. You will add the remaining flour during the kneading process. It's best to add flour gradually and knead it in so that you don't end up with dough that's too stiff and heavy. How much you need will vary with the weather and the type of flour.

Kneading the Dough

You knead the dough for three reasons: to develop the gluten in the flour (the long strands of protein that expand as the yeast multiplies and give the dough its volume and elasticity); to incorporate air into the dough and to generate warmth within it, which are both necessary if the dough is to rise properly. As the dough rises, the living yeast ferments, turning oxygen and sugars into carbon dioxide and alcohols. Trapped in the network of dough, the carbon dioxide forces the dough to expand, making the bread rise.

Use a pastry scraper or a spoon to scrape the dough out of the bowl. Before you begin kneading, wait a minute or two to allow the flour to absorb the moisture.

The Fold-Lean-Turn Method

The "fold-lean-and-push-turn" technique of kneading is easy and effective. Using a pastry scraper to facilitate turning the dough, which will be very wet at first, fold the dough in half toward you. With floured hands, lean into the dough, beginning at the edge where the two folds come together, and press your weight from the heels of your palms out through your fingertips. Rock forward on your feet, and let your body push your hands into the dough, pushing the dough away from you rather than down into the work surface. (When you push the dough away instead of down, it has less tendency to stick to the surface, so you won't have the urge to add too much flour.)

At first, because the dough is sticky, you should press gingerly, or the dough will go all over the place. Now turn the dough a quarter turn to the left or right. Fold the dough in half toward you again and lean into it, pushing it away from you. The heels of your palms are doing most of the work here (with the help of the rest of your body), but the movement ends in the fingertips. Turn the dough again. Fold, lean, turn; fold, lean, turn. The dough will be amorphous and annoyingly sticky at first, but in just a few turns, it will begin to stiffen up. Sprinkle flour onto the surface of the dough as necessary to minimize sticking, but sprinkle most of the flour onto the work surface, and work it in sparingly.

Whole wheat dough absorbs moisture more slowly than white flour dough; you want to give it time to do this. If the dough seems very sticky, let it rest for 5 minutes so the moisture can be absorbed. If you add too much flour all at once, the bread will be too heavy, stiff and hard to handle, and it won't rise properly. Dough made with white flour begins to get tough, elastic and resistant after about 5 minutes of kneading. On the other hand, whole wheat doughs are always a little stickier and less tough. Many sourdough breads are hopelessly sticky, sometimes almost like taffy. As the dough toughens, I often find that I'm leaning into the dough a few times before turning it, to work it more thoroughly. So the rhythm is fold, lean (push), lean (push), lean (push), turn.

The Lifting-and-Slapping Method

You can also grab the entire piece of dough and slap it down on the table, slapping it down, lifting it up as high as your head and slapping it down over and over again. As you lift the dough, you will also be stretching it and folding it over itself to incorporate air into the dough. I find that I begin slapping the dough onto the work surface after I've been folding and leaning for a while, when the dough has become resistant.

The way you knead will be partially determined by the amount of dough you're working with. A large amount is easier to knead using the fold-lean-turn method than the lifting-and-slapping method. Whatever way you knead, try not to tear the dough, as this breaks the strands of gluten that you are working so hard to develop. You can avoid tearing the dough by being gentle when you knead. You don't have to knead violently to develop the dough, just firmly. A steady, peaceful rhythm is best and can be very relaxing.

Your fingertips and hands will tell you when the dough has been sufficiently kneaded. After you've made bread a few times, you'll begin to recognize the point at which dough is ready to rise. It should be bouncy and elastic. White flour doughs will have a few bubbles on the surface. As several writers aptly say, "It should feel as if it has a mind of its own." It's a living thing, after all, and there is something both friendly and lively about properly kneaded dough.

It usually takes about 10 minutes of kneading to develop the gluten and get the dough into shape, but the time—and the amount of flour you have to add to your kneading surface—can vary. If it is very humid or hot, the dough may be stickier than it is in dry weather and take longer to stiffen. Doughs with lots of grains will be dense and slightly tacky on the surface; those with rye flour will be very tacky.

The way to tell if the dough has been sufficiently kneaded is to shape it into a ball and plunge a few fingers into it. If the dough springs back, it is ready to rise. It won't necessarily spring back quickly or all the way, but it does not remain indented and passive. If it doesn't spring back, knead some more.

Once you have finished kneading and are ready to shape the dough, place it into the bowl quickly because it will soon begin to stick to the work surface.

Kneading With an Electric Mixer

Heavy-duty electric mixers with dough-hook attachments, such as the Rival and the KitchenAid, can be extremely convenient, especially if you make a lot of bread. When there is more than 2 pounds of dough, I don't use a dough hook because too much dough strains the motor. If you are a beginner, even if you have a machine, it's important initially to knead by hand, in order to familiarize yourself with the way dough should feel.

When using an electric mixer, dissolve the yeast in the liquid in the bowl of your mixer and let stand for 5 to 10 minutes, until creamy. Add the oil, if using. Mix together the smaller amount of flour called for with the salt in a separate bowl and add this all at once to the bowl. Mix together briefly using the mixing or paddle attachment, just to amalgamate the ingredients. Then change to the dough hook, scraping all of the dough that clings to the paddle into the bowl. Knead on low speed for 2 minutes, then turn to medium speed and knead for 8 to 10 minutes. Do not overwork the dough, or it will become too hot (as will the machine). The dough should come away from the sides of the bowl and form a ball around the dough hook, which will be working air into the dough and slapping it around to develop the gluten. If the dough continues to adhere to the sides of the bowl, add flour as necessary. After 8 to 10 minutes, I use a pastry scraper to scrape the dough out of the bowl onto a floured surface, flour my hands and finish off the kneading by hand, 30 to 60 seconds. This way, I can be sure that the dough has been properly kneaded: Contact with the dough is important.

Shaping the Dough Into a Ball

When the dough has been kneaded sufficiently, shape it into a ball. Do this by folding it over itself, toward you, and turning, without leaning, all the way around. Pinch together the seam on the bottom.

First Rise

Before you put the dough back in the mixing bowl, it's a good idea to rinse the bowl because bits of dough that adhere to it can spoil the dough's texture. Washing the bowl now is also easier than later, when the dough hardens.

Some people don't oil the bowl, claiming that unabsorbed oil can make holes in the finished loaf. I've never had problems with oil, which I use to prevent the surface of the dough from drying out and to make it easier to turn out the dough without tearing it later. If you'd prefer not to coat the bowl with oil, that's okay, since plastic wrap will keep the surface moist.

If you have oiled the bowl, place the dough in it, rounded side down first, then turn the dough over so the rounded side is up. If you have not oiled the bowl, place the dough in rounded side up. Cover the bowl tightly with plastic wrap to keep drafts off the dough and trap the heat that will be generated as the yeast multiplies. I also place a towel over the plastic wrap to help prevent drafts from reaching the dough, just in case the plastic wrap comes loose at the sides. You can also secure the plastic with a rubber band and do without the towel.

Set the bowl in a warm spot. If it's a warm day or your kitchen is warm, anywhere will do.

Allow the dough to rise until more or less doubled in volume, usually 1½ to 2 hours, depending on the recipe. Don't feel that you have to be a prisoner to your dough. If you want to go out to a movie, put the dough in the refrigerator to slow the rising. Refrigerated dough can rise overnight or all day, so you can mix and knead the dough before going to bed or before going to work, and finish it off later. Then, before baking, allow some time for the dough to return to room temperature.

Dough can also be frozen, which, in effect, puts the yeast to sleep for a while. Shape it into a ball, and seal in a plastic bag. Remove the dough from the bag when you thaw it, and place it in a lightly oiled bowl. Like refrigerated dough, frozen dough behaves just like freshly made dough when it returns to room temperature, although you may have to get it going again with a little kneading.

Punching Down the Dough

When the dough has more or less doubled in volume and has risen into a soft, spongy mass, with a smooth, usually slightly domed but sometimes billowy or bubbly surface, it needs to be deflated, or "punched down," to release the gas created by the yeast and to slow down the yeast's action. (With free-form sourdough breads, just shaping them is enough to deflate the dough sufficiently.)

If you let the dough rise too long, the yeast will produce too much carbon dioxide and alcohol, suffocate in its own by-products and fall. This is why the dough should be shaped as soon as it has doubled in volume. This said, I have left dough for hours at room temperature—either forgotten about it or had unexpected things happen that prevented me from punching it down at the designated time—and the bread has still been fine. If the dough overrises, knead it for a couple of minutes and then shape.

A good way to tell if the dough is ready for punching down is to wet your finger and stick it gently, about ½ inch deep, into the center of the dough. The dough should feel spongy and the hole should not fill in at all. If it does, the dough needs to rise a little more. If it doesn't, it's time to punch it down and/or shape the loaves.

Punching down isn't really violent, but it's called "punching" because most people deflate the dough by sticking their fist into it. Sprinkle the surface of the dough with a little flour, and stick your fist or fingertips into the middle of the dough. The dough will sigh and collapse, and you will see that it has been transformed into hundreds of little glutenous strands separated by airy bubbles. Don't be hard on the dough: you just want to release the gases without tearing the strands of gluten.

Some recipes—those for hearty, whole grain breads—call for a second rise in the bowl. This second rising helps to achieve a lighter loaf. For other breads, the dough is shaped before the second rising.

Shaping Techniques

Round Loaves

Using a spatula or a pastry scraper, carefully scrape the dough out of the bowl onto a lightly floured work surface, being careful not to tear it. Moisten your hands so the dough won't stick to them. Knead for about a minute, and shape the dough into a ball. If you are making more than one loaf, use a metal or plastic pastry scraper or a sharp knife to cut the dough into equal-size pieces, according to the number of loaves or rolls you wish to make. If you wish, weigh the pieces to make sure they're equal.

Shape the dough into tight balls (or one tight ball for one large loaf). Do this the same way you did at the end of kneading, by pulling the edge of the dough up and folding it over itself, turning and folding all the way around. Cup your hands around the ball, lightly flouring the dough if it is sticky, and gently lift and bounce the dough, turning it inside the dome of your hands, to get a very round, tight ball. Let it rest for 5 minutes.

After you have let the dough rest, cup your hands around it again and give it another turn, just to make sure it is smooth. Now the loaf is ready for a second rise; see page 25.

Pan Loaves

While the dough is resting, oil the loaf pans. It is important to oil the pans well—I oil non-stick pans as well as regular ones—so that the loaves can be removed easily after baking.

Press a ball of dough into a rectangle about 1 inch thick and a little longer than the loaf pan. There are three different ways to form the loaves:

Roll up the rectangle tightly, like a sausage, and pinch it together firmly along the lengthwise crease. Rock the loaf gently on the board to give it a rounded shape. Fold in the two ends toward the center and pinch the folds.

or

Fold the rectangle of dough lengthwise like a business letter, folding in one edge to the middle and the remaining edge over the first fold. Rock the loaf gently back and forth on the board. Pinch it together firmly along the lengthwise crease, and fold in the short ends, as above.

or

Fold the rectangle of dough in half, and gently pinch together the edges, using the heel of your hand. Flatten out the rectangle slightly, fold it over once more, and then pinch the edges of the lengthwise seam. Rock back and forth to give it a rounded log shape, and fold in the short ends.

Place the loaf, crease side up, in the oiled loaf pan. Gently push it into the pan with the backs of your hands to shape it and coat it with oil. Turn over the loaf so that the smooth side is up, and gently press it into the sides of the pan again. It will spring back, which is a good sign. The dough should fill the pan by about two-thirds to three-quarters (some will fill the pan only by half, depending on the recipe and the size of the pan). Cover the pan loosely with a towel, and set it in a warm spot for the dough to rise. It is ready to bake when it rises above the edge of the pans.

Baguettes

Baguette dough is often quite sticky, so work quickly on a lightly floured surface. Moisten your hands to prevent the dough from sticking. Two techniques work well:

French technique: Press or roll the dough into a small rectangle about 1 inch thick. Fold one long side all the way over to the other edge, and gently pat the seam together, using the heel of your hand or your fingertips. Now take the rounded edge you have just folded and fold it over again to the other edge of the dough. Pinch or pat the edges together, and placing both hands together at the center of the log, roll it gently but firmly back and forth under your hands on your work surface, while you move your hands away from each other, out toward the edges of the dough. The dough will stretch out into a long, tight, evenly shaped cylinder. Fold under the ends, and pinch the seams.

or

You can fold the rectangle of dough like a business letter. Fold the long edge toward the center, and gently pat the seam together with the heel of your hand or your fingertips. Fold this rounded piece toward the remaining edge,

and pinch or pat together at the seam. Place your hands together in the middle of the log shape, and roll back and forth to stretch out, folding the ends in and pinching the seams.

Sausage-Shaped Loaves— Bloomers or Batards

These long free-form loaves are wider than baguettes. Shaped like pan loaves, they are then lengthened like a baguette.

Small Round Rolls

Divide the dough into small, equal-size pieces and create tight, round balls by cupping your hand over the pieces and rolling them around and around under the dome of your hand on the table. Or you can shape the balls by pulling one side of the dough over to the opposite side and pinching underneath, then turning the dough and continuing all the way around. Pinch the bottoms together well. Place on an oiled, cornmeal-dusted baking sheet.

Second Rise

For the second rising, you have a choice of methods. You can let the dough rise upside down in a towel-lined basket or bowl called a banneton (see page 16); you can let the dough rise in the bowl and reshape it once more; or you can let it rise on a baking sheet.

If using the banneton method: If you are assembling your own banneton, dust a clean, dry dish towel with flour and line a bowl or a basket with it. Form the dough into a ball, dust the surface with flour, and place it, rounded side down, in the towel-lined bowl or basket. Sprinkle a little flour over the surface of the dough. Cover the bowl with a damp dish towel, and set in a warm spot to rise.

If using an oiled bowl or a baking sheet: Form the dough into a ball, and let rise in an oiled bowl until nearly doubled in bulk. Reshape the dough by cupping your hands around it and gently propping it up, without pressing hard enough to deflate it. Move your hands quickly around the edges of the dough. Place it on a baking sheet that has been oiled and sprinkled with cornmeal. Or, shape the dough into a tight ball, and let rise directly on the oiled, cornmeal-sprinkled baking sheet. The dough will probably spread out and will have to be reshaped gently before baking, or baked before it spreads out too much.

If you let the baguettes rise on baking sheets, they will spread out and flatten. For this reason, I recommend using bannetons or special baguette pans. You can create a banneton for baguettes by placing the dough on a generously floured, stiff towel (linen is good) or a heavy piece of muslin and pleating the towel up along the sides of the baguette so that the towel becomes a makeshift baguette pan. If you are using baguette pans, oil them generously and dust them with cornmeal. Baguettes should rise for about 45 minutes, until just about doubled in volume.

The time for the second rise varies with the type of bread and the shape of the loaf. It is important to allow the dough to develop its full potential, but it's also very important not to allow it to rise for too long. If it does, it will spread out too much on a baking sheet, and it will collapse during baking because there will be too many air bubbles in the dough and not enough structure. If the dough has risen too much, knead and reshape, then let rise again until nearly doubled.

Slashing and Brushing

Most loaves need to be slashed before baking. The slashes are escape hatches for steam, which quickly develops as the loaves bake. Unreleased steam can cause the loaves to crack or break apart. The best tool for slashing is a ra-zor blade, dipped in water. A sharp knife dipped in water will also work, but a razor blade is sharper and more efficient. Slash the loaves just before putting them into the oven, and as they bake, the slashes will open, giving the loaves an attractive appearance.

Some breads are brushed with a glaze made from beaten egg, or egg beaten with water (egg wash), so that they will have a shiny surface. You also brush them just before baking, but be careful to brush lightly, as you can deflate the loaves at this delicate stage.

Baking

When you bake bread, the high heat kills the yeast, stopping its action—but only after one last burst of life, when the dough is exposed to the oven heat, causing the final, satisfying rise.

Preheat the oven for at least 15 minutes and preferably 30 to 60 minutes. It's important that your oven be hot when the bread goes in. The temperature varies with the bread. Breads baked in loaf pans tend to bake at medium heat, 350 to 375 degrees F. Crusty loaves need a higher heat, 400 to 425 degrees. Some recipes have you bake the loaves at a very high heat, 450 to 500 degrees for the first 10 minutes, then turn the heat down to 350 to 400 degrees. All breads should be baked in the middle or the upper third of the oven. (If you are making two loaves at once, you will usually be able to get them both on a single baking sheet if they are round, or you will be able to fit two loaf pans side by side in the oven, so both will be at the same position.) If they are too low and close to the flame, the bottoms will burn before the loaves are cooked through.

Achieving a Good Crust

Breads that are brushed with a glaze should be brushed again halfway through the baking for a shiny crust.

Baguettes and country loaves should have a thick, hard crust, achieved by introducing steam into the oven (see page 17).

Tiles or a baking stone also helps give a crusty finish. Preheat them for at least 30 minutes in the oven. If baking directly on the baking stone, dust it with cornmeal or semolina and transfer the dough carefully to the hot stone. Spray, slash and place in the hot oven at once.

Baking Times

Rolls usually take about 20 minutes to bake; round country breads generally require 40 to 60 minutes; pan loaves need 45 to 60 minutes.

Bread is done when the crust is dark brown (or black for black breads) and hard. The best way to tell is to tap the bottom of the bread; it should produce a hollow sound. If the bottom seems soft or doesn't sound hollow, bake a little longer.

Cooling and Storing

Remove breads at once from pans or baking sheets (some quick breads are exceptions). To remove a loaf from a pan, run a knife around the edge of the pan, then carefully turn it upside down. Tap the bottom of the pan; the loaf should come out easily. Cool the bread on racks: it will sweat as it cools, and if there is no air circulating underneath it, it will become soggy. Allow the bread to cool for at least 1 hour, and preferably longer, before slicing. If you cut it too soon, it won't develop a proper crumb and won't slice as well as it could.

For the first couple of days, keep bread in the open air, just covering the cut parts with aluminum foil. Country breads made with whole wheat flours will keep like this for up to a week; after 3 or 4 days, whole grain breads should be wrapped in foil and refrigerated. They will dry out a bit, but the cooler temperature will prevent them from molding. Except for sourdough country breads, which last longer, white breads usually dry out in a day or two.

With the exception of some of the whole grain breads and loaf breads that do not have hard crusts, breads should never be stored in plastic bags, as they tend to sweat and lose their hard crust.

If you do store bread in plastic, it should be refrigerated after 2 days to prevent mold from forming. I also do not keep bread in breadboxes, because they too are warm and humid, encouraging mold.

Quick breads and muffins can be stored in plastic but should be refrigerated after a day or two unless otherwise instructed.

Freezing

Most breads freeze very well, especially if they have oil, butter, milk or eggs in them. Even without added fats, I find that whole wheat breads freeze well. To freeze, tightly wrap in aluminum foil, and then seal in a plastic bag. Frozen bread will keep for up to 6 months. It takes about 2 hours to thaw at room temperature or, if wrapped in foil, 30 to 45 minutes in a warm oven.

Basic Yeast Breads

Basic Whole Wheat Loaf

2 LOAVES

THIS IS A LOVELY, MOIST, DENSE LOAF that slices well. The dough is sticky and heavy. At the end of kneading, it will be just about smooth and slightly tacky on the surface. It's an excellent basic recipe that can be modified by substituting different kinds of flours for portions of the whole wheat flour.

This dough will vary depending on the coarseness of the flour. If the flour is coarsely ground, you might want to substitute up to 2 cups of unbleached white flour or whole wheat pastry flour for the whole wheat flour.

2	teaspoons active dry yeast
3	cups lukewarm water
2	tablespoons mild-flavored honey, or 1 tablespoon malt extract (page 15)
	About 7-8 cups whole wheat flour
2½	teaspoons salt
2	tablespoons sunflower, safflower or canola oil
1	egg, beaten with 2 tablespoons water, for egg wash (optional)
2	tablespoons sesame seeds

Dissolve the yeast in the water in a large bowl and let stand for 5 to 10 minutes, until creamy. Stir in the honey or malt extract.

Mix together 3¾ cups of the flour and the salt in a medium bowl. With a wooden spoon, gradually beat this mixture, 1 cup at a time, into the liquid mixture until smooth. Beat in the oil, and gradually fold in 3¼ cups flour.

Place a generous amount of the remaining flour on the work surface and turn out the dough. Begin kneading, using a pastry scraper to facilitate folding the dough, and adding flour to the work surface as needed.

Knead for 15 to 20 minutes, dusting your hands and the work surface often. The dough will be sticky at first, and you will need to add a lot of flour, but it will stiffen after about 5 minutes. At the end of the kneading, the dough will be dense and elastic, though still tacky on the surface. Sprinkle a little flour on the work surface and shape the dough into a ball.

Rinse, dry and lightly oil the bowl. Place the dough in it and turn to coat with the oil. Cover tightly with plastic wrap and a towel and let rise in a warm spot for 1½ to 2 hours, or until doubled in size.

Punch down the dough and let rise again, covered, for 1 hour or until nearly doubled. (*This rise can be omitted; the loaves will be slightly more dense.*)

Turn out the dough onto a lightly floured surface. Moisten your hands. Shape the dough into a ball and cut in half. Shape into 2 balls, and let relax for 10 minutes.

Now form the loaves (see page 24). Oil two 8-x-4-inch loaf pans and place the loaves in them, first upside down, then right side up, to coat with the oil. If you are using the egg wash, brush the loaves with it, sprinkle them with the sesame seeds, and brush again with the egg wash. Cover with a damp towel and set in a warm place to rise for 20 to 45 minutes, if this is the third rising; or for 45 to 90 minutes, if this is the second rising, until the tops of the loaves curve up above the sides of the pans.

About 30 minutes before baking, preheat the oven to 350 degrees F, with a rack in the middle.

Just before baking, slash the loaves across the top with a razor blade or sharp knife. Bake for 50 to 55 minutes, or until the loaves are nutty brown and respond to tapping with a hollow sound.

Unmold, running a knife around the pans to loosen the loaves, if necessary. Cool on racks.

Basic White Loaf

2 SMALL LOAVES

THIS BREAD HAS A LIGHT, MOIST CRUMB and a pleasing flavor. The dough is easy to knead and very elastic.

2   teaspoons active dry yeast
2   cups lukewarm water
     About 4-5 cups unbleached white flour
2   teaspoons salt

Dissolve the yeast in the water in a large bowl and let sit for 5 to 10 minutes, or until creamy.

Mix together 3½ cups of the flour and the salt in a medium bowl. Gradually beat the flour mixture, 1 cup at a time, into the liquid mixture, with a wooden spoon; the dough should be stiff enough to turn out onto the work surface.

Dust the work surface with flour and turn out the dough. Knead, using a pastry scraper to facilitate folding, for 10 to 15 minutes, adding flour to the work surface and to your hands as needed. At first the dough will be sticky, but it will become resilient after the first 5 minutes, and by the end of the kneading, it should be smooth and elastic. Sprinkle the work surface and your hands with more flour and shape the dough into a ball.

Rinse, dry and lightly oil the bowl. Place the dough in it and turn to coat with the oil. Cover tightly with plastic wrap and a towel and let rise in a warm spot for 1½ to 2 hours, until doubled in bulk.

Punch down the dough and let rise, covered, for another 1½ hours, or until nearly doubled in bulk.

Turn the dough out of the bowl, moisten your hands, knead it a couple of times, and shape it into a ball. Cut the ball in half and shape into 2 balls. Let rest for 10 minutes.

Now form the loaves (see page 24). Oil or butter two 8-x-4-inch loaf pans, and place the loaves in the pans, first upside down, then right side up, to coat with the oil. Let rise until the tops curve up above the sides of the pans.

About 30 minutes before baking, preheat the oven to 375 degrees F, with a rack in the middle.

Slash the loaves across the top with a razor blade or sharp knife. Bake for 50 to 55 minutes, until the loaves are brown and respond to tapping with a hollow sound.

Remove from the pans and cool on a rack.

Mixed Grain Bread, page 50

French Sourdough Country Bread, page 104

Black Bread with Poppy Seeds, page 68

English Muffins, page 238

Pizza with Sweet Peppers, page 185

Cottage Loaf, page 88

Fruit-Filled Bread, page 166

Sourdough Walnut Bread, page 120

White Country Loaf

1 LARGE ROUND LOAF

THIS BEAUTIFUL CRUSTY BREAD isn't a country loaf in the traditional sense, in that it doesn't use a sourdough starter. But the large round loaf, baked at high heat in a steamy oven, will have a hard crust and a dense crumb. The dough is altogether unlike whole wheat bread dough; it's resistant and bubbly and is very smooth at the end of kneading. A bit of rye flour is added to the dough for flavor, giving it a slightly acidic tang.

1	teaspoon active dry yeast
2	cups lukewarm water
	About 4-5 cups unbleached white flour
¼	cup rye flour
2	teaspoons salt

Dissolve the yeast in the water in a large bowl and let stand for 5 to 10 minutes, until creamy. Beat in 2½ cups of the white flour with a wooden spoon and mix until thoroughly blended. Cover with plastic wrap and a towel and let rise in a warm place for 1 hour, or until light and bubbly.

To knead by hand: Mix together the rye flour and salt in a medium bowl. Fold this mixture into the yeast mixture. Fold in 1½ cups of the white flour. Dust the work surface generously with some of the remaining flour, and turn out the dough.

Begin to knead, using a pastry scraper to facilitate folding, for 10 to 15 minutes, adding more flour to the work surface and to your hands as needed. The dough will become resilient after the first 5 minutes and by the end of the kneading, it should be smooth and elastic. Sprinkle the work surface and your hands with more flour and shape the dough into a ball.

To knead with an electric mixer: In a medium bowl, combine the rye flour, salt and 1½ cups of the remaining white flour; add to the yeast mixture all at once. Mix together with the paddle attachment. Change to the dough hook and mix on low speed for 2 minutes. Mix on medium speed for 8 to 10 minutes, adding up to 1 cup more of the flour if the dough seems very sticky. Scrape out the dough onto a floured work surface, knead a couple of times and shape into a ball.

Rinse, dry and lightly oil the bowl. Place the dough in it, turning to coat it with the oil. Cover tightly with plastic wrap and a towel and let rise in a warm spot for 2 to 3 hours, until doubled in bulk.

Lightly flour the work surface and turn out the dough. Knead a couple of times and shape into a ball.

Return the dough to the bowl, rounded side up, cover and let rise for 1 to 1½ hours, or until nearly doubled. (*Alternatively, place the dough in a banneton or a towel-lined bowl to rise and reverse out onto a baking stone; see page 100.*)

About 30 minutes before baking, preheat the oven to 400 degrees F, with a rack in the middle. Sprinkle a baking sheet or baking stone with cornmeal. Turn out the dough, reshape it into a ball and place it on the baking sheet. Let rise again slightly, about 15 minutes.

Slash the loaf across the top with a razor blade or sharp knife. Bake for 45 to 50 minutes, spraying with water a couple of times during the first 10 minutes of baking, until the loaf is dark brown and responds to tapping with a hollow sound.

Cool on a rack.

Whole Wheat Country Loaf

1 LARGE ROUND LOAF

Baked at high heat in a steamy oven, this large round loaf has a hard crust and a dense crumb. It is a marvelously hearty everyday bread, with a rich, grain-filled flavor.

1	teaspoon active dry yeast
2	cups lukewarm water
1	teaspoon malt extract (optional, page 15)
3½	cups whole wheat flour
1	tablespoon sunflower, safflower or canola oil
2	teaspoons salt
¼	cup rye flour
	About ½-1½ cups unbleached white flour

Dissolve the yeast in the water in a large bowl and let stand for 5 to 10 minutes, until creamy. Stir in the malt extract, if using. With a wooden spoon, beat in about 2½ cups of the whole wheat flour and mix until thoroughly blended. Cover with plastic wrap and a towel and set in a warm place to rise for 1 hour, or until light and bubbly.

To knead by hand: With a wooden spoon, fold the oil and the salt into the yeast mixture; fold in the rye flour. Add the remaining 1 cup of the whole wheat flour to the dough and fold in; the dough should be stiff enough to turn out onto the work surface. Dust the work surface generously with some white flour, and turn out the dough.

Knead, using a pastry scraper to facilitate folding, for 10 to 15 minutes, adding white flour to the work surface and to your hands as needed. The dough will become resilient after the first 5 minutes of kneading, and by the end of the kneading, it should be elastic and somewhat smooth. Sprinkle the work surface and your hands with more flour and shape the dough into a ball.

To knead with an electric mixer: In a medium bowl, combine the remaining 1 cup of the whole wheat flour, the salt, the rye flour and ½ cup of the white flour. Stir into the yeast mixture and add the oil. Mix together with the paddle. Change to the dough hook, and mix on low speed for 2 minutes. Mix on medium speed for 8 to 10 minutes. If the dough seems very sticky, add up to 1 cup white flour. Scrape out of the bowl onto a lightly floured work surface, knead a few times and shape into a ball.

Rinse, dry and lightly oil the bowl. Place the dough in it, turning to coat with the oil. Cover tightly with plastic wrap and a towel and let rise in a warm place for 2 to 3 hours, until doubled in bulk.

Punch down the dough and turn out onto the work surface. Knead a couple of times, and shape into a ball.

Return the dough to the bowl, rounded side up, cover and let rise for 1 to 1½ hours, or until nearly doubled. (*Alternatively, place the dough in a banneton or a towel-lined bowl to rise and reverse it onto a baking stone; see page 100.*)

About 30 minutes before baking, preheat the oven to 400 degrees F, with a rack in the middle. Sprinkle a baking sheet with cornmeal. Turn out the dough onto the baking sheet, reshape it into a ball and let rise again slightly, about 15 minutes.

Slash across the top with a razor blade or sharp knife. Bake for 45 to 50 minutes, spraying with water a couple of times during the first 10 minutes of baking, until the loaf is dark brown and responds to tapping with a hollow sound.

Cool on a rack.

Whole Grain and Whole Wheat Breads

Making Whole Grain Breads
The Sponge Technique

MANY OF THE RECIPES for hearty whole grain breads in this chapter use the sponge method of breadmaking. In this method, half of the flour is added to the yeast, liquid and sweetener, and the mixture is allowed to stand in a warm place for 1 hour. The salt, which would interfere with the yeast action, is added later.

I first learned this method following a book called *The Tassajara Bread Book*, by Edward Espe Brown, who popularized the technique by explaining it in a particularly clear and sensible way. As Brown says, "Gluten is formed when the sponge stretches in rising, which would otherwise be the product of *your* labor in kneading. This added elasticity makes the remaining ingredients more easily incorporated and kneading more easily accomplished."

The remaining flour and any other ingredients are then added, and the dough is allowed to rise two more times before the loaves are shaped and allowed to rise again. Sponge breads take longer to make than other loaves because of the extra rising at the beginning and another rising before the loaves are formed (there are four risings in all). This extra time is particularly beneficial to dense grain breads, which otherwise would be leaden.

Sponge breads don't really require more work than other breads, just more time—about 5 hours from start to finish. But don't feel that you have to stick around the house for the entire period. If you have to go out for longer than the specified rising time, you can let the dough rise in the refrigerator. Then if you leave it and it goes for an extra 30 minutes or even an extra hour, it won't adversely affect the bread.

I find that I have better luck with sponge breads if I do the kneading by hand. One of the reasons is that electric mixers don't deal very well with quantities of flour or flour and grains greater than 2 pounds, and these breads weigh about 2 pounds each. Also, the loaves are very dense, and it's important that you "get the feel" of them so that you don't add too much flour and so that you knead them sufficiently.

Mixing the Sponge

Dissolve the yeast in the water, and add the sweetener. Let sit for 5 to 10 minutes, until creamy. Using a wooden spoon or a large whisk, stir in the flour, 1 cup at a time. After all of the flour required for the sponge has been added, you will have a mixture that has the consistency of very thick mud. At this point, stir the sponge thoroughly to blend the flour and to begin the gluten-forming process.

In these recipes, I suggest stirring 100 times, changing directions a couple of times throughout the stirring. This is not as strenuous as it might sound and takes only about 1½ minutes.

Cover the bowl with plastic and a towel, and set in a warm place to rise for 1 hour. By the end of this time, the sponge should be bubbly, and you can continue adding the remaining ingredients and kneading.

Hearty Whole Wheat Bread
(Sponge Technique—Basic Recipe)

2 LOAVES

THESE LOAVES ARE NUTTY, somewhat sweet and marvelously chewy. When you mix up the dough, you'll first dissolve the yeast in the water with the sweeteners, then stir in half the flour. The resulting mud-like mixture is called a "sponge." It will rise for about an hour, allowing the yeast to begin to do its work, so that the gluten is easily developed when you add the remaining ingredients and knead the dough. Breads that rely on this method have a rich, almost cakey texture.

For the sponge

1	tablespoon active dry yeast
3	cups lukewarm water
2	tablespoons mild-flavored honey
2	tablespoons molasses, or 2 tablespoons additional honey
2	cups unbleached white flour
2	cups whole wheat flour

For the dough

¼	cup sunflower, safflower or canola oil
1	tablespoon salt
	About 3½-4½ cups whole wheat flour

For the loaves

1	egg, beaten with 2 tablespoons water, for egg wash
1	heaping tablespoon sesame seeds

To make the sponge: Dissolve the yeast in the warm water in a large bowl. Stir in the honey and molasses. With a wooden spoon or large whisk, gradually stir in the white and whole wheat flours, 1 cup at a time; the mixture will be the consistency of mud.

When all of the flour has been added, stir by hand about 100 times, changing directions every once in awhile and scraping down the sides, about 2 minutes; the sponge will be the consistency of thick mud.

Cover with plastic wrap and a towel and set in a warm place for 1 hour, until bubbly.

To make the dough: Pour the oil onto the sponge, sprinkle on the salt and fold with a wooden spoon, turning the bowl between folds. Do not stir, because this tears the dough, reducing the elasticity that results from the sponge.

Begin folding in the whole wheat flour, sprinkling it onto the dough, 1 cup at a time, and folding it in the same way, turning the bowl a quarter turn after each fold. Each cup should take about 4 turns to be incorporated.

After you've added about half of the flour, the dough should begin to pull away from the sides of the bowl in a sticky, formless mass. As soon as it is more or less cohesive, place the next cup of flour on the work surface and scrape out the dough onto it.

Flour your hands, and using a pastry scraper to facilitate folding, fold the mass of dough in half toward you. Because it will be very wet at first, just pat it together at the beginning and turn it a quarter turn. Continue to fold the dough over and gently press it together, adding flour to the work surface, to the dough and to your hands as needed. After a few turns, the dough will begin to stiffen. After 3 to 5 minutes of kneading, add flour only to the work surface, not to the surface of the dough. As you continue to knead, the dough will become stiff, elastic and resistant—harder to fold and press together. Continue kneading for at least 10 minutes, adding only small amounts of flour to the work surface and to your hands, until the dough is stiff, dense and elastic. The surface may be slightly tacky and should spring back when you press it with your finger. Shape the dough into a ball by folding it toward you and turning it a quarter turn, 4 times, without kneading. Pinch together the folds at the bottom.

Rinse, dry and lightly oil the bowl. Place the dough in it, turning to coat it with the oil. Cover again with plastic wrap and a towel and let rise in a warm place for 1 hour, until doubled in bulk.

Gently punch down the dough, cover again and let rise in a warm place for 45 to 60 minutes, until nearly doubled in bulk. (*This rise can be omitted if you are short on time; the loaves will be slightly more dense. Just punch down the dough and go on to the next step.*)

Turn out the dough onto a lightly floured work surface. Moisten your hands. Knead a couple of times and shape into a ball. Using a sharp knife, cut it in half. Shape into 2 balls and let rest for 5 minutes. Meanwhile, generously butter or oil 2 loaf pans.

To make the loaves: Form the dough into 2 loaves (see page 24) and place them in the loaf pans, first upside down, then right side up to coat with the oil. Brush the loaves with the egg wash, sprinkle with the sesame seeds and brush again with the egg wash. Cover and let rise in a warm place for 15 to 30 minutes (longer if you omitted the third rise), or until the tops of the loaves curve above the sides of the pans.

About 30 minutes before baking, preheat the oven to 350 degrees F, with a rack in the middle.

Using a razor blade or sharp knife, cut two or three ½-inch-deep slashes across the top of each loaf. Bake for 50 to 60 minutes, brushing halfway through with the egg wash. The bread is done when it is golden brown and responds to tapping with a hollow sound.

Remove from the pans and cool on a rack.

Mixed Grain Bread

2 LOAVES

I've been making this bread for about 22 years. It is dense, cakey, slightly sweet, chewy and wholesome, with a variation of flavors and textures from the different grains.

You can substitute one kind of grain for another in this bread, using wheat or rye instead of oats, cornmeal for ground millet, chickpea flour for soy flour.

This bread takes about 5 hours from start to finish, but the dough can be refrigerated after you knead it or punch it down, so you needn't feel tied to the house for all that time. Although dense and heavy, the dough is not difficult to work with. (See photograph, page 33.)

For the sponge

1	tablespoon active dry yeast
3	cups lukewarm water
2	tablespoons mild-flavored honey
2	tablespoons molasses
2	cups unbleached white flour
2	cups whole wheat flour

For the dough

¼	cup sunflower, safflower or canola oil
1	tablespoon salt
¾	cup flaked or rolled oats
¾	cup barley flakes
¾	cup bulgur or cracked wheat
⅔	cup millet, ground to a flour in a blender or spice mill, or cornmeal
½	cup soy flour or chickpea flour
	About 1½-2 cups whole wheat flour

For the loaves

1	egg, beaten with 2 tablespoons water, for egg wash
1	heaping tablespoon sesame seeds

To make the sponge: Dissolve the yeast in the warm water in a large bowl. Stir in the honey and molasses. With a wooden spoon or large whisk, stir in the white and whole wheat flours, 1 cup at a time.

When all of the flour has been added, stir by hand about 100 times, changing directions every once in awhile and scraping down the sides; the sponge will be the consistency of thick mud.

Cover with plastic wrap and a towel and set in a warm place for 1 hour, until bubbly.

To make the dough: Fold the oil, and then the salt, into the sponge, using a large wooden spoon and turning the bowl between folds. Fold in the grains and soy or chickpea flour, one at a time.

Fold in 1 cup of the whole wheat flour; the dough should hold together in a sticky mass. Place a large handful of flour on the work surface and scrape out the dough onto it. Flour your hands and begin kneading the dough, adding flour as needed. After a few minutes, the dough will begin to stiffen and become easier to work with. Knead for 10 to 15 minutes, adding more flour as necessary. The dough will be dense, but it should become stiff and elastic as you knead, with a slightly tacky surface. Shape into a ball. Rinse, dry and lightly oil the bowl. Place the dough in it, turning to coat it with the oil. Cover with plastic wrap and a towel and let rise in a warm spot for 1 hour, or until doubled in bulk.

Punch down the dough, cover again and let rise in a warm place for 45 to 60 minutes, or until nearly doubled in bulk. (*This rise can be omitted; the loaves will be slightly more dense.*) Generously butter or oil 2 loaf pans.

To make the loaves: Turn out the dough onto a lightly floured work surface. Knead a couple of times and divide the dough in half. Form into 2 loaves (see page 24) and place in the loaf pans, first upside down, then right side up, to coat with the oil.

Brush the loaves lightly with the egg wash, sprinkle with the sesame seeds and brush again. Cover and let rise until the tops of the loaves curve above the sides of the pans, 20 to 45 minutes, depending on the weather and the stage at which you shaped the loaves.

About 30 minutes before baking, preheat the oven to 350 degrees F, with a rack in the middle.

Slash the loaves across the top with a razor blade or sharp knife. Bake for 50 to 60 minutes, brushing them halfway through the baking with the egg wash. The bread is done when it is golden brown and responds to tapping with a hollow sound.

Remove from the pans and cool on a rack.

Cornmeal and Millet Bread

2 LOAVES

THIS LOVELY, GOLDEN BREAD has a rich flavor and a grainy texture. The cornmeal and millet make the bread slightly crumbly. It makes good toast.

For the sponge

1	tablespoon active dry yeast
3	cups lukewarm water
3	tablespoons mild-flavored honey
2	cups unbleached white flour
2	cups whole wheat flour

For the dough

¼	cup sunflower, safflower or canola oil or melted unsalted butter
1	scant tablespoon salt
¾	cup flaked or rolled oats
1	cup plus 1 tablespoon millet, ground (you should have 1⅓ cups ground millet)
1	cup cornmeal
	About 1½-2½ cups whole wheat flour or a mixture of whole wheat and unbleached white flours

For the loaves

1	egg, beaten with 2 tablespoons water, for egg wash
1	heaping tablespoon sesame seeds

To make the sponge: In a large bowl, dissolve the yeast in the warm water, and stir in the honey. With a wooden spoon or large whisk, stir in the white and whole wheat flours, 1 cup at a time.

When all of the flour has been added, stir by hand about 100 times, changing directions every once in a while and scraping down the sides; the sponge will be the consistency of thick mud.

Cover with plastic wrap and a towel and set in a warm place for 1 hour, until bubbly.

To make the dough: With a wooden spoon, fold the oil or butter and the salt into the sponge, turning the bowl between folds. Mix in the oats, ground millet and cornmeal. Begin folding in the whole wheat flour, 1 cup at a time. As soon as the dough is cohesive, scrape it out onto a floured work surface. Knead the dough, adding flour as needed, for

10 minutes, or until stiff and elastic. Shape into a ball. Rinse, dry and lightly oil the bowl. Place the dough in it, turning to coat it with the oil. Cover and let rise in a warm place for 1 hour, or until doubled in bulk.

Punch down the dough; cover again and let rise in a warm place for 45 to 60 minutes until nearly doubled in bulk. (*This rise can be omitted; the loaves will be somewhat more dense.*) Generously butter or oil 2 loaf pans.

To make the loaves: Turn out the dough onto a floured surface. Knead for a minute or two, then divide in half and form into 2 loaves (see page 24). Place the loaves in the loaf pans, first upside down, then right side up, to coat with the oil. Brush the loaves with the egg wash; sprinkle with the sesame seeds and brush again. Cover and let rise in a warm spot for 20 to 40 minutes, or until the tops of the loaves curve above the sides of the pans.

About 30 minutes before baking, preheat the oven to 350 degrees F, with a rack in the middle.

Slash the loaves across the top with a razor blade or sharp knife. Bake for 50 to 60 minutes, brushing halfway through with the egg wash. The bread is done when it is golden brown and responds to tapping with a hollow sound.

Remove from the pans and cool on a rack.

Sesame-Grain Bread

2 LOAVES

THIS NUTTY BREAD IS RICH, CRUNCHY and fragrant with sesame seeds and grains; it's slightly lighter than Mixed Grain Bread on page 50. It slices well.

For the sponge

1	tablespoon active dry yeast
3	cups lukewarm water
2	tablespoons mild-flavored honey
2	tablespoons molasses
2	cups unbleached white flour
2	cups whole wheat flour

For the dough

¾	cup sesame seeds
¼	cup sunflower, safflower or canola oil
1	tablespoon salt
¾	cup flaked or rolled oats
1	cup cornmeal
	About 2-2½ cups whole wheat flour

For the loaves

1	egg, beaten with 2 tablespoons water, for egg wash
1	heaping tablespoon sesame seeds

To make the sponge: Dissolve the yeast in the warm water in a large bowl. Mix in the honey and molasses. With a wooden spoon or large whisk, stir in the white and whole wheat flours, 1 cup at a time.

When all of the flour has been added, stir by hand 100 times, changing directions every once in awhile and scraping down the sides; the sponge will be the consistency of thick mud.

Cover with plastic wrap and a towel and set in a warm place for 1 hour, until bubbly.

To make the dough: Place the sesame seeds in a mortar or a food processor fitted with the steel blade and pound or process just until cracked. Do not overprocess.

Fold the oil and then the salt into the sponge, using a wooden spoon, and turning the bowl between folds. Fold in the oats and the cornmeal; fold in the sesame seeds.

Begin folding in the whole wheat flour. After about 1½ cups have been added, the dough should hold together in a sticky mass. Place a large handful of flour on the work surface and turn out the dough onto it. Flour your hands and begin kneading. Knead, adding more flour as necessary, for 10 to 15 minutes. The dough will be dense, but should become stiff and elastic as you knead, with a slightly tacky surface. Shape into a ball. Rinse, dry and lightly oil the bowl. Place the dough in it, turning to coat it with the oil. Cover and let rise in a warm place for 1 hour, until doubled in bulk.

Punch down the dough, cover and let rise in a warm place for 45 to 60 minutes, or until nearly doubled. Generously butter or oil 2 loaf pans. (*This rise can be omitted; the loaves will be slightly more dense.*)

To make the loaves: Turn out the dough onto a lightly floured work surface. Knead a couple of times and divide the dough in half. Form into 2 loaves (see page 24) and place in the loaf pans, first upside down, then right side up, to coat with the oil.

Brush the loaves lightly with the egg wash, sprinkle with the sesame seeds and brush again. Cover and let rise until the tops of the loaves curve above the sides of the pans, 20 to 45 minutes, depending on the weather and the stage at which you shaped the loaves.

About 30 minutes before baking, preheat the oven to 350 degrees F, with a rack in the middle.

Slash the loaves across the top with a razor blade or sharp knife. Bake for 50 to 60 minutes, brushing halfway through with the egg wash. The bread is done when it is golden brown and responds to tapping with a hollow sound.

Remove from the pans and cool on a rack.

Oatmeal Bread

2 LOAVES

A RICH, MOIST BREAD made with cooked flaked or rolled oats, this is one of my favorites. It makes good sandwich bread and great toast.

Leftover hot cereal makes a terrific addition to any whole wheat bread. You may have to reduce the liquid correspondingly, depending on how much you add to the dough.

For the sponge

1	cup flaked or rolled oats
2½	cups boiling water
1	tablespoon active dry yeast
½	cup lukewarm water
3	tablespoons mild-flavored honey
1	cup unbleached white flour
1	cup whole wheat flour

For the dough

¼	cup sunflower, safflower or canola oil
1	tablespoon salt
	About 2-3 cups whole wheat flour

For the loaves

1	egg, beaten with 2 tablespoons water, for egg wash
1	tablespoon sesame seeds

To make the sponge: Place the oats in a small bowl and pour the boiling water over them. Cover and let stand for at least 4 hours, or overnight.

Dissolve the yeast in the warm water in a large bowl and let stand for 10 minutes, until creamy. Stir in the soaked oats and their liquid and the honey. With a wooden spoon or large whisk, gradually stir in the white and the whole wheat flours.

When all of the flour has been added, stir by hand 100 times, changing directions every once in awhile and scraping down the sides; the sponge will be the consistency of very thick mud.

Cover with plastic wrap and a towel and set in a warm spot to rise for 1 hour, until bubbly.

To make the dough: Fold the oil and the salt into the sponge with a wooden spoon. Fold in 2 cups of the whole wheat flour, 1 cup at a time, turning the bowl between folds. When the dough coheres, scrape it out onto a floured work surface, and begin to knead, flouring your hands and adding small amounts of whole wheat flour as necessary. Knead for 10 minutes; the dough will stiffen but will still be tacky.

Shape the dough into a ball. Rinse, dry and lightly oil the bowl. Place the dough in it, turning to coat with the oil. Cover and let rise in a warm place for 1 to 1½ hours, until doubled in bulk.

Punch down the dough, cover and let rise in a warm place for 45 minutes, or until nearly doubled. (*This rise can be omitted; the loaves will be slightly more dense.*) Generously butter or oil 2 loaf pans.

To make the loaves: Turn out the dough onto a lightly floured work surface. Knead a couple of times and divide the dough in half. Form into 2 loaves (see page 24) and place them in the loaf pans, first upside down, then right side up, to coat with the oil.

Brush the loaves with the egg wash, sprinkle with the sesame seeds, and then brush again with egg wash. Cover and let rise in a warm place until the tops of the loaves curve above the sides of the pans, 20 to 40 minutes.

About 30 minutes before baking, preheat the oven to 375 degrees F, with a rack in the middle.

Slash across the tops of the loaves with a razor blade or sharp knife. Bake for 50 minutes, brushing halfway through with the egg wash. The bread is done when it is golden brown and responds to tapping with a hollow sound.

Remove from the pans and cool on a rack.

Whole Wheat Bread with Oat Bran

2 LOAVES

THE FIBER IN OATS IS SOLUBLE fiber, and research has shown that it helps lower blood cholesterol and control blood sugar levels. This bread slices and toasts beautifully.

For the sponge

1	tablespoon active dry yeast
3	cups lukewarm water
2	tablespoons mild-flavored honey
2	tablespoons molasses
2	cups unbleached white flour
2	cups whole wheat flour

For the dough

¼	cup sunflower, safflower or canola oil
1	tablespoon salt
1⅔	cups oat bran
	About 1½-2 cups whole wheat flour

For the loaves

1	egg, beaten with 2 tablespoons water, for egg wash
1	heaping tablespoon sesame seeds

To make the sponge: Dissolve the yeast in the warm water in a large bowl. Mix in the honey and molasses. With a wooden spoon or large whisk, mix in the white and whole wheat flours, 1 cup at a time.

When all of the flour has been added, stir by hand 100 times, changing directions every once in awhile and scraping down the sides; the sponge should be the consistency of thick mud.

Cover with plastic wrap and a towel and set in a warm place for 1 hour, until bubbly.

To make the dough: Fold the oil and then the salt into the sponge with a wooden spoon, turning the bowl between folds. Fold in the oat bran.

Begin folding in the whole wheat flour. After you have added about 1 cup, the dough should hold together in a sticky mass. Place a large handful of flour on the work surface and scrape out the dough onto it. Flour your hands and begin kneading, adding flour as needed. After a few minutes, the dough will begin to stiffen and will become easier to work with. Knead, adding more flour as necessary, for 10 to 15 minutes; the dough will be dense, but should become stiff and elastic as you knead, with a slightly tacky surface. Shape into a ball. Rinse, dry and lightly oil the bowl. Place the dough in it, turning to coat with the oil. Cover and let rise in a warm place for 1 hour, or until doubled in bulk.

Punch down the dough. Cover and let rise in a warm place for 45 to 60 minutes, until nearly doubled. (*This rise can be omitted; the loaves will be slightly more dense.*) Generously butter or oil 2 loaf pans.

To make the loaves: Turn out the dough onto a lightly floured work surface. Knead a couple of times and divide the dough in half. Form into 2 loaves (see page 24) and place in the loaf pans, first upside down, then right side up, to coat with the oil.

Brush the loaves lightly with the egg wash; sprinkle with the sesame seeds and brush again. Cover and let rise until the tops of the loaves curve above the sides of the pans, 20 to 45 minutes, depending on the weather and the stage at which you shaped the loaves.

About 30 minutes before baking, preheat the oven to 350 degrees F, with a rack in the middle.

Slash the loaves across the top with a razor blade or sharp knife. Bake for 50 to 60 minutes, brushing halfway through with the egg wash. The bread is done when it is golden brown and responds to tapping with a hollow sound.

Remove from the pans and cool on a rack.

Sprouted Wheatberry Bread

2 LOAVES

WHEN WHOLE WHEATBERRIES ARE SPROUTED, they become sweet and chewy. Added to bread, they make a moist loaf. Whole wheatberries can be purchased in health food stores.

To sprout wheatberries: Soak 1 cup whole wheatberries in 2 cups water for at least 10 hours or overnight. Drain and spread in a bowl, a sprouting box or a clay plant dish. Cover with a plate and set in a cool place. Water and drain twice a day for 2 days. When the berries grow short white sprouts, they are ready to use.

For the sponge

1	tablespoon active dry yeast
3	cups lukewarm water
2-3	tablespoons mild-flavored honey
2	cups unbleached white flour
2	cups whole wheat flour

For the dough

¼	cup sunflower, safflower or canola oil
1	tablespoon salt
	Sprouted wheatberries (from 1 cup whole wheatberries), coarsely chopped in a food processor or by hand
	About 4-5 cups whole wheat flour

For the loaves

1	egg, beaten with 2 tablespoons water, for egg wash
1	heaping tablespoon sesame seeds

To make the sponge: Dissolve the yeast in the warm water in a large bowl. Mix in the honey. With a wooden spoon or large whisk, mix in the white and whole wheat flours, 1 cup at a time.

When all of the flour has been added, stir by hand 100 times, changing directions every once in awhile and scraping down the sides of the bowl; the sponge should be the consistency of thick mud.

Cover and let rise in a warm place for 1 hour, until bubbly.

To make the dough: With a wooden spoon, fold the oil and then the salt into the sponge, turning the bowl between folds. Fold in the chopped sprouted wheatberries.

Begin folding in the whole wheat flour. After about 1½ cups have been added, the dough should hold together in a sticky mass. Place a large handful of flour on the work surface and turn out the dough onto it. Flour your hands and begin kneading, adding flour as needed. Knead, adding more flour as necessary, for 10 to 15 minutes. The dough will be dense, but should become stiff and elastic as you knead, with a slightly tacky surface. Shape into a ball. Rinse, dry and lightly oil the bowl. Place the dough in it, turning to coat with the oil. Cover and let rise in a warm place for 1 hour, until doubled in bulk.

Punch down the dough, cover and let rise in a warm place for 45 to 60 minutes, or until doubled. (*This rise can be omitted; the loaves will be slightly more dense.*) Generously butter or oil 2 loaf pans.

To make the loaves: Turn out the dough onto a lightly floured work surface. Knead a couple of times and divide the dough in half. Form into 2 loaves (see page 24) and place in the loaf pans, first upside down, then right side up, to coat with the oil.

Brush the loaves lightly with the egg wash, sprinkle with the sesame seeds and brush again. Cover and let rise until the tops of the loaves curve above the sides of the pans, 20 to 45 minutes, depending on the weather and the stage at which you shaped the loaves.

About 30 minutes before baking, preheat the oven to 350 degrees F, with a rack in the middle.

Slash the loaves across the top with a razor blade or sharp knife. Bake for 50 to 60 minutes, brushing halfway through with the egg wash. The bread is done when it is golden brown and responds to tapping with a hollow sound.

Remove from the pans and cool on a rack.

Buckwheat and Whole Wheat Bread

2 LOAVES

BUCKWHEAT FLOUR ADDS A DISTINCTIVE FLAVOR to this rich, earthy, slightly sour bread. It goes nicely with cheese and smoked fish.

For the sponge

1	tablespoon active dry yeast
2	cups lukewarm water
2	tablespoons mild-flavored honey
1	tablespoon molasses
1	cup low-fat plain yogurt
2	cups unbleached white flour
2	cups whole wheat flour

For the dough

¼	cup sunflower, safflower or canola oil
½	cup semolina or cracked wheat
1¼	cups buckwheat flour
1	tablespoon salt
	About 2-2½ cups whole wheat flour

For the loaves

1	egg, beaten with 2 tablespoons water, for egg wash

To make the sponge: Dissolve the yeast in the warm water in a large bowl. Stir in the honey and molasses. With a wooden spoon or large whisk, stir in the yogurt, and then the white and whole wheat flours, 1 cup at a time.

When all of the flour has been added, stir by hand 100 times, changing directions every once in awhile and scraping down the sides; the sponge should be the consistency of thick mud.

Cover with plastic wrap and a towel and set in a warm place for 1 hour, until bubbly.

To make the dough: With a wooden spoon, fold in the oil, turning the bowl between folds. In a medium bowl, mix together the semolina or cracked wheat, the buckwheat flour and the salt. Fold the mixture into the sponge. Begin folding in the whole wheat flour. As soon as the dough coheres, scrape it out of the bowl onto a floured work surface.

Flour your hands and begin to knead. Knead for 10 minutes, or until the dough is stiff and elastic, adding flour as needed. The dough will remain a bit tacky. Rinse, dry and lightly oil the bowl. Shape the dough into a ball and place it in the bowl, turning to coat with the oil. Cover and let rise in a warm place for 1 hour, or until doubled in bulk.

Punch down the dough, cover and let rise in a warm place for 45 to 60 minutes, or until nearly doubled. (*This rise can be omitted; the loaves will be slightly more dense.*) Generously butter or oil 2 loaf pans.

To make the loaves: Turn out the dough onto a lightly floured work surface. Knead a few times, then divide the dough in half. Form into 2 loaves (see page 24). Place in the loaf pans, first upside down, then right side up, to coat with the oil. Cover and let rise for 25 to 45 minutes, or until the tops of the loaves curve above the sides of the pans.

About 30 minutes before baking, preheat the oven to 375 degrees F, with a rack in the middle.

Gently brush the tops of the loaves with the egg wash. Slash the loaves across the top with a razor blade or sharp knife. Bake for 50 to 60 minutes, until the loaves are golden brown and respond to tapping with a hollow sound.

Remove from the pans and cool on a rack.

Rye-Oatmeal Bread

2 LOAVES

T HE RYE AND CARAWAY SEEDS give this bread an unmistakable savory flavor. Like Mixed Grain Bread (page 50), this one is dense. Since rye flour doesn't have gluten as does wheat flour, the bread will be somewhat heavier than an all-wheat loaf.

For the sponge

1	tablespoon active dry yeast
2½	cups lukewarm water
½	cup lukewarm coffee, or ½ cup additional lukewarm water
¼	cup molasses
2	cups unbleached white flour
2	cups whole wheat flour

For the dough

¼	cup sunflower, safflower or canola oil
1	scant tablespoon salt
2-3	tablespoons caraway seeds
1	cup flaked or rolled oats
¾	cup rye flakes, or ¾ cup additional flaked or rolled oats
1⅔	cups rye flour
	About 1-2 cups whole wheat flour

For the loaves

1	egg, beaten with 2 tablespoons water or cold coffee, for egg wash
1	heaping tablespoon caraway seeds (optional)

To make the sponge: Dissolve the yeast in the warm water in a large bowl. Mix in the coffee or additional warm water and the molasses. With a wooden spoon or large whisk, stir in the white and whole wheat flours, 1 cup at a time.

When all of the flour has been added, stir by hand 100 times, changing directions every once in awhile and scraping down the sides; the sponge should be the consistency of thick mud.

Cover with plastic wrap and a towel and set in a warm place for 1 hour, until bubbly.

To make the dough: With a wooden spoon, fold the oil and then the salt and caraway seeds into the sponge, turning the bowl between folds. Fold in the oats and rye flakes, one at a time, and the rye flour.

Begin folding in the whole wheat flour. After about ¾ cup has been added, the dough should hold together in a sticky mass. Place a generous amount of flour on the work surface and scrape out the dough. Flour your hands and begin kneading, adding flour as needed. After a few minutes, the dough will begin to stiffen and will become easier to work with. Knead, adding more flour as necessary, for 10 to 15 minutes; the dough will be dense and sticky, but should become stiff and elastic as you knead, with a slightly tacky surface. Shape the dough into a ball. Rinse, dry and lightly oil the bowl. Place the dough in the bowl, turning to coat with the oil. Cover and let rise in a warm place for 1 hour, or until doubled in bulk.

Punch down the dough, cover and let rise in a warm place for 45 to 60 minutes, until nearly doubled. (*This rise can be omitted; the loaves will be slightly more dense.*) Generously butter or oil 2 loaf pans.

To make the loaves: Turn out the dough onto a lightly floured work surface. Knead a couple of times and divide the dough in half. Form into 2 loaves (see page 24) and place in the loaf pans, first upside down, then right side up to coat with the oil.

Brush the loaves lightly with the egg wash; sprinkle with the optional caraway seeds and brush again. Cover and let rise until the tops of the loaves curve above the sides of the pans, 20 to 45 minutes, depending on the weather and the stage at which you shaped the loaves.

About 30 minutes before baking, preheat the oven to 350 degrees F, with a rack in the middle.

Slash the loaves across the top with a razor blade or sharp knife. Bake for 50 to 60 minutes, brushing halfway through with the egg wash. The bread is done when it is golden brown and responds to tapping with a hollow sound.

Remove from the pans and cool on a rack.

Rye-Oatmeal Bread with Anise and Raisins

2 LOAVES

THIS BREAD IS DELICIOUS for breakfast and with tea.

Proceed as directed but use 2 tablespoons honey and 2 tablespoons molasses instead of the ¼ cup molasses in the sponge. Replace the caraway seeds in the dough with 2 tablespoons crushed anise seeds, omit the rye flakes, increase the flaked or rolled oats to ½ cups, and add 1 cup raisins. Omit the topping of caraway seeds.

Barley Bread

2 LOAVES

Barley flour, which can be purchased in health food stores, gives this bread a malty, slightly acidic flavor. The bread has a beautiful close crumb and toasts nicely. It slices well and makes a good sandwich bread.

For the sponge

1	tablespoon active dry yeast
2½	cups lukewarm water
½	cup buttermilk or low-fat plain yogurt
2	tablespoons mild-flavored honey, or 1 tablespoon malt extract (page 15)
2	cups unbleached white flour
2	cups whole wheat flour

For the dough

¼	cup sunflower, safflower or canola oil
1	tablespoon salt
1¾	cups barley flour
	About ½-1 cup whole wheat flour

For the loaves

1	egg, beaten with 2 tablespoons water, for egg wash
1	heaping tablespoon sesame seeds

To make the sponge: Dissolve the yeast in the warm water in a large bowl. Mix in the buttermilk or yogurt and the honey or malt extract. With a wooden spoon or large whisk, mix in the white and whole wheat flours, 1 cup at a time.

When all of the flour has been added, stir by hand 100 times, changing directions every once in awhile and scraping down the sides; the sponge should be the consistency of thick mud.

Cover with plastic wrap and a towel and let stand in a warm place for 1 hour, until bubbly.

To make the dough: Fold the oil and then the salt into the sponge with a wooden spoon, turning the bowl between folds. Fold in 1 cup of the barley flour, and then the remaining ¾ cup barley flour. Gradually fold in the whole wheat flour. As soon as the dough holds together, scrape it out onto a lightly floured work surface. Flour your hands and begin kneading, adding flour to the work surface as necessary. Knead, adding more flour, for 10 minutes; the dough will be fairly stiff and elastic, with a slightly tacky surface. Shape into a ball. Cover and let rise in a warm place for 1 to 1½ hours, or until doubled in bulk.

Punch down the dough, cover and let rise again in a warm place for 45 to 60 minutes, or until nearly doubled. (*This rise can be omitted; the loaves will be slightly more dense.*) Generously butter or oil 2 loaf pans.

To make the loaves: Turn the dough out onto a lightly floured work surface. Knead a couple of times and divide the dough in half. Form into 2 loaves (see page 24) and place in the loaf pans, first upside down, then right side up, to coat with the oil.

Brush the loaves lightly with the egg wash; sprinkle with the sesame seeds and brush again. Cover and let rise until the tops of the loaves curve above the sides of the pans, 20 to 45 minutes, depending on the weather and the stage at which you shaped the loaves.

About 30 minutes before baking, preheat the oven to 350 degrees F, with a rack in the middle.

Just before baking, slash the loaves across the top with a razor blade or sharp knife. Bake for 50 to 60 minutes, or until the loaves are golden brown and respond to tapping with a hollow sound.

Remove from the pans and cool on a rack.

Black Bread with Poppy Seeds

2 LONG OR ROUND LOAVES

T HE ADDITION OF BREAD CRUMBS makes for a delightfully chewy texture in this lovely, slightly sweet, dark loaf with a close crumb. I often make it for parties and catering, because it slices nicely and the long loaf yields a lot of slices. This bread goes well with savory dips and smoked salmon. You can use the electric mixer here since there is less dough than in the other breads in this chapter. (See photograph, page 35.)

For the sponge

1	tablespoon active dry yeast
1½	cups lukewarm water
½	cup strong black coffee (can be instant), cooled to lukewarm
3	tablespoons blackstrap molasses
½	teaspoon ground ginger
1	cup fresh whole wheat bread crumbs
2	cups unbleached white flour

For the dough

¼	cup sunflower, safflower or canola oil
2½	cups rye flour
2½	teaspoons salt
¾	cup whole wheat flour
	About ¼-¾ cup unbleached white flour

For the topping

1	large egg
¼	cup coffee, cooled
	Sesame seeds or poppy seeds (optional)

To make the sponge: Dissolve the yeast in the warm water in a large bowl and let stand for 5 minutes, or until creamy. Stir in the coffee and molasses. Add the ginger and bread crumbs and mix well. With a wooden spoon or large whisk, stir in the white flour, 1 cup at a time. Stir by hand 100 times, changing directions every once in awhile and scraping down the sides, or beat with an electric mixer for 2 minutes; the sponge should be the consistency of thick mud.

Cover with plastic wrap and a towel and set in a warm place for 50 to 60 minutes, until bubbly.

To knead by hand: With a wooden spoon, fold the oil into the sponge, turning the bowl between folds. Mix together the rye flour and salt in a medium bowl; fold in. Fold in the whole wheat flour. Lightly flour the work surface and turn out the dough. Knead for 10 to 15 minutes, using a pastry scraper to help turn the dough and adding white flour as needed. At the beginning, the moistness of the dough will be discouraging, but the dough will stiffen quickly and by the end of kneading, will be very stiff and somewhat elastic but still tacky on the surface.

To knead with an electric mixer: Mix together the rye flour, salt and whole wheat flour in a medium bowl. Add the oil and the flour mixture to the sponge and mix together using the paddle. Change to the dough hook, and mix on low speed for 2 minutes. Mix on medium speed for 8 to 10 minutes, adding white flour if the mixture seems too sticky. Turn out onto a floured work surface and knead for 1 minute.

Shape the dough into a ball. Rinse, wipe dry and lightly oil the bowl. Place the dough in the bowl, turning to coat with the oil. Cover and let rise for about 1½ hours, or until doubled in bulk.

To make the loaves: Punch down the dough and turn it out onto a lightly floured work surface. Moisten your hands. Divide it in half and shape into 2 long or round loaves (see pages 24 to 25). Make the loaves high, as the dough will spread out. You can place the loaves directly into oiled baguette pans, if you are using them.

Prepare an egg wash by beating the egg into the coffee. Brush the loaves with the egg wash and sprinkle with poppy seeds or sesame seeds, if you wish. Let rise for 40 minutes, or until nearly doubled.

About 30 minutes before baking, preheat the oven to 400 degrees F, with a rack in the middle.

Slash the loaves across the top with a razor blade or sharp knife. Bake for 40 to 45 minutes, brushing halfway through with the egg wash, until the loaves are dark blackish brown and respond to tapping with a hollow sound.

Remove from the pans, if using, and cool on a rack.

Portuguese Yeast-Raised Cornbread
(*Broa*)

2 SMALL ROUND LOAVES

THE CORNMEAL GIVES THIS PORTUGUESE COUNTRY BREAD a heavenly, slightly sweet flavor and heavy, crunchy texture. It's moist with a thick, hard crust. The dough is slightly sticky but resilient and not very difficult to handle. This bread toasts well and is wonderful with soups and salads.

1	tablespoon active dry yeast
1½	cups lukewarm water
1	tablespoon sugar or mild-flavored honey
2	cups stone-ground yellow cornmeal
	About 4-4½ cups unbleached white flour
1	cup lukewarm milk
2	tablespoons olive oil
2½	teaspoons salt

Dissolve the yeast in the warm water in a large bowl. Stir in the sugar or honey and let stand for 5 minutes, until creamy.

With a wooden spoon or large whisk, stir in 1 cup of the cornmeal and 1 cup of the white flour. Stir by hand 100 times, changing directions every once in awhile and scraping down the sides; the sponge should be the consistency of thick mud.

Cover with plastic wrap and a towel and set in a warm spot for 45 minutes, until bubbly.

Stir the milk into the sponge, and then fold in the oil and salt. Fold in the remaining 1 cup cornmeal, and begin folding in the remaining 3 to 3½ cups white flour. As soon as the dough holds together, scrape it out onto a well-floured work surface, and begin to knead, using a pastry scraper to facilitate folding. Knead for 10 minutes, until the dough is smooth and elastic, flouring your hands and the work surface often. Shape into a ball.

Rinse, dry and lightly oil the bowl. Place the dough in it, turning to coat it with the oil. Cover with plastic wrap and a towel, and set in a warm place to rise for 1½ hours, or until doubled in bulk.

Punch down the dough, turn out onto the board and knead for 5 minutes. Shape into a ball again, place in the bowl, cover and let rise in a warm place for about 1 hour, or until doubled.

Turn out the dough onto a floured surface. Moisten your hands. Knead for a few minutes and divide in half. Shape into 2 tight, round loaves (see page 24). Oil 2 cake pans or a baking sheet and dust with cornmeal. Place the loaves in the pans and sprinkle the tops with cornmeal or flour. Cover loosely with a towel and let rise for 30 to 45 minutes, or until nearly doubled.

About 30 minutes before baking, preheat the oven to 450 degrees F, with a rack in the middle.

Slash the loaves across the top with a razor blade or sharp knife. Bake for 15 minutes, spraying the loaves with water a couple of times during the first 10 minutes of baking.

Reduce the heat to 400 degrees, and bake for another 15 minutes, until the loaves are dark brown and respond to tapping with a hollow sound.

Remove from the pans, if using, and cool on a rack.

Strong Black Pumpernickel

3 SMALL ROUND OR OVAL LOAVES OR 2 LARGE LOAVES

ANOTHER BLACK BREAD, this one is heavy, with a strong, spicy flavor because of the addition of vinegar, chocolate and caraway seeds. Like all rye breads, the dough is sticky, dense, heavy and unwieldy. Bear with it; the bread is delicious. Thinly slice it and eat with cheese, ham or salads.

2½	cups lukewarm water
¼	cup cider vinegar
¼	cup blackstrap molasses
1	ounce (1 square) unsweetened chocolate, chopped
2	tablespoons caraway seeds
2	teaspoons instant coffee
2	tablespoons active dry yeast
1	teaspoon sugar
3⅓	cups rye flour
1	cup bran
1	tablespoon salt
	About 2½-3½ cups unbleached white flour, or a combination of whole wheat pastry flour and unbleached white flour
1	egg, beaten with 2 tablespoons water, for egg wash
1	tablespoon poppy seeds (optional)

Combine 2 cups of the warm water, the vinegar, molasses, chocolate, caraway seeds and instant coffee in a heavy-bottomed saucepan or in the top of a double boiler and heat, stirring, until the chocolate and coffee thoroughly dissolve. Remove from the heat and let cool to lukewarm.

Dissolve the yeast in the remaining ½ cup warm water in a large bowl; add the sugar and let stand for 5 to 10 minutes, until creamy. When the water-chocolate mixture has cooled to lukewarm, stir it into the yeast mixture.

Mix together the rye flour, bran and salt in a medium bowl. Fold into the yeast mixture, 1 cup at a time. Let sit for 10 minutes.

With a wooden spoon, begin stirring in the white flour (or the combination of whole wheat pastry flour and white flour), and as soon as you can, scrape out the dough onto the work surface. Knead, adding flour as needed, for 10 minutes; the dough will be dense and tacky.

(continued on page 81)

Sourdough Country Bread with Sun-Dried Tomatoes, page 122

Brioche and Challah, pages 152 and 156

Quick Irish Tea Bread, page 217

Buttermilk Drop Scones, Stilton Scones and Fig and Orange Drop Scones, pages 224, 226 and 227

Focaccia, page 192

Sourdough Country Bread with Olives, page 124

Cheese Muffins with Sweet Red Pepper, Lemon Muffins and Orange-Date Muffins, pages 230, 232 and 234

Whole Wheat Bagels, page 94

Shape the dough into a ball. Rinse, dry and lightly oil the bowl. Place the dough in the bowl, turning to coat with the oil. Cover the bowl with plastic wrap and a towel, and set in a warm place to rise for 1½ hours, or until doubled in size.

Oil 2 baking sheets and sprinkle with cornmeal.

Lightly flour the work surface and turn out the dough. Moisten your hands. Shape the dough into a ball. Cut into 2 or 3 pieces, depending on the size loaf you desire, and shape into round or oval loaves (see page 24). Set the loaves on the baking sheet, cover with a towel and let rise until nearly doubled, about 1 hour; the dough may spread considerably. Reshape gently before preheating the oven.

About 30 minutes before baking, preheat the oven to 375 degrees F, with a rack in the middle.

Brush the loaves lightly with the egg wash, sprinkle with poppy seeds, if desired, and brush again with the egg wash. Slash the loaves across the top with a razor blade or sharp knife. Bake for about 45 minutes, brushing the loaves halfway through with the egg wash, until they are blackish brown and respond to tapping with a hollow sound.

Remove from the baking sheets and cool on a rack.

Bran Bread

1 ROUND LOAF

THIS IS MY VERSION OF A DELICIOUS BRAN BREAD made by an excellent baker in Apt, a Provençal town in the valley of the Luberon mountains. The bread is a good every-day bread. It toasts well.

This is a very wet dough, best kneaded in an electric mixer; if you don't have a mixer, knead it right in the bowl, using a pastry scraper and flouring your hands generously.

2	teaspoons active dry yeast
2	cups lukewarm water
1	teaspoon honey
1	tablespoon olive oil
½	cup bran
2½	cups whole wheat flour
2	teaspoons salt
1½-2½	cups unbleached white flour

Dissolve the yeast in the warm water in a large bowl. Stir in the honey, and let stand for 5 to 10 minutes, until creamy.

To knead by hand: Fold the oil and bran into the yeast mixture. Mix together the whole wheat flour and the salt in a medium bowl. Fold in, 1 cup at a time. Begin adding the white flour and knead the dough right in the bowl, adding white flour as needed, for 10 minutes; the dough will continue to be sticky.

To knead with an electric mixer: Combine the bran, whole wheat flour, 1½ cups of the white flour and the salt in a medium bowl. Add all at once to the yeast mixture, along with the oil. Mix together with the paddle. Change to the dough hook, and mix on low speed for 2 minutes. Mix on medium speed for 8 to 10 minutes. If the dough seems very wet and sticky, sprinkle in up to 1 cup white flour. Scrape out the dough onto a lightly floured surface and shape into a ball.

Rinse, dry and lightly oil the bowl. Place the dough in it, turning to coat with the oil. Cover with plastic wrap and a towel, and set in a warm place to rise for about 2 hours, or until doubled in bulk.

Flour the work surface; moisten your hands and scrape out the dough. Knead for a minute or so, moistening your hands and flouring the work surface as necessary, and shape the dough into a ball.

Let the dough rise again, rounded side up, in the oiled bowl, for 1 to 1½ hours, until nearly doubled in bulk. (*Alternatively, place the dough in a banneton or a towel-lined bowl to rise; see page 100.*)

About 30 minutes before baking, preheat the oven to 425 degrees F, with a rack in the middle. Oil a baking sheet and sprinkle it with cornmeal.

Gently turn out the dough onto the baking sheet or a baking stone (page 17). Moisten your hands and reshape the dough gently. Shortly before baking, slash the loaf across the top with a razor blade or sharp knife. Bake for 40 to 45 minutes, spraying the loaf with water during the first 10 minutes of baking, until the crust is hard and brown and responds to tapping with a hollow sound.

Remove from the baking sheet or stone and cool on a rack.

Scottish Whole Wheat Rolls with Sesame Seeds

8 ROLLS

THESE ARE THE TRADITIONAL MORNING ROLLS of Scotland, where they are known as baps. They have a particularly rich, buttery flavor. Serve them toasted with jam or use them as sandwich rolls.

2	teaspoons active dry yeast
¾	cup lukewarm water
½	cup lukewarm milk
1	teaspoon honey
1¾	cups whole wheat flour
¾-1¼	cups unbleached white flour
2	teaspoons salt
¼	cup (½ stick) unsalted butter, softened
	Milk, for brushing the rolls
2	tablespoons sesame seeds

In a small bowl or the bowl of your electric mixer, dissolve the yeast in the warm water and add the warm milk and honey. Let stand for 5 to 10 minutes, until creamy.

To knead by hand: Mix together the whole wheat flour, ¾ cup of the white flour and the salt in a large bowl. Rub in the butter by taking up the flour and rubbing briskly between the palms of your hands or use a food processor fitted with the steel blade, pulsing several times. Add the yeast mixture, and stir together into a soft dough. Scrape out the dough onto a floured work surface and knead, adding white flour as needed, for 10 minutes; the dough will be soft and pliable.

To knead with an electric mixer: Combine the whole wheat flour, ¾ cup of the white flour and salt in a medium bowl. Add all at once to the yeast mixture, along with the butter. Mix together with the paddle. Change to the dough hook, and mix on low speed for 2 minutes. Mix on medium speed for 8 to 10 minutes. If the dough seems very wet and sticky, sprinkle in up to ½ cup white flour. Scrape out the dough onto a lightly floured surface and knead for a minute or so by hand. Shape into a ball.

Rinse, dry and lightly oil the bowl. Place the dough in it, turning to coat with the oil. Cover with plastic wrap and a towel, and set in a warm place to rise for 1½ hours, or until doubled in bulk.

Punch down the dough and turn out onto a work surface. Moisten your hands and shape the dough into a ball. Divide into 8 equal pieces and form each into a tight, round ball (see page 25). Oil a baking sheet, dust it with cornmeal and place the rolls on the baking sheet. Brush the rolls with milk and sprinkle them with the sesame seeds, pressing the seeds lightly into the dough.

Cover with a towel and let rise in a warm place for 30 to 40 minutes, or until nearly doubled. Meanwhile, preheat the oven to 400 degrees F, with a rack in the middle.

Bake the rolls for 15 to 20 minutes, until puffed and golden.

Remove from the pan and cool on a rack.

Baguettes with Wheat Germ

4 SLENDER BAGUETTES

THE ADDITION OF WHEAT GERM and a little bit of whole wheat flour to this French bread gives it a sweet, nutty flavor. It is light and delicate. If you use the egg wash, the crust will be shiny, but not as hard as if you omit it.

2½   teaspoons active dry yeast
2½   cups lukewarm water
     Pinch of sugar
1   tablespoon melted unsalted butter or sunflower, safflower or canola oil
1   cup wheat germ
1   cup whole wheat flour
     About 5-6 cups unbleached white flour
1   scant tablespoon salt
1   egg, beaten with 3 tablespoons water, for egg wash (optional)

Dissolve the yeast in the warm water in a large bowl. Add the sugar and let stand for 10 minutes, until creamy.

To knead by hand: Fold the melted butter or oil into the yeast mixture with a wooden spoon. Mix together the wheat germ, whole wheat flour, 5 cups of the white flour and the salt in a medium bowl. Fold into the yeast mixture, 1 cup at a time. Scrape out the dough onto a lightly floured surface and knead, adding white flour as needed, for 10 minutes. The dough will be sticky at first but will become very elastic, though it will remain tacky on the surface.

To knead with an electric mixer: Combine the wheat germ, whole wheat flour, 5 cups of the white flour and salt in a medium bowl. Add all at once to the yeast mixture, along with the melted butter or oil. Mix together with the paddle. Change to the dough hook, and mix on low speed for 2 minutes. Mix on medium speed for 8 to 10 minutes. If the dough seems very wet and sticky, sprinkle in up to 1 cup more white flour. Scrape out the dough onto a lightly floured surface and knead for a minute or so by hand.

Shape the dough into a ball. Rinse, dry and lightly oil the bowl. Place the dough in it, turning to coat with the oil. Cover with plastic wrap and a towel, and set in a warm place to rise for 1½ hours, or until doubled in bulk.

Punch down the dough and let rise again until nearly doubled, about 1 hour. Meanwhile, butter or oil a baking sheet or baguette pans and sprinkle with cornmeal.

Lightly flour the work surface and turn out the dough; it will be soft and sticky. Moisten your hands and working quickly, divide the dough into 4 equal pieces. Shape each into a ball. Cover the balls you are not working on with plastic wrap, while you shape each into a baguette (see page 25). Place in the baguette pans or on the baking sheets. Brush with the egg wash, if using.

Cover the loaves with a towel and let rise for 20 to 30 minutes, or until nearly doubled. Meanwhile, preheat the oven to 400 degrees F, with a rack in the middle.

Slash the loaves across the top with a razor blade or sharp knife. Bake for 35 to 45 minutes, spraying the loaves a couple of times during the first 10 minutes of baking, until they are golden brown and respond to tapping with a hollow sound. For extra-shiny loaves, brush with the egg wash several times during the baking.

Remove from the pans, if using, and cool on a rack.

Cottage Loaf

1 LARGE ROUND LOAF

THIS IS A LOAF WITH A TOPKNOT, adapted from Elizabeth David's *English Bread and Yeast Cookery*. It's a country-type bread; the dough is enriched with a bit of whole wheat flour. It toasts well and makes a good all-purpose bread. The dough should be quite dense; don't let it rise too much the second time, or the loaf won't retain its shape. (See photograph, page 38.)

2½ teaspoons active dry yeast
2½ cups lukewarm water
   About 4½-5½ cups unbleached white flour
1⅔ cups whole wheat flour
1 tablespoon salt

Dissolve the yeast in the warm water in a large bowl. Let stand for 5 to 10 minutes, until creamy.

To knead by hand: In a medium bowl, mix together 4½ cups of the white flour, the whole wheat flour and the salt. With a wooden spoon, fold the flour mixture into the yeast mixture, 1 cup at a time. Scrape the dough out onto the work surface. Knead, adding white flour as needed, for 10 minutes; the dough should be stiff and elastic.

To knead with an electric mixer: In a medium bowl, combine 4½ cups of the white flour, the whole wheat flour and the salt, and add all at once to the yeast mixture. Mix together with the paddle. Change to the dough hook, and mix on low speed for 2 minutes. Mix on medium speed for 8 to 10 minutes. If the dough seems very wet and sticky, sprinkle in up to 1 cup more white flour. Scrape out the dough onto a lightly floured surface and knead for a minute or so by hand.

Shape the dough into a ball. Rinse, dry and oil the bowl. Return the dough to the bowl, turning to coat with the oil. Cover with plastic wrap and a towel, and set in a warm place to rise for 1½ hours, or until doubled.

Punch down the dough and turn it out onto the work surface. Moisten your hands and shape the dough into a ball. Cut the dough into 2 unequal pieces, one twice as large as the other. Shape these pieces into tight balls.

Oil a baking sheet and dust it with cornmeal. Place the larger ball of dough on the baking sheet, rounded side up; leave the smaller one in the bowl, rounded side down. Cover both pieces with plastic wrap and set in a warm spot to rise for 40 minutes, or until nearly doubled. Do not allow the dough to double in size completely, or it will collapse when you assemble the bread.

Preheat the oven to 450 degrees F, with the rack just below the middle. Flatten the top of the larger piece slightly, and using a razor blade or sharp knife, slash it with an X across the middle, about 1½ inches wide. Flatten the seam side of the smaller piece of dough slightly, and gently place it on top of the bottom piece to form a topknot.

Cover with a towel and let rest for about 10 minutes. Do not let the loaf sit for too long, or it will spread out and lose its shape; if it begins to do so, put it directly into the oven.

Bake for 40 minutes, or until the loaf is golden brown and responds to tapping with a hollow sound.

Remove from the baking sheet and cool on a rack.

Sicilian Bread

1 LARGE ROUND OR 2 SMALL LOAVES

A PALE YELLOWISH WHITE LOAF with a hard crust covered with sesame seeds, this loaf is one of the many gastronomic pleasures of Sicily. Sicilian bakers shape the loaves in a number of ways: rolled into a long cylinder and curled back and forth over itself, shaped like a small ladder, shaped like a coiled S or, as in this recipe, simply shaped into a baguette or round loaf, which is the easiest. Use finely ground semolina for this—the kind used in making pasta. Coarse semolina will be too heavy, and the loaves won't rise.

This finished bread has a dense, grainy texture and a satisfying, nutty taste. It's especially nice toasted.

2½	teaspoons active dry yeast
1	teaspoon malt extract (page 15) or honey
1½	cups lukewarm water
1	tablespoon olive oil
2	cups finely ground semolina
2	teaspoons salt
	About 1½-2 cups unbleached white flour
¼	cup sesame seeds

Dissolve the yeast and malt extract or honey in the warm water in a large bowl. Let stand for 5 to 10 minutes, until creamy. Stir in the olive oil.

To knead by hand: In a small bowl, mix together the semolina and salt. With a wooden spoon, stir the semolina mixture, 1 cup at a time, into the yeast mixture. Fold in ½ cup of the white flour. Place 1 cup of the white flour on the work surface, turn out the dough and knead, adding white flour as necessary, until smooth and firm, about 10 minutes.

To knead with an electric mixer: Mix together the semolina, 1½ cups of the white flour and the salt in a medium bowl. Add the flour mixture to the yeast mixture and mix together with the paddle. Change to the dough hook, and beat on low speed for 2 minutes. Mix on medium speed for 8 minutes, adding white flour if the dough is sticky. Scrape the dough out of the bowl onto a lightly floured surface and knead for 1 minute by hand.

Form the dough into a ball. Rinse, dry and lightly oil the bowl. Place the dough in the bowl, turning to coat with the oil. Cover with plastic wrap and a towel and let rise in a warm place for about 1½ hours, until doubled.

Lightly flour the work surface and scrape out the dough. Moisten your hands. Shape the dough into 1 large round loaf, 2 sausage-shaped loaves or 2 round loaves (see pages 24 to 25).

Lightly oil a baking sheet. Place the loaves on the baking sheet and brush thoroughly with water. Sprinkle with the sesame seeds and gently press the seeds into the dough. Brush again with water. Cover lightly with a towel and let rise for 40 minutes, or until nearly doubled. Gently reshape the dough and let rest for 10 minutes.

Meanwhile, preheat the oven to 425 degrees F, with a rack in the middle.

Slash the loaves across the top with a razor blade or sharp knife. Place the bread in the oven and bake for 10 minutes, spraying the oven with water a couple of times.

Reduce the heat to 400 degrees and bake for 25 to 30 minutes longer for 2 loaves, 40 to 50 minutes for 1 large loaf, until the loaves are golden brown and respond to tapping with a hollow sound.

Remove from the baking sheet and cool on a rack.

Fougasse

Usually made with either baguette dough or a brioche-like dough, *fougasse* is a ladder-shaped bread that is a specialty of southern France. French bakers often add anchovies, olives, nuts or herbs to their *fougasse* dough. My version incorporates a small amount of whole wheat flour into the dough, giving it a nutty flavor.

2½	teaspoons active dry yeast
1½	cups lukewarm water
1	tablespoon olive oil
2½-3	cups unbleached white flour
1¼	cups whole wheat flour
2½	teaspoons salt
⅔	cup imported black olives, pitted and chopped, *or* 1 can anchovy fillets, drained, rinsed and chopped, *or* ½ cup chopped walnuts, *or* ¼ cup chopped fresh rosemary or thyme

Dissolve the yeast in the warm water in a large bowl, and let stand for 5 to 10 minutes, until creamy. Stir in the olive oil.

To knead by hand: Mix together 2½ cups of the white flour, the whole wheat flour and the salt in a medium bowl. With a wooden spoon, fold the flour mixture into the yeast mixture, 1 cup at a time. As soon as the dough holds together, scrape it out onto a floured work surface. Knead, adding white flour as needed, for 10 minutes.

To knead with an electric mixer: Combine 2½ cups of the white flour, the whole wheat flour and the salt in a medium bowl. Add the flour mixture all at once to the yeast mixture. Mix together with the paddle. Change to the dough hook, and mix on low speed for 2 minutes. Mix on medium speed for 8 to 10 minutes. If the dough seems very wet and sticky, sprinkle in up to ½ cup more white flour. Scrape out the dough onto a lightly floured surface and knead for a minute or so by hand.

Shape the dough into a ball. Rinse, dry and lightly oil the bowl. Place the dough in the bowl and turn to coat it with the oil. Cover with plastic wrap and a towel, and set in a warm place to rise for 1½ hours, or until doubled in bulk.

Scrape out the dough onto a floured work surface. Moisten your hands. If adding any of the optional ingredients, sprinkle them over the dough and knead in for a couple of minutes.

Press or roll out the dough into a rectangle, about 12 inches long and 6 to 8 inches wide. Place the rectangle with the long sides in front of you on your work surface. Starting 2 inches from the top, make 3 parallel incisions, spacing them evenly, and cutting to within 2 inches of the edges of the dough. Pull the dough apart at these incisions so that it looks like a ladder (see illustrations, right).

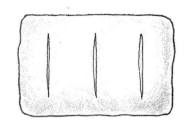

Oil a baking sheet and dust it with cornmeal. Transfer the bread to the baking sheet, lifting it gently by the ends. Cover with a damp towel. Let rise for 45 minutes, or until nearly doubled.

About 30 minutes before baking, preheat the oven to 400 degrees F, with a rack in the middle.

Bake the bread for 45 minutes, spraying with water a couple of times during the first 10 minutes, until it is golden and crusty and responds to tapping with a hollow sound.

Remove from the pan and cool on a rack.

Whole Wheat Bagels

1 DOZEN

I WAS WEANED ON BAGELS, but I never made one until I moved to Paris. Then I got homesick for them and found that making them was extremely easy. Now that I'm back in the United States, I still make my own.

The dough is easy to work with and requires only one long rise. Shaping the bagels is a snap. You simply divide the dough into small pieces, shape them into balls, flatten them slightly and stick your thumb through the middle to make the hole.

Bagels can be varied with a number of toppings, such as sesame seeds, poppy seeds, chopped onion or caraway. The dough can be made with white flour, whole wheat or rye. My standard recipe combines whole wheat and white flours. (See photograph, page 80.)

For the dough

2	tablespoons active dry yeast
1½	cups lukewarm water
1	tablespoon honey or malt extract (page 15)
2½	cups whole wheat flour or whole wheat pastry flour
2	teaspoons salt
	About ½-1 cup unbleached white flour

For the boiling

2½	quarts water
1	tablespoon sugar or malt extract

For the topping

1	egg white, mixed with 1 tablespoon water, for egg wash
2	tablespoons sesame seeds, poppy seeds, coarse salt, minced onion *or* caraway seeds (optional)

To make the dough: Dissolve the yeast in the warm water in a large bowl. Stir in the honey or malt extract and let stand for 5 to 10 minutes, until creamy.

Stir in 1¼ cups of the whole wheat flour and beat vigorously with a wooden spoon or large whisk or at medium speed with an electric mixer fitted with the paddle attachment for about 5 minutes.

To knead by hand: With a wooden spoon, fold the remaining 1¼ cups whole wheat flour and the salt into the yeast mixture. Place ½ cup white flour on the work surface and scrape out the dough onto it. Knead, adding white flour as needed, for 10 minutes, until stiff and elastic.

To knead with an electric mixer: Add the remaining 1¼ cups whole wheat flour and ½ cup white flour to the yeast mixture. Mix together with the paddle. Change to the dough hook, and mix on low speed for 2 minutes. Mix on medium speed for 8 to 10 minutes. If the dough seems very sticky, sprinkle in up to ½ cup white flour. Scrape out the dough onto a lightly floured surface and knead for about 1 minute by hand, or until stiff and elastic.

Shape the dough into a ball. Rinse, dry and lightly oil the bowl. Place the dough in it, turning to coat it with the oil. Cover with plastic wrap and a towel, and set in a warm place to rise for 1½ hours, or until doubled in bulk.

Punch down the dough and turn out onto the work surface. Divide into 12 equal pieces, shape into balls, cover lightly with plastic wrap and let rest for 5 minutes.

To shape and boil the bagels: Meanwhile, combine the 2½ quarts water and the sugar or malt extract and bring to a boil in a large pot over high heat.

Gently flatten each ball slightly and make a hole in the center by sticking your thumb through and spreading the center apart with your fingers. Stretch the hole so that it's a little larger than you want it to look when the bagels are done; as the bagels rise and bake, the holes will shrink. Place the bagels on a lightly floured surface and cover lightly with plastic wrap or a towel. Let sit for 10 minutes; the bagels will rise slightly.

Preheat the oven to 425 degrees F, with one rack in the middle and another in the upper third.

With the water at a gentle boil and using a wide spatula or a skimmer, gently lower the bagels, in batches of two or three, into the simmering water. After 30 seconds, flip them over so that they cook on both sides. Simmer for 30 more seconds, then carefully lift them out of the water and drain on a towel. Repeat with the remaining bagels.

To bake the bagels: Oil 2 baking sheets and sprinkle with cornmeal. Gently brush the bagels with the egg wash. Sprinkle with the topping of your choice and transfer the bagels to the baking sheets.

Bake for 25 to 30 minutes, switching the position of the sheets halfway through the baking, and turning the bagels after about 20 minutes, so that the bottom sides won't brown too much. The bagels are done when dark brown and shiny.

Remove from the baking sheets and cool on a rack.

Variations

Plain Bagels: Use unbleached white flour in place of the whole wheat flour.

Pumpernickel Bagels: Dissolve 2 teaspoons instant coffee and 2 tablespoons molasses in the water along with the yeast (omit the honey or malt extract). Omit the whole wheat flour, and use 1⅔ cups rye flour and 1⅔ to 2 cups unbleached white flour, as needed.

Sourdough Country Breads

Sourdough Country Breads

YOU MAY NOT KNOW IT, but right at this moment, spores of different types of wild yeast are floating around in the air of your kitchen, waiting to be cultured. When flour and water are mixed together and left out at room temperature, they attract these wild yeasts, which bakers call "friendly strains" because they encourage bread to rise. After a day at room temperature, the mixture will take on a slightly sour aroma and will expand. That is because the wild yeasts from the air feed on the sugars in the flour and multiply, releasing alcohol and carbon dioxide in the process, causing the mixture to ferment. By adding more flour and water to this "sour dough," which allows more fermentation to take place, and exposing the mixture to high heat, some enterprising human discovered breadmaking thousands of years ago.

Until the invention of active dry yeast in the nineteenth century, fermented doughs, or sourdoughs, were the only leavenings used in yeast bread. Lately, these most primitive of breads have become wildly popular—and with good reason. Breads made with sourdough leavening are slow-rising breads that are distinguishable from other breads because of their deep, rich, often acidic flavor, their thick, hard crusts and their long shelf life.

I got hooked on sourdough country breads when I lived in France, where I find them to be consistently superior to the ever-deteriorating baguette. There, I made my first sourdough mixture, which has traveled with me, in a covered jar, over the years. Every once in a while, I forget to retain a bit of dough from a batch of bread, or my starter becomes too sour for my taste, and I begin it all over again. Each one is slightly different from the one before and changes with each batch of bread, but it is always powerful and pungent. Sourdough can go neglected in the refrigerator for a few weeks, but it always comes back to life after a flour-and-water replenishment. Even after years of working with these flour-and-water leavens, I still find them miraculous, awe-inspiring. How can flour and water turn into something that makes such wonderful bread?

THERE ARE PROBABLY as many different sourdough starters and techniques for making bread with this natural leaven as there are countries. In this chapter, I've concentrated on French- and Italian-style country breads because these are the sourdoughs I like the best. In France, sourdough starter is made with flour and water only—no yeast. Called *chef*, or *levain*, breads made from these starters can be quite acidic. (Technically, the *chef* is the initial mixture of flour and water that has attracted wild yeasts; once this starter has been replenished, either by adding more flour and water to it or by saving a piece of the dough, it is referred to as *levain*.)

The starter used in Italy, called *biga*, contains a small amount of yeast and requires less time than the *levain*. Lately, inspired by Carol Field, whose *The Italian Baker* is one of my most cherished reference books, I've been using *biga* for my breads. The starter isn't replenished but is started anew each time you get ready to bake. Breads made with *biga* are less acidic than the French sourdoughs, making them slightly more convenient. I like both.

Most sourdough breads have great staying power (baguettes, which are the exception, go hard after a day or two). They can last up to a week if kept in a fairly cool place.

The starter should be refrigerated if you aren't baking every day or two. Keep it in a covered jar or bowl and bring it to room temperature before you use it. If it sits for more than a week, feed it with about ½ cup flour and ¼ cup water the day before baking, to give the yeast a boost and to render it less acidic.

General Techniques for Sourdough Country Breads

MOST OF THE RECIPES in this chapter make a large round loaf (or 2 smaller loaves) from 4 to 5 cups of flour, about 1 cup of starter and 2 cups of water. The doughs have a very different texture than those in the preceding chapter. Generally, they are not as bulky and dense, and they're much stickier, because the ratio of water to flour is higher. They can be unwieldy, but it is partly this wet quality that results in a chewy texture and rich flavor. Especially when rye flour is present, you have to resign yourself to sticky dough (it helps to wet your hands with a small amount of water when you're shaping the loaves). If you have an electric mixer with a dough hook, you'll really appreciate it with these breads.

Most of the loaves here use a combination of sourdough and commercial yeast. However, you can make most of them with no yeast at all, just the starter. The first rising time is only 1 hour, and the second one is much longer, lasting from 6 to 10 hours. This bread will have a more acidic flavor than bread made with yeast.

One of the nice things about the yeasted sourdough breads is that they are very easy to mix and require relatively little rising time. In many recipes, you can choose between 1 and 2 teaspoons of yeast. If you use only 1 teaspoon, the rising time will be longer, but the dough will develop a richer flavor. Let your tastes and time constraints be your guide. In any case, there are only two rises involved, one after mixing up the dough and kneading, the other after removing some of the starter and shaping the loaf. The breads are baked at high heat in a moist oven.

Mixing the Dough

If you're using yeast, dissolve it in the water and let it sit until the mixture is creamy (5 to 10 minutes), then stir in the sourdough. The sourdough will be quite viscous, and it will not dissolve completely. Stirring until it is partially dissolved is sufficient; don't worry if there are strands floating through the water. Kneading the dough will evenly distribute them.

If You Are Kneading the Dough by Hand

Add any oil called for, mix together the flour(s) and salt, and fold in, 1 cup at a time. As soon as you can, scrape out the dough onto the work surface. Knead, adding white flour as necessary, for 10 minutes.

If You Are Using an Electric Mixer

Combine the flour(s)—using the smaller amount if a range is given—and the salt, and add all at once to the bowl, along with the oil. Mix together with the paddle. Change to the dough hook, and mix at low speed for 2 minutes. Mix at medium speed for 8 to 10 minutes. In most of the recipes here, the dough will form a ball on the dough hook after about 5 minutes of kneading. If the dough seems very wet and sticky, sprinkle in up to ½ cup more white flour. Scrape out the dough onto a lightly floured surface and knead a few times by hand, using a pastry scraper, if necessary, to help turn the dough.

When the dough is stiff and resilient but not necessarily smooth, shape it into a ball and place in the bowl (which you have washed, dried and, in some recipes, lightly oiled). Tightly cover the bowl with plastic wrap (you can secure it with a rubber band) and a towel, and set it in a warm place to rise for no less than 2 hours and, if you are using less than 2 teaspoons yeast, at least 3, until the dough has doubled in size.

If you are replenishing your sourdough with flour and water rather than a piece of the dough, add ½ cup flour and ¼ cup water to your starter and mix together well.

Shaping the Loaves, Second Rising

My breadmaking life changed considerably quite recently when I attended a workshop given by Carol Field, who says that punching down country loaves prevents them from rising properly. Just turn out the dough and gently shape the loaves. Handling them will make them sigh and collapse a bit and develop spring for the last rise.

Sprinkle the work surface with a very small amount of flour. Moisten your hands so they won't stick to the dough. Turn out the dough onto the floured work surface. If you are replenishing your starter from the dough, remove about 1 cup (8 ounces) of the starter, and place it in a large covered jar, a crock or a bowl with a cover. Let it sit for an hour or so before refrigerating.

Shape the remaining dough into 1 or 2 balls. Make sure the balls are very tight. To do this, pull the dough from one side all the way over itself to the other, turn it a quarter turn, and continue to do this all the way around. Pinch together the seams at the bottom, cup your hands around the dough and gingerly turn it around, bouncing it lightly on the surface to get a ball. It will be sticky and unwieldy. Keep your hands moistened and use a pastry scraper, if necessary.

Using a Banneton

For the next rising, you can use what the French call a banneton, a canvas-lined basket that can be improvised by lining a bowl with a heavily floured dish towel (see page 16). The dough rises upside down in the banneton, and at the time of baking, it is reversed onto a hot baking stone or sheet. Because the dough is moist, it has a tendency to stick to the towel; be sure to dust both the dough and the towel very heavily. Form the dough into a tight ball and place upside down in the banneton. Lightly dust the bottom of the dough with flour. Cover loosely with a damp dish towel, and let rise anywhere from 45 minutes to 2 hours, depending on the recipe, until doubled in bulk.

You can also use a heavily oiled, cornmeal-dusted bowl for the second rising. The dough rises, rounded side down, in the bowl for anywhere from 45 minutes to 2 hours, depending on the recipe and until doubled in bulk.

Reshape the dough gently (it will be sticky again; oil or moisten your hands), and place it on a baking sheet that has been oiled and sprinkled with cornmeal. Let rise slightly, for 15 to 20 minutes. The loaf will spread out quickly on the baking sheet. If you use this method, your loaf won't have the floured country look of a bread that has risen in a banneton.

Baking

If you are using a baking stone, preheat it in the oven for 30 minutes to 1 hour and dust it with cornmeal. If you are using a baking sheet, brush it with oil and sprinkle with cornmeal. Place a rack in the middle and preheat the oven to 400 degrees for at least 30 minutes before baking. To achieve a really hard crust, spray the loaf or loaves with water just before putting them into the oven, and spray the oven a couple of times during the first 10 minutes of baking.

If you have used a banneton, reverse the loaf gently onto the baking sheet or hot baking stone and slash it with a razor blade or sharp knife dipped in water, making an X, several crisscross patterns or a kind of tic-tac-toe square across the top. When you reverse the bread from the banneton onto the baking stone or sheet, it may spread out quite a bit. It will rise considerably in the hot oven, but even so, your first loaves may look a little flattened. They will, though, still have a lovely crumb, texture and taste.

If the loaves have risen on baking sheets, they may have spread out too much; gently bolster up the sides with moistened or oiled hands. Spray with water and place immediately in the preheated oven.

Bake a large loaf for 45 to 50 minutes, smaller loaves for 35 to 40 minutes, or until the bread is dark brown and responds to tapping with a hollow sound. Remove from the stone or pan and cool on a rack.

Cut long slices and cut these slices into pieces, or cut the bread in half or into quarters and slice. (*Pain de Campagne* is often sold in large quarter loaves in France.)

Storing Sourdough Breads

Don't store these crusty country loaves in a breadbox. The crust will soften because of the moisture. Just keep the cut side covered with foil. To freeze, add a tablespoon of oil to the recipe if no oil is called for, and when the bread is cool, wrap it tightly in foil and seal in a plastic bag. If you don't have a large bread-eating family, you can also cut these country loaves into quarters and freeze.

French Sourdough Starter
(*Chef* or *Levain*)

ENOUGH FOR 2 LARGE LOAVES

THIS IS THE STARTER I'VE BEEN USING OVER THE YEARS for my sourdough breads. It is based on Patricia Wells' version of the starter, or *chef*, used by the famous French baker Lionel Poîlane. Unlike many sourdough starters, this *chef* isn't runny but is more like a spongy dough. You can keep it going either by saving about 1 cup of dough every time you make country bread or by "feeding" the starter, adding ½ cup flour and ¼ cup water to the starter left in the bowl after you make bread. If you use the first method, your *chef* will always be changing, especially if you vary the flours in your breads. Most of the breads in this chapter rely on a *chef* that originated with this recipe. But you can also use the Italian Sourdough Starter (*Biga*) on page 109. The *chef* travels well in a covered bowl or jar. It takes 4 days to develop.

    2   cups unbleached white flour
    1   cup water

Days 1-4: Stir together ½ cup flour and ¼ cup water in a medium bowl. Stir with a wooden spoon or knead gently until the mixture is uniform; it will be sticky and soft. Place in a bowl and cover with plastic wrap, or place in a large jar or crock and cover. Leave overnight at room temperature.

Every day for the next 3 days, add ½ cup flour and ¼ cup water to the mixture and stir or knead together until smooth. Return to the bowl or jar and cover. The starter will expand slightly and begin to take on an acidic aroma after the second day.

Day 5: Now you are ready to make bread. Proceed with the recipe of your choice. Try making bread with no yeast (page 103) first. If you do, use all of the *chef* the first time, then use only 1 cup in subsequent loaves. (The *chef* gets stronger with time, so you need less of it.)

If you bake bread less than once or twice a week, feed the starter every few days by stirring in ½ cup white flour and ¼ cup water.

No-Yeast Sourdough Country Bread
(*Pain de Campagne*)

1 LARGE ROUND LOAF

Many bakers add no yeast to their country bread, because the starter it-self gives enough leaven. Whether or not you get good bread without using yeast depends on the strength of your starter. If you bake bread often, the *chef* will be powerful. But if it sits for over 5 days, it loses some of its strength.

1   cup French Sourdough Starter (page 102)
2   cups water, at room temperature
     About 4-5 cups unbleached white flour, or use half white flour and half
         whole wheat flour
2   teaspoons salt

Whisk together the sourdough starter and the water in a large bowl until the starter is thoroughly dissolved.

To knead by hand: Combine 3½ cups flour and the salt in a medium bowl. Using a wooden spoon, gradually fold the flour mixture into the sourdough starter mixture. Flour the work surface and scrape out the dough. Using a pastry scraper to help fold the dough, knead for 10 to 15 minutes, adding more flour as needed. Shape into a ball.

To knead with an electric mixer: Combine 4 cups flour and the salt and add to the sourdough mixture all at once. Mix together briefly using the paddle, until combined. Scrape off the paddle, replace it with the dough hook, and knead on low speed for 2 minutes. Mix at medium speed for 8 to 10 minutes, adding up to 1 cup of flour if the dough seems liquid (it will be slightly sticky). Scrape onto a floured work surface, knead a few times and shape into a ball.

Rinse, dry and lightly oil the bowl. Place the dough in it and cover with plastic wrap and a towel. Let rise in a warm spot for 2 hours. It will rise slightly.

Scrape the dough onto a lightly floured work surface. (*If you are replenishing the sour-dough starter, remove 1 cup of the dough and place in a bowl to use for your next loaf. Cover the starter and refrigerate after a few hours, if not using again in a day's time.*) Moisten your hands. Form a tight, round loaf with the remaining dough (see page 100).

Generously oil a 2-quart bowl and dust with cornmeal. Dust the top of the loaf with flour and place, rounded side down, in the bowl. Cover with a towel and let rise in a warm place for 8 to 12 hours, until nearly doubled in bulk. (*Alternatively, place the dough in a banneton or a towel-lined bowl to rise; see page 100.*)

About 30 minutes before baking, preheat the oven to 400 degrees F, with a rack in the middle.

Gently turn out the dough onto an unoiled baking sheet or a hot baking stone. Slash across the top with a razor blade or sharp knife. Bake for 45 to 50 minutes, spraying a couple of times with water during the first 10 minutes of baking, until the loaf is brown and responds to tapping with a hollow sound.

Remove from the stone or pan and cool on a rack.

French Sourdough Country Bread

1 LARGE ROUND OR 2 SMALL LOAVES

Bakers in France are required by law to use 5 percent rye flour in their country breads. Because I find white flour a little bland, I use a tiny bit more than 5 percent rye flour and I sometimes add a small amount of semolina; but this is optional. This very sticky dough yields a chewy, resilient, slightly sour loaf with a thick, hard crust. (See photograph, page 34.)

Note: Usually, I use only 1 teaspoon of yeast and let the dough rise for up to 3 hours. A long-rising, naturally fermenting dough will have a more complex flavor, a moister texture and a harder crust than a shorter-rising dough. But if you don't want such a long rising time, use 2 teaspoons of yeast.

1-2	teaspoons active dry yeast (see note above)
2	cups lukewarm water
1	cup French Sourdough Starter (page 102)
½	cup rye flour
½	cup finely ground semolina (optional; replace with unbleached white flour, if not using)
	About 4-5 cups unbleached white flour
2½	teaspoons salt

Dissolve the yeast in the warm water in a large bowl and let stand for 10 minutes, until creamy.

Stir in the sourdough starter; mix together well.

To knead by hand: Using a wooden spoon, stir the rye flour and the semolina into the yeast mixture. In a medium bowl, combine 4 cups white flour and the salt and gradually fold into the yeast mixture. Flour the work surface and scrape out the dough. Using a pastry scraper to help fold the dough, knead for 10 to 15 minutes, adding flour to the surface and to your hands as needed; the dough will be very sticky.

To knead with an electric mixer: Add the rye flour and the semolina to the yeast mixture. Combine 4 cups white flour and the salt in a medium bowl and add all at once to the yeast mixture. Mix together briefly using the paddle, until everything is combined. Scrape the dough off the paddle, replace it with the dough hook and knead on low speed for 2 minutes. Mix on medium speed for 8 to 10 minutes, adding up to 1 cup flour as needed. Turn out onto a floured surface and knead a few times.

Shape the dough into a ball. Rinse, dry and lightly oil the bowl. Place the dough in it, turning to coat with the oil. Cover with plastic wrap and a towel and let rise in a warm place for 1½ to 3 hours, or until doubled in bulk.

Scrape out the dough onto a lightly floured surface. Moisten your hands and knead for 1 minute, using a pastry scraper to manipulate the sticky dough. (*If you are replenishing the sourdough starter, remove a heaped cup of the dough and place in a bowl to use for your next loaf. Cover the starter and refrigerate after a few hours, if not using again in a day's time.*)

Shape the dough into 1 or 2 tight, round loaves (see page 100).

Dust the top of the bread with flour and let rise in an oiled bowl or bowls in a warm place for about 1½ hours, until nearly doubled in bulk. (*Alternatively, place the dough in a banneton or a towel-lined bowl to rise; see page 100.*)

About 30 minutes before baking, preheat the oven to 400 degrees F, with a rack in the middle.

If you are not using a baking stone, oil a baking sheet and dust it with cornmeal. Gently turn out the dough onto the baking sheet. Let rise slightly, about 15 minutes; omit this step if you are baking directly on a stone.

Slash across the top of the bread with a razor blade or sharp knife. Bake for 40 to 50 minutes, spraying the bread with water a couple of times during the first 10 minutes of baking, until the bread is brown and responds to tapping with a hollow sound.

Remove from the stone or pan and cool on a rack.

Whole Wheat Sourdough Country Bread

1 LARGE ROUND LOAF

THIS BREAD IS A MAINSTAY IN MY HOME. It has a tart, earthy flavor and a hard crust. Chewy and dense, it has great staying power. Sometimes I use all whole wheat flour, but more often I use two-thirds whole wheat flour and one-third unbleached white. Or I combine varying quantities of whole wheat, white and other flours, such as buckwheat or rye.

Note: I use only 1 teaspoon of yeast, and let the dough rise for up to 3 hours. But if you don't want such a long rising time, use 2 teaspoons.

> 1-2 teaspoons active dry yeast (see note above)
> 2 cups lukewarm water
> 1 cup French Sourdough Starter (page 102)
> 3⅓ cups whole wheat flour
> About 1-2 cups unbleached white flour
> 2½ teaspoons salt

Dissolve the yeast in the warm water in a large bowl and let stand for 10 minutes, until creamy.

Stir in the sourdough starter and mix together well.

To knead by hand: In a medium bowl, combine the whole wheat flour, 1 cup of the white flour and the salt. Gradually fold the flour mixture into the yeast mixture with a wooden spoon. Flour the work surface and scrape out the dough. Using a pastry scraper to help fold the dough, knead for 10 to 15 minutes, adding flour to the surface and to your hands as needed.

To knead with an electric mixer: Combine the whole wheat flour, 1 cup of the white flour and the salt in a medium bowl. Add all at once to the yeast mixture. Mix together briefly using the paddle, until everything is combined. Scrape the dough off the paddle, replace it with the dough hook and knead on low speed for 2 minutes. Mix on medium speed for 8 to 10 minutes, adding up to 1 cup white flour if the dough seems very moist (it should be sticky). Turn out onto a floured surface and knead a few times.

Shape the dough into a ball. Rinse, dry and lightly oil the bowl. Place the dough in the bowl, turning to coat with the oil. Cover with plastic wrap and a towel and let rise in a warm place for 1½ to 3 hours, until doubled in bulk.

Lightly flour the work surface and scrape out the dough. (*If you are replenishing the sourdough starter, remove a heaped cup and place in a bowl to use for your next loaf. Cover the starter, and refrigerate after a few hours, if not using again in a day's time.*)

Oil the bowl lightly, dust it with cornmeal and moisten your hands. Form the dough into a tight, round loaf (see page 100). Dust the surface with flour and return to the bowl, rounded side down. Cover with a towel and let rise in a warm place for about 1½ hours, or until nearly doubled in bulk. (*Alternatively, place the dough in a banneton or a towel-lined bowl to rise; see page 100.*)

About 30 minutes before baking, preheat the oven to 400 degrees F, with a rack in the middle.

If you are not using a baking stone, oil a baking sheet and dust it with cornmeal. Gently turn out the dough onto the baking sheet. Let rise slightly, about 20 minutes; omit this step if you are baking directly on a stone.

Slash across the top with a razor blade or sharp knife just before baking. Bake for 45 to 50 minutes, spraying the loaf with water a couple of times during the first 10 minutes, until it is brown and responds to tapping with a hollow sound.

Remove from the stone or pan and cool on a rack.

Sourdough Country Bread with Raisins

1 LARGE ROUND LOAF

I LOVE THE CONTRASTING FLAVORS of sweet raisins and sourdough bread. It's especially nice for breakfast or tea.

Proceed as for Whole Wheat Sourdough Country Bread (page 106), using 1¼ cups rye flour and 2 cups whole wheat flour with the white flour.

Before the first rise, turn out the dough as directed, and knead in 2 cups raisins or currants. Proceed as directed.

Dark Whole Wheat Sourdough Country Bread

1 LARGE ROUND LOAF

THE COFFEE AND THE MOLASSES in this dense bread make a very dark loaf.

2½	teaspoons active dry yeast
2	cups lukewarm water, or 1½ cups lukewarm water mixed with
	½ cup lukewarm coffee
1	cup French Sourdough Starter (page 102)
1	tablespoon molasses
2½	teaspoons salt
	About 4-5 cups whole wheat flour

Proceed as for Whole Wheat Sourdough Country Bread (page 106), adding the molasses after you stir in the starter. Begin with 4 cups whole wheat flour and gradually knead in the remainder, as needed. (Omit the white flour.)

Italian Sourdough Starter
(*Biga*)

MAKES 2 CUPS, ENOUGH FOR 2 LARGE LOAVES

UNLIKE FRENCH SOURDOUGH STARTER (page 102), this Italian starter contains a small amount of yeast. It allows the *biga* to ferment quickly, so that it can be used as soon as 4 hours after mixing it up. However, I like to let it develop for a day, and use half of it the first day and the other half the next, to make 1 large loaf at a time. The recipe is based on the *biga* in Carol Field's *The Italian Baker*.

¼	teaspoon active dry yeast
¼	cup lukewarm water
¾	cup water, at room temperature
2¼	cups unbleached white flour

Dissolve the yeast in the warm water in a medium bowl and let stand for 5 minutes, or until it begins to cloud.

Add the room-temperature water. Gradually stir in the flour, using a wooden spoon or an electric mixer fitted with the paddle. Stir or knead until the mixture is uniform. It will be a slightly sticky dough. Tightly cover the bowl with plastic wrap and a towel and set in a warm place for 4 to 24 hours before using. It will be quite bubbly after 1 day.

Italian Sourdough Country Loaf

1 LARGE ROUND LOAF

THIS HEARTY, CRUSTY BREAD, made with a combination of whole wheat and white flours, calls for less yeast than the other sourdough breads in this chapter and consequently has a longer rising time. It makes a moist loaf with a rich, nutty flavor and slices very nicely.

1	teaspoon active dry yeast
2	cups lukewarm water
1	teaspoon malt extract (page 15, optional)
1	cup Italian Sourdough Starter (page 109)
2½	cups whole wheat flour, preferably finely ground
2½	teaspoons salt
	About 2-2½ cups unbleached white flour

Dissolve the yeast in the warm water in a large bowl and let stand for 5 to 10 minutes, until creamy. Stir in the malt extract, if using, and the sourdough starter.

To knead by hand: Combine the whole wheat flour and salt in a medium bowl and gradually stir into the yeast mixture with a wooden spoon. Fold in 1 cup of the white flour and place a large handful of white flour on the work surface. Scrape out the dough and begin to knead, using a pastry scraper to facilitate folding, flouring your hands and the work surface often. Knead for 10 to 15 minutes, until the dough is stiff, elastic and somewhat smooth.

To knead with an electric mixer: Combine the whole wheat flour, the salt and 2 cups of the white flour in a medium bowl. Add to the yeast mixture all at once. Mix together with the paddle. Change to the dough hook and knead for 2 minutes on low speed. Mix for 8 to 10 minutes on medium speed, adding up to ½ cup more flour if the dough seems very sticky. Finish kneading on a floured work surface for about 2 minutes.

Shape the dough into a ball. Rinse, dry and lightly oil the bowl. Place the dough in it, turning to coat with the oil. Cover with plastic wrap and a towel and let rise in a warm place for 3 hours, or until doubled.

Lightly flour the work surface and scrape out the dough. (*If you are replenishing the sour-dough starter, remove a heaped cup and place in a bowl to use for your next loaf. Cover and refrigerate after a few hours, if not using again in a day's time.*) Moisten your hands and shape the dough into a tight, round loaf (see page 100). Return the dough to the bowl. Let rise for 1 to 2 hours, until nearly doubled in bulk. (*Alternatively, place the dough on a banneton or a towel-lined bowl to rise; see page 100.*)

About 30 minutes before baking, preheat the oven to 400 degrees F, with a rack in the middle.

If you are not using a baking stone, oil a baking sheet and sprinkle it with cornmeal. Gently turn out the dough on the baking sheet. Let rise slightly for 15 to 20 minutes; omit this step if you are baking directly on the stone.

Slash across the top of the dough with a razor blade or sharp knife just before baking. Bake for 45 to 55 minutes, spraying the loaf with water during the first 10 minutes of baking, until it is dark brown and responds to tapping with a hollow sound.

Remove from the stone or pan and cool on a rack.

Sourdough Country Bread with Cornmeal and Oats

1 ROUND LOAF

Dense, hearty and delicious, this bread has a thick, hard crust, a yellowish color and a close crumb.

 2 teaspoons active dry yeast
 2 cups lukewarm water
 1 cup French or Italian Sourdough Starter (page 102 or 109)
 1 cup rolled or flaked oats
 1 cup cornmeal
 2½ teaspoons salt
 About 3-4 cups unbleached white flour

Dissolve the yeast in the warm water in a large bowl and let stand for 10 minutes, until creamy.

Stir in the sourdough starter and combine thoroughly.

To knead by hand: With a wooden spoon, stir the oats, cornmeal and salt into the yeast mixture. Gradually add the white flour and fold in. By the time you have added 2 cups, you should be able to knead. Add ½ cup white flour to the work surface and scrape out the dough. Using a pastry scraper to help fold the dough, knead for 10 to 15 minutes, adding white flour as needed; the dough should be smooth and resilient.

To knead with an electric mixer: Combine the oats, cornmeal and salt and add to the yeast mixture. Add 2 cups white flour and mix together briefly, using the paddle, until everything is combined. Scrape off the paddle and replace it with the dough hook. Knead on low speed for 2 minutes. Mix on medium speed for 8 to 10 minutes, adding up to 2 cups white flour if the dough seems very wet (it will be sticky). Scrape out onto a floured work surface, knead a few times and shape into a ball.

Rinse, dry and lightly oil the bowl. Place the dough in it, turning to coat with the oil. Cover with plastic wrap and a towel and let rise in a warm place for 1½ to 2 hours, until doubled in bulk.

Lightly flour the work surface and scrape out the dough. Moisten your hands and knead the dough for a minute, using a pastry scraper to help manipulate it. (*If you are replenishing the sourdough starter, remove a heaped cup and place it in a bowl. Cover the starter, and refrigerate after a few hours, if not using again in a day's time.*)

Form the dough into a tight, round loaf (see page 100). Return it to the bowl and let rise for about 1½ hours, until nearly doubled in bulk. (*Alternatively, place the dough in a banneton or a towel-lined bowl to rise; see page 100.*)

Preheat the oven to 400 degrees F, with a rack in the middle.

If you are not using a baking stone, oil a baking sheet and sprinkle it with cornmeal. Gently turn out the dough onto the baking sheet. Let rise slightly, about 20 minutes; omit this step if you are baking directly on a stone.

Slash across the top of the loaf with a razor blade or sharp knife. Bake for 45 to 50 minutes, spraying with water a couple of times during the first 10 minutes of baking, until the loaf is brown and responds to tapping with a hollow sound.

Remove from the stone or pan and cool on a rack.

Sourdough Baguettes

2 LOAVES

THESE BAGUETTES ARE CHEWY AND CRUNCHY. They won't keep as well as round sourdough loaves because of their long, thin shape. They go well with any meal and are good for making croutons.

2	teaspoons active dry yeast
1	cup lukewarm water
1	teaspoon malt extract (page 15)
1	tablespoon sunflower, safflower or canola oil
½	cup French or Italian Sourdough Starter (page 102 or 109)
1½	cups whole wheat flour
1½	teaspoons salt
	About ½-1 cup unbleached white flour

Dissolve the yeast in the warm water in a large bowl and let stand for 5 to 10 minutes, until creamy. Stir in the malt extract and oil. Stir in the sourdough starter.

To knead by hand: Mix together the whole wheat flour and the salt in a medium bowl and stir gradually into the yeast mixture with a wooden spoon. Place ½ cup of the white flour on the work surface and scrape out the dough. Begin to knead, adding flour as needed. Knead for 10 minutes. Shape into a ball; the dough will be slightly sticky.

To knead with an electric mixer: Combine the whole wheat flour, salt and ½ cup of the white flour and add to the yeast mixture all at once. Mix together with the paddle. Scrape off the dough and change to the dough hook. Knead on low speed for 2 minutes. Mix on medium speed for 8 to 10 minutes. Add more white flour as needed. Scrape out of the bowl onto a floured work surface, knead a few times and shape into a ball.

Rinse, dry and lightly oil the bowl. Place the dough in it, turning to coat with the oil. Cover with plastic wrap and a towel and set in a warm place to rise for 2 hours, or until doubled.

Turn out the dough onto a lightly floured surface. Knead for a few minutes. (*If you are replenishing the sourdough starter, remove a heaped cup and place it in a bowl. Cover the starter, and refrigerate after a few hours, if not using again in a day's time.*)

Divide dough in half. Shape into 2 long, slender baguette-shaped loaves (see page 25).

Oil baguette pans or a baking sheet and dust with cornmeal. Place the loaves in the pans, cover and let rise for about 1 hour, until nearly doubled in bulk.

About 30 minutes before baking, preheat the oven to 400 degrees F, with a rack in the middle.

Slash the loaves 3 or 4 times across on the diagonal with a razor blade or sharp knife. Bake for 30 to 35 minutes, spraying with water a couple of times during the first 10 minutes of baking, until the loaves are brown and respond to tapping with a hollow sound.

Remove from the pan(s), if using, and cool on a rack.

Whole Wheat and Buckwheat Sourdough Bread

1 LARGE ROUND LOAF

A LITTLE BIT OF BUCKWHEAT FLOUR added to the dough gives this bread a distinctive earthy flavor. Buckwheat flour has a strong taste, so you don't need much.

2	teaspoons active dry yeast
2	cups lukewarm water
1	cup French or Italian Sourdough Starter (page 102 or 109)
3⅓	cups whole wheat flour
½	cup buckwheat flour
2½	teaspoons salt
	About ¾-1¼ cups unbleached white flour

Dissolve the yeast in the warm water in a large bowl and let stand for 10 minutes, until creamy.

Stir in the sourdough starter and combine thoroughly.

To knead by hand: Combine the whole wheat flour, buckwheat flour and salt in a medium bowl. Using a wooden spoon, gradually fold the flour mixture into the yeast mixture. By the time you have added all of it, you should be able to knead. Add about ½ cup white flour to the work surface and scrape out the dough. Using a pastry scraper to help fold the dough, knead for 10 to 15 minutes, adding white flour as needed.

To knead with an electric mixer: Combine the whole wheat flour, buckwheat flour, salt and ½ cup white flour in a medium bowl; add to the yeast mixture. Mix together briefly using the paddle, until everything is combined. Scrape off the paddle, replace it with the dough hook and knead on low speed for 2 minutes. Mix on medium speed for 8 to 10 minutes, adding up to ¾ cup more white flour if the dough seems very wet (it will be sticky). Scrape out onto a floured surface, knead a few times and shape into a ball.

Rinse, dry and lightly oil the bowl. Place the dough in it, turning to coat with the oil. Cover and let rise in a warm place for 2 hours, until doubled in bulk.

Lightly flour the work surface and scrape out the dough. (*If you are replenishing the sourdough starter, remove a heaped cup and place in a bowl. Cover and refrigerate after a few hours, if not using again in a day's time.*) Moisten your hands and knead the dough a few times.

Form the dough into a tight, round loaf (see page 100). Return it to the bowl and let rise for about 1½ hours, or until nearly doubled in bulk. (*Alternatively, place the dough in a banneton or a towel-lined bowl to rise; see page 100.*)

Preheat the oven to 400 degrees F, with a rack in the middle.

If you are not using a baking stone, oil a baking sheet and dust it with cornmeal. Gently turn out the dough onto the baking sheet. Let rise slightly, about 20 minutes; omit this step if you are baking directly on a stone.

Shortly before baking, slash across the top with a razor blade or sharp knife. Bake for 45 to 50 minutes, spraying with water a couple of times during the first 10 minutes of baking, until the loaf is brown and responds to tapping with a hollow sound.

Remove from the stone or pan and cool on a rack.

Sourdough Bran Bread

1 LARGE ROUND LOAF

THIS HIGH-FIBER BREAD HAS A GREAT, DENSE, CHEWY TEXTURE and a moist crumb. If you use the molasses, it will be quite dark and somewhat sweet. A hearty morning bread, it is hefty and sticks to your ribs.

2½	teaspoons active dry yeast
2	cups lukewarm water
1	tablespoon molasses (optional)
1	cup French or Italian Sourdough Starter (page 102 and 109)
2	cups bran
2½	cups whole wheat flour
2½	teaspoons salt
	About ¼-½ cup unbleached white flour

Dissolve the yeast in the warm water in a large bowl. Let stand for 5 to 10 minutes, until creamy.

Stir in the molasses, if using, and the sourdough starter.

To knead by hand: Stir in the bran. Mix together the whole wheat flour and the salt in a medium bowl, and fold into the yeast mixture, 1 cup at a time. As soon as you can, scrape out the dough onto the work surface. Add a handful of white flour to the work surface and knead for 10 minutes; the dough will be dense and tacky.

To knead with an electric mixer: Combine the bran, whole wheat flour and salt in a medium bowl, and add all at once to the yeast mixture. Mix together with the paddle, then change to the dough hook. Mix on low speed for 2 minutes. Mix on medium speed for 8 to 10 minutes. If the dough seems very wet and sticky, sprinkle in up to ½ cup of the white flour. Scrape out the dough onto a lightly floured surface and knead for a minute or so by hand.

Shape the dough into a ball. Rinse, dry and lightly oil the bowl. Place the dough in it, turning to coat with the oil. Cover with plastic wrap and a towel, and set in a warm place to rise for 1½ to 2 hours, or until doubled in bulk.

Lightly flour the work surface and turn out the dough. Moisten your hands and shape the dough into a tight, round loaf (see page 100). Oil a baking sheet and dust it with cornmeal. Place the loaf on the baking sheet. Cover lightly with a towel and let rise for 45 to 60 minutes, or until nearly doubled. (*Alternatively, place the dough in a banneton or a towel-lined bowl to rise; see page 100.*)

About 30 minutes before baking, preheat the oven to 400 degrees F, with a rack in the middle.

Shortly before baking, slash across the top with a razor blade or sharp knife. Bake for 45 to 50 minutes, spraying with water a couple of times during the first 10 minutes of baking, until the loaf is brown and responds to tapping with a hollow sound.

Remove from the pan and cool on a rack.

Sourdough Walnut Bread

1 LARGE ROUND OR 2 SMALL LOAVES

ONE OF MY FAVORITE FRENCH BREADS is this country bread with walnuts. It is a fairly dark bread made with whole wheat flour. It goes especially well with cheese. (See photograph, page 40.)

2	teaspoons active dry yeast
2	cups lukewarm water
1	cup French or Italian Sourdough Starter (page 102 or 109)
1	tablespoon walnut oil (optional)
3⅓	cups whole wheat flour
2½	teaspoons salt
	About 1-2 cups unbleached white flour
2	cups broken walnut pieces

Dissolve the yeast in the warm water in a large bowl and let stand for 5 to 10 minutes, until creamy.

Stir in the sourdough starter and the walnut oil, if using, and combine thoroughly.

To knead by hand: Combine the whole wheat flour and the salt in a medium bowl, and gradually fold into the yeast mixture. Add ½ cup white flour to the work surface and scrape out the dough. Using a pastry scraper to help fold the dough, knead for 10 to 15 minutes, adding white flour as needed.

To knead with an electric mixer: Combine the whole wheat flour, salt and 1 cup white flour in a medium bowl. Add to the yeast mixture all at once, and mix together briefly using the paddle, until everything is combined. Scrape the dough off the paddle, replace it with the dough hook and knead on low speed for 2 minutes. Mix on medium speed for 8 to 10 minutes, adding up to 1 cup white flour as necessary. Scrape out onto a floured surface and knead a few times.

Rinse, dry and lightly oil the bowl. Shape the dough into a ball and place the dough in it, turning to coat with oil. Cover with plastic wrap and a towel and let rise in a warm place for 1½ to 2 hours, or until doubled in bulk.

Lightly flour the work surface and scrape out the dough. Moisten your hands and knead the dough for a minute or so, using a pastry scraper to help. (*If you are replenishing the sourdough starter, remove a heaped cup and place in a bowl. Cover and refrigerate after a few hours, if not using again in a day's time.*)

Press out the dough to an approximately 1-inch-thick round and sprinkle the walnuts over the surface. Fold the dough over and knead for a couple of minutes, until the walnuts are evenly distributed.

Form the dough into 1 or 2 tight, round loaves (see page 100). Return the large ball to the bowl and cover with a towel; if making smaller loaves, let them rise directly on oiled, cornmeal-dusted baking sheets. (*Alternatively, place the dough in a banneton or a towel-lined bowl to rise; see page 100.*) Let rise in a warm place for 45 to 60 minutes, or until nearly doubled in bulk.

Preheat the oven to 400 degrees F, with a rack in the middle.

If you are not using a baking stone, oil a baking sheet and dust it with cornmeal. Gently turn out the dough onto the baking sheet. Let rise slightly, about 20 minutes; omit this step if you are baking directly on a stone.

Shortly before baking, slash across the top with a razor blade or sharp knife. Bake for 40 to 50 minutes, spraying with water a couple of times during the first 10 minutes, until the bread is brown and responds to tapping with a hollow sound.

Remove from the stone or pan and cool on a rack.

Sourdough Country Bread with Sun-Dried Tomatoes

1 LARGE ROUND OR 2 SMALL LOAVES

THIS IS A LOVELY, SAVORY COUNTRY BREAD brimming with sun-dried tomatoes that perfume the entire loaf. It goes nicely with pasta and with goat cheese. (See photograph, page 73.)

2½	teaspoons active dry yeast
2	cups lukewarm water
1	cup French or Italian Sourdough Starter (page 102 or 109)
1	cup whole wheat flour
½	cup finely ground semolina
	About 3-4 cups unbleached white flour
2½	teaspoons salt
1½	cups sun-dried tomatoes (preferably marinated in olive oil and drained), chopped

Dissolve the yeast in the warm water in a large bowl and let stand for 5 to 10 minutes, until creamy.

Stir in the sourdough starter; mix together well.

To knead by hand: Combine the whole wheat flour, semolina, 3 cups of the white flour and the salt in a medium bowl. Gradually fold the flour mixture into the yeast mixture. Flour the work surface and scrape out the dough. Using a pastry scraper to help fold the dough, knead for 10 to 15 minutes, adding flour to the surface and to your hands as necessary.

To knead with an electric mixer: Combine the whole wheat flour, semolina, 3 cups of the white flour and the salt in a medium bowl. Add all at once to the yeast mixture. Mix together briefly using the paddle, until everything is combined. Scrape the dough off the paddle and replace it with the dough hook. Knead on low speed for 2 minutes. Mix on medium speed for 8 to 10 minutes, adding up to 1 cup more white flour if the dough seems very liquid (it should be sticky). Turn out onto a floured surface and knead a few times.

Rinse, dry and lightly oil the bowl. Place the dough in it, turning to coat with the oil. Cover with plastic wrap and a towel and let rise in a warm place for 1½ to 2 hours, until doubled in bulk.

Sprinkle the work surface lightly with flour and scrape out the dough. Moisten your hands, and knead the dough a few times, using a pastry scraper to make folding easier. (*If you are replenishing the sourdough starter, remove a heaped cup and place in a bowl. Cover and refrigerate after a few hours, if not using again in a day's time.*)

Form the dough into 1 or 2 balls. Press out the dough to an approximately 1-inch-thick round and spread the sun-dried tomatoes over the surface. Fold over the dough and knead until the tomatoes are evenly distributed.

Form the dough into a tight, round loaf (see page 100). Return it to the bowl and let rise in a warm place for 45 to 60 minutes, or until nearly doubled in bulk. (*Alternatively, place the dough in a banneton or a towel-lined bowl to rise; see page 100.*)

Preheat the oven to 400 degrees F, with a rack in the middle.

If you are not using a baking stone, oil a baking sheet and dust with cornmeal. Gently turn out the dough on the baking sheet. Let rise slightly, about 15 minutes; omit this step if you are baking directly on a stone.

Shortly before baking, slash across the top with a razor blade or sharp knife.

Bake for 40 to 50 minutes, spraying with water a couple of times during the first 10 minutes, until the bread is brown and responds to tapping with a hollow sound.

Remove from the stone or pan and cool on a rack.

Sourdough Country Bread with Olives

1 VERY LARGE LOAF OR 2 SMALL LOAVES

THIS OLIVE BREAD IS UNBEATABLE. The dough is not as sour as the other breads in this chapter. This bread is made over 3 days. You mix the starter on the first day, the sponge on the second and the dough on the third. The result is a huge loaf with a rich, earthy flavor; the olives add whatever acidity may be lacking in the dough. I serve this bread with Mediterranean meals, salads and cheese. (See photograph, page 78.)

For the starter

2½	teaspoons active dry yeast
1	cup lukewarm water
1	cup whole wheat flour

For the sponge

2	cups lukewarm water
2½	cups whole wheat flour

For the dough

1	tablespoon olive oil
2½	cups whole wheat flour
1	scant tablespoon salt
	About 1¾-3 cups unbleached white flour
1⅓	cups imported Provençal or Greek olives, pitted and halved or coarsely chopped

Day 1—To make the starter: Two days before you wish to bake, dissolve the yeast in the warm water in a large bowl and stir in the whole wheat flour. Mix thoroughly, cover with plastic wrap and set in a warm place for 24 hours.

Day 2—To make the sponge: Stir the warm water into the starter. Whisk in the whole wheat flour, 1 cup at a time. Mix well, cover again and set in a warm place for another 24 hours.

Day 3—To knead by hand: Stir the olive oil into the sponge with a wooden spoon. Mix together the whole wheat flour and salt in a medium bowl and gradually fold into the sponge. Place 1 cup of white flour on the work surface and scrape the dough out of the bowl. Knead, flouring your hands often and adding white flour to the work surface, for 10 minutes, or until the dough is elastic. It will be sticky; use a pastry scraper to help turn the dough.

To knead with an electric mixer: Add the olive oil to the sponge. Mix together the whole wheat flour, salt and 1¾ cups of the white flour. Add to the dough all at once, and mix together using the paddle. Scrape the dough off the paddle and change to the dough hook. Knead on low speed for 2 minutes. Mix on medium speed for 8 to 10 minutes, adding up to 1¼ cups white flour if the dough is very sticky. Scrape out of the bowl onto a floured work surface. Knead a few times.

Shape the dough into a ball. Rinse, dry and lightly oil the bowl. Place the dough in it, turning to coat with the oil. Cover and let rise in a warm place for 1½ hours, or until doubled in bulk.

Lightly flour the work surface and scrape out the dough. Moisten your hands and press out the dough to an approximately 1-inch-thick round. Spread the olives over the surface, fold the dough in half, and knead for a couple of minutes, until the olives are evenly distributed. Shape the dough into 1 or 2 tight, round loaves (see page 100). Work quickly and keep your hands moistened; the dough will be sticky.

Return the dough to the bowl and let rise in a warm place for about 1½ hours, or until nearly doubled in bulk. (*Alternatively, place the dough in a banneton or a towel-lined bowl to rise; see page 100.*)

Preheat the oven to 400 degrees F, with a rack in the middle.

If you are not using a baking stone, oil a baking sheet and dust it with cornmeal. Gently turn out the dough onto the baking sheet. Let rise slightly, about 20 minutes; omit this step if you are baking directly on a stone.

Shortly before baking, slash across the top with a razor blade or sharp knife. Bake for 45 to 60 minutes, spraying with water a couple of times during the first 10 minutes, until the bread is brown and responds to tapping with a hollow sound.

Remove from the stone or pan and cool on a rack.

Sourdough Country Rye Bread with Raisins

2 LARGE LOAVES OR 3 SMALL LOAVES

ONLY SLIGHTLY ACIDIC, THIS RYE BREAD has a dense crumb, and it's packed with raisins. I like it best thinly sliced and lightly toasted, for breakfast. It requires 2½ or 3 days from start to finish. If you begin the starter in the afternoon or evening, you will mix up the sponge the following evening and finish the bread the following day. If you mix the starter in the morning, you will mix the sponge the following morning and finish the bread that night.

For the starter

1	teaspoon active dry yeast
1	cup lukewarm water
1	cup rye flour

For the sponge

1¼	cups lukewarm water
2	tablespoons molasses
1	cup unbleached white flour
1¾	cups rye flour

For the dough

½	cup lukewarm water
1	tablespoon salt
1	cup whole wheat flour
1	cup rye flour
	About 1½-2 cups unbleached white flour

For the loaves

2⅔	cups raisins or currants
1	egg yolk, beaten with 1 tablespoon water or milk, for egg wash (optional)

Day 1—To make the starter: In a small bowl, dissolve the yeast in the water and whisk in the flour. Combine well, cover with plastic and set in a warm spot to rise for 24 hours.

Day 2—To make the sponge: Stir down the starter and scrape into a large bowl. Whisk in the water, molasses, white flour and rye flour. Blend well; the mixture will be quite thick and sticky. Cover with plastic wrap and set the bowl in a warm place for 12 hours.

Day 3—To knead by hand: Fold the warm water, salt, whole wheat flour and the rye flour into the dough with a wooden spoon. Fold in the white flour, ½ cup at a time, until the dough can be turned out of the bowl. Place ½ cup of white flour on the work surface and scrape out the dough. The dough will be very sticky. Flour your hands well. If the dough is too sticky to handle, use a pastry scraper to fold the dough. Knead for about 10 minutes, adding white flour by the handful, as needed. After about 5 minutes, the dough should become easier to work with.

To knead with an electric mixer: Stir the warm water into the sponge. Mix together the salt, whole wheat flour, rye flour and 1 cup of the white flour in a medium bowl. Add to the mixture all at once, and mix together using the paddle. Scrape the dough off the paddle and change to the dough hook. Knead on low speed for 2 minutes. Mix on medium speed for 8 to 10 minutes, adding up to 1 cup more white flour as necessary. Scrape out of the bowl onto a floured work surface. The dough will be very sticky.

Rinse, dry and lightly oil the bowl. Shape the dough into a ball and place the dough in the bowl, turning to coat with the oil. Cover with plastic wrap and a towel and set in a warm place to rise for 2 hours, or until doubled.

Lightly flour the work surface and turn out the dough. Moisten your hands. Press out the dough to a 1-inch thickness and spread the raisins or currants over the surface. Fold the dough over and knead several times, until the fruit is evenly distributed.

Oil a baking sheet. Divide the dough into 2 or 3 equal pieces (or for rolls, see below). Shape into tight, round loaves (see page 100) and place on the baking sheet. Cover with plastic wrap or a towel and set in a warm place to rise slightly, 30 to 45 minutes.

Meanwhile, preheat the oven to 400 degrees F, with a rack in the middle.

Brush the loaves with the egg wash, if using. Slash the top with 2 intersecting Xs, using a razor blade or sharp knife, so that 8 intersecting lines radiate out from the center like a star.

Bake for 40 to 50 minutes, turning the baking sheet around and brushing halfway through with the egg wash. The bread is done when it is dark brown and responds to tapping with a hollow sound.

Remove from the pan and cool on a rack.

Variation

To make rolls: Divide the dough into 18 to 24 equal pieces and roll each into a ball (see page 25). Place on oiled baking sheets, cover with plastic wrap and a towel and let rise for about 1 hour, or until nearly doubled in size.

Brush the rolls with egg wash and slash an X across the tops. Bake for 25 to 30 minutes, turning the sheets around and brushing the rolls halfway through.

Savory Yeast Breads

Potato Bread

2 MEDIUM ROUND LOAVES

POTATOES ENRICH BREAD, giving it an earthy taste and a moist, hearty texture. This bread, made with half whole wheat flour and half white, has a distinctive potato flavor. *Note*: Knead this dough by hand since there is a lot of it.

> 2 medium potatoes, peeled and quartered
> 2 teaspoons active dry yeast
> ½ cup lukewarm water
> 1 large egg, at room temperature
> 1 cup low-fat plain yogurt or buttermilk
> 1 tablespoon sunflower, safflower or canola oil
> 3 cups whole wheat flour
> 2½ teaspoons salt
> About 3-4 cups unbleached white flour

Boil the potatoes until tender. Drain and reserve the cooking water. Mash the potatoes and let cool.

Dissolve the yeast in the warm water in a large bowl and let stand for 5 to 10 minutes, until creamy.

Beat the egg in a large measuring cup. Add 1 cup of the reserved potato water and the yogurt or buttermilk. Add warm water as necessary to make 2½ cups.

Add the egg mixture and the oil to the yeast mixture, and beat in the mashed potatoes. Mix together the whole wheat flour and salt in a medium bowl, and stir into the potato-yeast mixture with a wooden spoon. Stir in the white flour, 1 cup at a time. As soon as the dough coheres, scrape it out onto a lightly floured work surface.

Knead the dough, using a pastry scraper, if necessary, to help turn it, and adding white flour as needed, for about 15 minutes. It will be slightly dense but resilient, and at the end of kneading, it should be soft, elastic and somewhat sticky.

Shape the dough into a ball. Rinse, dry and lightly oil the bowl. Place the dough in it, turning to coat with the oil. Cover with plastic wrap and a towel, and set in a warm place to rise for about 1½ hours, or until doubled in bulk.

Punch down the dough and turn out onto a lightly floured surface. Moisten your hands and knead for a couple of minutes; divide in half. Oil a baking sheet and dust with corn-meal. Form the dough into 2 round loaves (see page 24) and place, rounded sides up, on the baking sheet. Dust the tops with flour. Cover with a towel and let rise in a warm place for about 45 minutes, or until nearly doubled.

About 30 minutes before baking, preheat the oven to 400 degrees F, with a rack in the middle.

Slash the loaves across the top with a razor blade or sharp knife. Bake for 45 to 60 minutes, spraying the loaves with water a couple of times during the first 10 minutes, until they are brown and respond to tapping with a hollow sound.

Remove from the baking sheet and cool on racks.

Potato Bread with Caraway Seeds

1 VERY LARGE ROUND LOAF OR 2 SMALL ROUND LOAVES

Made with three-quarters white flour and one-quarter whole wheat flour, this bread has a close crumb and slices beautifully. Caraway seeds add pungent flavor.

2	medium potatoes, peeled, scrubbed and quartered
2½	teaspoons active dry yeast
2½	cups lukewarm water
1½	cups whole wheat flour
2½	teaspoons salt
1½	teaspoons caraway seeds
	About 4-5 cups unbleached white flour

Boil the potatoes until tender. Drain and mash; let cool.

Dissolve the yeast in ½ cup of the water in a large bowl. Stir in 3 tablespoons of the whole wheat flour. Loosely cover with plastic wrap, and let stand in a warm place for 30 minutes.

To knead by hand: Stir the remaining 2 cups of the warm water into the yeast mixture. Add the mashed potatoes and mix well. Mix together the remaining 1¼ cups plus 1 tablespoon whole wheat flour, salt and caraway seeds in a medium bowl; stir into the water-and-yeast mixture.

With a wooden spoon, begin to add the white flour, 1 cup at a time. As soon as the dough coheres, scrape it onto a floured work surface and begin to knead, adding flour as needed; the dough will soon become resistant and elastic. Knead for about 15 minutes. At the end of the kneading, it will be soft and sticky.

To knead with an electric mixer: Stir the remaining 2 cups of the warm water into the yeast mixture. Using the paddle attachment, beat in the potatoes. Combine 1¼ cups plus 1 tablespoon whole wheat flour, salt and caraway seeds in a medium bowl. Add all at once to the bowl and mix in. Change to the dough hook and add 4 cups of the white flour. Knead on low speed for 2 minutes, then on medium speed for 8 to 10 minutes. If the dough seems too sticky, sprinkle in up to 1 cup white flour. Scrape out the dough onto a lightly floured surface and knead for a minute or so by hand.

Shape the dough into a ball. Rinse, dry and lightly oil the bowl. Place the dough in it, turning to coat with the oil. Cover with plastic wrap and a towel, place in a warm spot, and let rise for 1 to 2 hours, or until doubled in bulk.

Punch down the dough and knead for about 5 minutes on a lightly floured surface. Oil a baking sheet and dust it with cornmeal. Moisten your hands and shape the dough into 1 or 2 tight balls (see page 24). Place on a baking sheet and let rise again for 45 minutes, or until nearly doubled. (*Alternatively, place the dough in a banneton or a towel-lined bowl to rise; see page 100.*)

About 30 minutes before baking, preheat the oven to 400 degrees F, with a rack in the middle.

Reshape the dough if necessary and let rise, if you've had to reshape it, for another 15 minutes.

Slash across the top with a razor blade or sharp knife. Bake for 1 hour for a large loaf, 40 to 45 minutes for smaller loaves, spraying with water a couple of times during the first 10 minutes, until the bread is a nice brown color and responds to tapping with a hollow sound.

Remove from the pan and cool on a rack.

French Herb Bread

4 BAGUETTES OR 4 SMALL ROUND LOAVES

THIS BREAD IS FULL OF rosemary, thyme, garlic and onion. It goes very nicely with cheese.

For the herb-and-onion mixture

1 medium onion, minced

1 tablespoon melted unsalted butter or sunflower, safflower or canola oil

3 garlic cloves, minced or put through a press

3 tablespoons finely chopped fresh parsley

1 tablespoon chopped fresh dill (optional)

2 teaspoons chopped fresh rosemary, or ¾ teaspoon dried

1 tablespoon fresh thyme, or 1½ teaspoons dried

For the dough

2½ teaspoons active dry yeast

2½ cups lukewarm water

Pinch of sugar

1 tablespoon melted unsalted butter or sunflower, safflower or canola oil

1 cup whole wheat flour

About 5-6 cups unbleached white flour

1 cup wheat germ

2½ teaspoons salt

1 egg, beaten with 3 tablespoons water, for egg wash

To make the herb-and-onion mixture: Sauté the onion in the butter or oil until tender; remove from the heat. Pound together the garlic, parsley, dill (if using), rosemary and thyme in a mortar or puree in a food processor.

To make the dough: Dissolve the yeast in the warm water in a large bowl. Add the sugar and let stand for 5 to 10 minutes, until creamy.

To knead by hand: Fold in the melted butter or oil, the sautéed onion and the herb mixture. Mix together the whole wheat flour, 5 cups of the white flour, the wheat germ and salt in a medium bowl. Fold in, 1 cup at a time, with a wooden spoon. As soon as you can, scrape out the dough onto a lightly floured work surface. Knead, adding white flour as needed, for 10 minutes. The dough will be sticky at first but will become very elastic, though it will remain tacky on the surface.

To knead with an electric mixer: Combine the whole wheat flour, 5 cups of the white flour, the wheat germ and salt in a medium bowl. Add all at once to the bowl, along with the melted butter or oil, the sautéed onion and the herb mixture. Mix together with the paddle until combined. Change to the dough hook, and mix on low speed for 2 minutes. Mix on medium speed for 8 to 10 minutes. If the dough seems very wet and sticky, sprinkle in up to 1 cup white flour. Scrape out the dough onto a lightly floured surface and knead for a minute or so by hand.

Rinse, dry and lightly oil the bowl. Shape the dough into a ball and place in the bowl, turning to coat with the oil. Cover with plastic wrap and a towel, and set in a warm place to rise for 1½ hours, or until doubled in size.

Punch down the dough and let rise again until doubled in bulk, about 1 hour. Meanwhile, butter or oil a baking sheet or baguette pans and sprinkle with cornmeal.

Lightly flour a work surface and turn out the dough; it will be soft and sticky. Keeping your hands and the surface lightly floured, divide the dough into 4 equal pieces. Shape into balls, and cover lightly with plastic wrap. Shape into baguettes or round loaves (see pages 24 to 25), and place in the baguette pans or on the baking sheets. Brush with the egg wash.

Cover the loaves with a towel and let rise for 20 to 30 minutes, or until nearly doubled.

Meanwhile, preheat the oven to 400 degrees F, with a rack in the middle.

Slash across the top of the loaves 3 or 4 times with a razor blade or sharp knife. Bake for 35 to 45 minutes, spraying a couple of times with water during the first 10 minutes, until the loaves are golden brown and respond to tapping with a hollow sound. For extra-shiny loaves, brush several times during the baking with the egg wash.

Remove from the pan(s) and cool on a rack.

Herbed Cottage Cheese Bread

1 LOAF

THIS IS A HIGH-PROTEIN, very easy-to-make bread. It requires only one rising, and the finished bread has a firm texture. It slices very well and works well for sandwiches. The dough is firm and elastic.

1	tablespoon active dry yeast
¼	cup lukewarm water
1	teaspoon sugar or mild-flavored honey
1¾	cups cottage cheese, at room temperature
1	large egg, at room temperature
1	tablespoon grated onion
2	tablespoons olive oil
¼	teaspoon baking soda
¼	cup chopped fresh dill or parsley
1⅔	cups whole wheat flour
1½	teaspoons salt
	About ¾-1¼ cups unbleached white flour
1	tablespoon melted unsalted butter or oil, for brushing the loaf

Dissolve the yeast in the warm water in a large bowl, and stir in the sugar or honey. Let stand for 5 to 10 minutes, until creamy.

Press the cottage cheese through a sieve, or puree in a food processor. Stir into the yeast mixture. Beat in the egg and add the onion, olive oil, baking soda and the dill or parsley; mix together well.

To knead by hand: Mix together the whole wheat flour and salt in a medium bowl, and fold in, 1 cup at a time, with a wooden spoon. As soon as you can, scrape out the dough onto a floured work surface. Knead, adding white flour as needed, for 10 minutes; the dough should be fairly smooth and elastic and spring back when indented with the fingers.

To knead with an electric mixer: Combine the whole wheat flour, salt and ¾ cup of the white flour. Add all at once to the bowl, and mix together with the paddle. Change to the dough hook, and mix on low speed for 2 minutes. Mix on medium speed for 8 to 10 minutes. If the dough seems very wet and sticky, sprinkle in up to ½ cup white flour. Scrape out the dough onto a lightly floured surface and knead for a minute or so by hand.

Generously butter a loaf pan. Shape the dough into a loaf (see page 24) and place in the pan, seam side up first, then seam side down, to coat with the oil. Brush the top of the loaf with the melted butter or oil. Cover with a lightly floured towel and let rise in a warm spot until nearly doubled in bulk, about 2 hours, or until the top of the loaf curves above the side of the pan.

About 30 minutes before baking, preheat the oven to 375 degrees F, with a rack in the middle.

Bake the bread for 35 to 40 minutes, until it responds to tapping with a hollow sound. Remove from the pan and cool on a rack.

Herbed Whole Wheat Bread

2 LOAVES

THE LOAVES OF THIS WHOLESOME BREAD have a close crumb and slice neatly. The bread makes a nice complement to dishes with Mediterranean flavors and is good for sandwiches.

1	tablespoon active dry yeast
2	cups lukewarm water
1	tablespoon mild-flavored honey
¼	cup plus 1 tablespoon sunflower, safflower or canola oil
1	small onion, minced
1	garlic clove, minced
1	cup low-fat plain yogurt, at room temperature
1	scant tablespoon salt
2	tablespoons chopped fresh dill
2	teaspoons dried thyme
2	teaspoons dried sage
5	cups whole wheat flour or whole wheat pastry flour
	About 1½-2½ cups unbleached white flour
1	egg, beaten with 2 tablespoons water, for egg wash
	Dill seeds, for decoration (optional)

Dissolve the yeast in the warm water in a large bowl. Stir in the honey and let stand for 5 to 10 minutes, until creamy.

Meanwhile, heat the 1 tablespoon oil in a skillet over medium-low heat. Sauté the onion with the garlic until the onion is tender. Remove from the heat.

Stir the yogurt into the yeast mixture, add the remaining ¼ cup oil, the salt, dill, thyme and sage. Stir in the sautéed onion and garlic. Stir in 2½ cups of the whole wheat flour with a wooden spoon. Gradually fold in the remaining 2½ cups. Fold in 1 cup of the white flour and place 1 cup on the work surface.

Scrape out the dough onto the work surface (you can also knead the dough in the bowl, if it is too sticky). Knead for 10 minutes, flouring your hands often and using a pastry scraper to fold the dough, adding more flour as needed. When the dough is stiff and elastic, shape into a ball. Rinse, dry and lightly oil the bowl. Place the dough in it, turning to coat with the oil. Cover with plastic wrap and a towel and set in a warm spot to rise for 1½ hours, or until doubled in bulk.

Punch down the dough and turn out onto a lightly floured work surface. Oil 2 loaf pans. Knead the dough for a minute or two; cut in half, and form each piece into a ball. Roll each ball into a loaf shape (see page 24) and place in the oiled pans, seam side up first, then seam side down, to coat with the oil. Cover with a damp towel and set in a warm place to rise for about 1 hour, or until the tops of the loaves curve above the sides of the pans.

About 30 minutes before baking, preheat the oven to 375 degrees F, with a rack in the middle.

Brush the loaves gently with the egg wash; sprinkle with the dill seeds, if using. Brush the loaves again, and slash across the top with a razor blade or sharp knife. Bake for 45 to 50 minutes, or until the loaves are golden brown and respond to tapping with a hollow sound.

Remove from the pans and cool on a rack.

Rosemary and Thyme Bread

2 SMALL ROUND LOAVES OR 1 LARGE LOAF

I WAS FIRST INSPIRED TO MAKE THIS BREAD IN PROVENCE, where these herbs grow into big bushes all over the countryside. The smell of the dough rising is enticing, and the baking loaves smell even better. This bread is best made with fresh herbs. But if you can't get them, use dried and halve the quantities. The dough is soft, elastic and easy to work with, the bread crusty and dense. (See photograph on the cover.)

2½	teaspoons active dry yeast
2	cups lukewarm water
2	tablespoons olive oil
¾	cup whole wheat flour
¼	cup finely chopped fresh rosemary, or 2 tablespoons chopped dried
2	tablespoons fresh thyme leaves, or 1 tablespoon dried
2½	teaspoons salt
	About 3½-4½ cups unbleached white flour

Dissolve the yeast in the warm water in a large bowl. Let stand for 5 to 10 minutes, until creamy.

To knead by hand: Stir the olive oil into the yeast mixture. Mix together the whole wheat flour, herbs and salt in a medium bowl, and fold into the yeast mixture with a wooden spoon. Begin adding the white flour, and as soon as you can, scrape the dough out onto the work surface. Knead, adding white flour as needed, for 10 minutes.

To knead with an electric mixer: Stir the olive oil into the yeast mixture. Combine the whole wheat flour, herbs, salt and 3½ cups of the white flour in a medium bowl. Add all at once to the yeast mixture, and mix together with the paddle. Change to the dough hook, and mix on low speed for 2 minutes. Mix on medium speed for 8 to 10 minutes. If the dough seems very wet and sticky, sprinkle in up to 1 cup white flour. Scrape out the dough onto a lightly floured surface and knead for a minute or so by hand; it will be soft, elastic and somewhat tacky.

Rinse, dry and lightly oil the bowl. Shape the dough into a ball and place it in the bowl, turning to coat with the oil. Cover the bowl with plastic wrap and a towel, and set in a warm place to rise for 1½ hours, or until doubled in bulk.

Punch down the dough, turn out onto a floured surface and shape into a large ball or divide in half and shape each half into a ball (see page 24). Oil and lightly dust a baking sheet with cornmeal, and place the loaves on the baking sheet. Cover with a towel and let rise for 45 to 60 minutes, or until nearly doubled. (*Alternatively, place the dough in a ban-neton or a towel-lined bowl to rise; see page 100.*) Reshape gently, if necessary.

About 30 minutes before baking, preheat the oven to 450 degrees F, with a rack in the middle.

Slash across the tops with a razor blade or sharp knife. Bake for 10 minutes, spraying with water a couple of times.

Reduce the heat to 400 degrees and bake for 30 to 35 minutes longer, until the loaves are brown and respond to tapping with a hollow sound.

Remove from the pan and cool on a rack.

Pesto Bread

1 LARGE ROUND LOAF OR 2 SMALL LOAVES

THIS GARLICKY BREAD is inspired by Carol Field's Pesto Bread, in her book, *The Italian Baker*. The bread makes a delicious addition to an Italian meal, and it's also great with cheese. Make this in spring and summer, when fresh basil is readily available.

For the pesto

2	cups fresh basil leaves, washed and dried, loosely packed
2	large garlic cloves, peeled
¼	teaspoon salt
⅓	cup olive oil
½	cup freshly grated Parmesan cheese

For the bread

2½	teaspoons active dry yeast
1	cup lukewarm water
1	cup whole wheat flour
1	teaspoon salt
	About 1½-2 cups unbleached white flour

To make the pesto: Combine the basil, garlic and salt in a food processor and puree, or pound together in a mortar. With the motor running, pour in the olive oil and process until smooth, or whisk the oil in. Add the Parmesan cheese and combine well; set aside.

To make the bread: Dissolve the yeast in the warm water in a large bowl. Let stand for 5 to 10 minutes, until creamy.

Stir the pesto into the yeast mixture and combine thoroughly.

To knead by hand: Combine the whole wheat flour and salt in a medium bowl, and fold into the yeast mixture with a wooden spoon. Fold in 1½ cups of the white flour and turn out onto a lightly floured surface. Knead for 10 minutes, or until the dough is smooth and elastic, adding more flour as needed.

To knead with an electric mixer: Combine the whole wheat flour, salt and 1½ cups of the white flour in a medium bowl. Add all at once to the yeast mixture, and mix together with the paddle. Change to the dough hook, and mix on low speed for 2 minutes. Mix on medium speed for 8 to 10 minutes. If the dough seems very wet and sticky, sprinkle in up to ½ cup white flour. Scrape out the dough onto a lightly floured surface and knead for a minute or so by hand.

Rinse, dry and lightly oil the bowl. Shape the dough into a ball and place in the bowl, turning to coat with the oil. Cover with plastic wrap and a towel and set in a warm place to rise for 1½ hours, or until doubled in bulk.

Punch down the dough and divide in half. Knead each piece briefly and shape each into a tight, round loaf (or you can make 1 large loaf; see page 24). Oil a baking sheet, and lightly dust with cornmeal. Place the dough on the baking sheet. Cover and let rise in a warm place for 45 to 60 minutes, or until nearly doubled in bulk. (*Alternatively, place the dough in a banneton or a towel-lined bowl to rise; see page 100.*)

About 30 minutes before baking, preheat the oven to 450 degrees F, with a rack in the middle.

Slash across the top with a razor blade or sharp knife. Immediately reduce the heat to 400 degrees. Bake for about 40 minutes for 2 loaves, 50 to 60 minutes for 1 large loaf, spraying with water a couple of times during the first 10 minutes, or until the loaves are deep brown and respond to tapping with a hollow sound.

Remove from the pan and cool on a rack.

Saffron Bread

1 VERY LARGE ROUND LOAF OR 2 SMALL LOAVES

Between the fourteenth and eighteenth centuries, saffron was widely cultivated in England, and the people who cultivated it were known as the Crokers of Saffron Walden. But because its cultivation is so labor-intensive—it takes 250,000 flowers to produce a pound of saffron, which are the dried stigmas of the *Crocus sativus* flower—it was abandoned as a profitable cash crop. What a pity.

This shiny-crusted saffron bread has a pungent flavor and gorgeous yellow hue. It goes well with fish and meat dishes and toasts well. The recipe comes from Elisabeth Luard, author of *The Old World Kitchen*.

¼-½	teaspoon saffron threads
⅓	cup boiling water
1½	teaspoons active dry yeast
1	cup plus 2 tablespoons lukewarm water
1	teaspoon sugar
	About 6½-7 cups unbleached white flour
1	teaspoon salt
½	cup lukewarm milk
¼	cup (½ stick) unsalted butter, melted and cooled
2	large eggs, beaten
	Milk or beaten egg, for egg wash

Place the saffron in a small bowl and pour the boiling water over it. Let stand for about 10 minutes, until the water turns yellow.

In a small bowl, dissolve the yeast in 1 cup of the warm water. Stir in the sugar and let stand for 5 to 10 minutes, until creamy.

Combine 6 cups of the flour and salt in a large bowl. Make a well in the center of the flour mixture and stir in the yeast mixture. Sprinkle ½ cup flour over the top, stir in and cover the bowl with plastic wrap. Let stand for about 20 minutes, or until beginning to bubble.

To knead by hand: Combine the saffron liquid with the remaining 2 tablespoons warm water and the warm milk in a medium bowl. Stir in the melted butter and beaten eggs. Add to the flour mixture and stir with a wooden spoon to form a soft dough. When the dough coheres, turn it out onto a lightly floured work surface, and knead until smooth, firm and uniformly yellow, 10 to 15 minutes. Add more flour as needed until the dough is stiff and elastic.

To knead with an electric mixer: Combine the saffron liquid with the remaining 2 tablespoons warm water and the milk in a medium bowl. Stir in the melted butter and beaten eggs. Add to the flour mixture and mix together using the paddle. Change to the dough hook, and mix on low speed for 2 minutes. Mix on medium speed for 8 to 10 minutes, until the dough is smooth and elastic. Add up to 1 cup more flour as needed. Turn out onto the work surface and knead for about 1 minute.

Rinse, dry and lightly oil the bowl. Shape the dough into a ball and place in the bowl, turning to coat with the oil. Cover with plastic wrap and a towel and set in a warm place to rise for 2 hours, or until doubled.

Oil a baking sheet and dust it with cornmeal. Punch down the dough. Knead for about 5 minutes on a well-floured surface. Shape the dough into a large ball or 2 smaller balls (see page 24). Place on the baking sheet, covered lightly with a towel, and let rise for about 45 minutes, or until nearly doubled. (*Alternatively, place the dough in a banneton or a towel-lined bowl to rise; see page 100.*)

About 30 minutes before baking, preheat the oven to 400 degrees F, with a rack in the middle.

Brush the top of the loaf lightly with the milk or beaten egg. Slash across the top with a razor blade or sharp knife. Bake for 50 to 60 minutes for a large loaf, or 40 to 45 minutes for smaller loaves, or until the loaves are golden brown and respond to tapping with a hollow sound.

Remove from the pan and cool on a rack.

Cheese and Mustard Bread

1 LOAF

THIS UNIQUE BREAD tastes like a cheese sandwich with the cheese and mustard baked right into the loaf. When you toast it, the fragrance of the mustard and cheese emerges, and it smells like a grilled cheese sandwich. I've made the bread with Dijon mustard and with a grainy English mustard and like both equally. The bread freezes well.

2½	teaspoons active dry yeast
½	cup lukewarm water
½	cup lukewarm milk
1	tablespoon mild-flavored honey
1	tablespoon olive oil
1	large egg, lightly beaten
¼-½	cup prepared mustard, such as Dijon, to taste
1	tablespoon grated onion (optional)
1	cup grated sharp Cheddar cheese
1	cup whole wheat flour
2-2¼	cups unbleached white flour
1¼	teaspoons salt
1	egg, beaten with 2 tablespoons water, for egg wash (optional)

Dissolve the yeast in the warm water in a large bowl. Let stand for 5 to 10 minutes, until creamy.

Stir in the warm milk, honey, oil, egg, mustard, onion, if using, and cheese.

To knead by hand: Mix together the whole wheat flour, 1⅔ cups of the white flour and the salt. Fold the flour mixture into the yeast mixture, 1 cup at a time, with a wooden spoon. As soon as you can, scrape out the dough onto a lightly floured work surface. Knead, adding white flour as needed, for 10 minutes; the dough will be smooth and elastic.

To knead with an electric mixer: Combine the whole wheat flour, 2 cups of the white flour and the salt in a medium bowl. Add all at once to the yeast mixture, and mix together with the paddle. Change to the dough hook, and mix on low speed for 2 minutes. Mix on medium speed for 8 to 10 minutes. If the dough seems very wet and sticky, sprinkle in up to ¼ cup white flour. Scrape out the dough onto a lightly floured surface and knead for a minute or so by hand.

Rinse, dry and lightly oil the bowl. Shape the dough into a ball and place in the bowl, turning to coat with the oil. Cover with plastic wrap and a towel, and set in a warm place to rise for 1½ hours, or until doubled in bulk. (*Alternatively, you can further develop the flavor of the dough by letting it rise overnight. Let rise in the oiled bowl in a warm place for 30 minutes. Shape into a loaf and place in an oiled bread pan. Cover loosely with plastic wrap and refrigerate overnight. In the morning, remove from the refrigerator and let stand in a warm place for 45 minutes.*)

Punch down the dough and turn out onto your work surface. Knead for 1 minute and shape into a loaf (see page 24). Oil a bread pan and place the dough in it, seam side up first, then seam side down, to coat it with the oil.

Cover with a towel and let rise in a warm place for about 1 hour, or until the top of the loaf curves above the sides of the pan.

About 30 minutes before baking, preheat the oven to 350 degrees F, with a rack in the middle.

Brush the top of the loaf with the egg wash, if desired. Slash across the top with a razor blade or sharp knife. Bake for about 50 minutes, or until the loaf is golden brown and responds to tapping with a hollow sound.

Remove from the pan and cool on a rack.

Cumin and Cornmeal Bread

2 LOAVES

CORNMEAL GIVES THIS BREAD A MARVELOUS TEXTURE, and though it has a rich, buttery taste, there's no butter in it. It's convenient to make because it doesn't require much rising time.

2½	teaspoons active dry yeast
1½	cups lukewarm water
1	tablespoon honey
1	cup low-fat plain yogurt
1	large egg
2	tablespoons sunflower, safflower or canola oil
2	tablespoons cumin seeds
2½	teaspoons salt
1	cup stone-ground cornmeal
2½	cups whole wheat flour
1-1¾	cups unbleached white flour
1	egg, beaten, for egg wash

Dissolve the yeast in the warm water in a large bowl. Stir in the honey, and let stand for 5 to 10 minutes, until creamy.

Stir in the yogurt, egg, oil, cumin seeds and salt and mix well. Fold in the cornmeal; gradually fold in the whole wheat flour. Add ½ cup of the white flour and place a large handful of white flour on the work surface. Scrape out the dough onto the work surface and knead, adding white flour as necessary, for 10 minutes; the dough will be quite sticky.

Rinse, dry and lightly oil the bowl. Place the dough in it, turning to coat with the oil. Cover with plastic wrap and a towel, and set in a warm place to rise for about 1½ hours, or until doubled in bulk.

Punch down the dough, turn it out and divide in half. Form into 2 loaves (see page 24). Oil 2 bread pans, and place the loaves in them, seam side up first, then seam side down, to coat with the oil. Cover with a towel and let rise again in a warm place for about 1 hour, or until the tops of the loaves curve above the sides of the pans.

About 30 minutes before baking, preheat the oven to 375 degrees F, with a rack in the middle.

Brush the loaves lightly with the egg wash. Slash across the top with a razor blade or sharp knife. Bake for about 50 minutes, or until the loaves are golden brown and respond to tapping with a hollow sound.

Remove from the pans and cool on a rack.

Rich and Sweet Yeast Breads

Cranberry-Orange Anadama Bread

2 SMALL LOAVES

ANADAMA BREAD IS A TRADITIONAL AMERICAN LOAF containing molasses and cornmeal. Legend has it that the bread originated in Massachusetts, when a woman named Anna, in the midst of preparing the evening meal of cornmeal mush and molasses, decided to abandon her husband. Her husband discovered she was gone, found the cornmeal mush and molasses and angrily mixed them together, adding yeast, flour and water and muttering all the while, "Anna, damn her."

There are several versions of the bread. This is a festive one, sweet with orange juice, honey and molasses and tart with cranberries. It has the same close crumb as traditional Anadama Bread.

2	cups orange juice
⅔	cup stone-ground yellow cornmeal
⅓	cup molasses
2	cups whole raw cranberries
1	tablespoon grated orange zest
1	tablespoon mild-flavored honey
2½	teaspoons active dry yeast
½	cup lukewarm water
2	tablespoons melted unsalted butter or sunflower, safflower or canola oil
2	teaspoons salt
	About 4-5 cups unbleached white flour
1	egg, beaten with 3 tablespoons water, for egg wash

About 1 hour before mixing the dough, warm the orange juice in a heavy-bottomed saucepan over medium heat until bubbles form around the edges. Gradually add the cornmeal in a slow stream, stirring constantly with a wooden spoon. Reduce the heat to low and stir constantly, scraping the cornmeal up from the sides and bottom of the pan, until the mixture is thick, about 3 minutes. Remove the pan from the heat, and stir in the molasses. Set aside to cool to lukewarm.

Meanwhile, put the cranberries, orange zest and honey in a blender or food processor and pulse until the cranberries are coarsely chopped; set aside.

Dissolve the yeast in the warm water in a large bowl. Let stand for 5 to 10 minutes, until creamy. When the cornmeal mixture has cooled, stir it into the yeast mixture.

To knead by hand: Fold the melted butter or oil into the cornmeal-yeast mixture. Fold in the cranberry mixture and the salt with a wooden spoon. Add enough white flour to make a dough stiff enough to scrape out onto a floured work surface. Knead, flouring your hands and the surface often, for 10 to 15 minutes, adding flour as necessary. By the end of the kneading, the dough will be stiff and elastic but may still be a bit tacky.

To knead with an electric mixer: Add the melted butter or oil, the cranberry mixture, the salt and 4 cups of the white flour to the cornmeal-yeast mixture. Beat with the paddle until combined. Change to the dough hook, and beat on low speed for 2 minutes. Mix on medium speed for 8 to 10 minutes. Add up to 1 cup more white flour if the dough seems too liquid. Scrape out the dough onto a floured surface and knead for 1 minute.

Rinse, dry and lightly oil the bowl. Shape the dough into a ball. Place in the bowl, turning to coat with the oil. Cover with plastic wrap and a towel, and set in a warm place to rise for 1 to 1½ hours, or until doubled in bulk.

Oil 2 loaf pans or a baking sheet and sprinkle with cornmeal.

Turn out the dough and divide in half. Form each piece into a ball and allow to rest for 5 minutes. (The dough will be so sticky that you may just have to pat it into the pans rather than forming loaves, which is fine.) Slash across the top with a razor blade or sharp knife. Set in a warm place to rise for 1 to 1½ hours, or until the tops of the loaves curve to the tops of the pans. Brush lightly with the egg wash.

About 30 minutes before baking, preheat the oven to 350 degrees F, with a rack in the middle.

Bake for 50 minutes, brushing halfway through with the egg wash, until the loaves are dark brown and respond to tapping with a hollow sound.

Remove from the pan(s) and cool on a rack.

Brioche

2 LARGE LOAVES OR 8 SMALL BRIOCHES

THE FIRST TIME I SAW A RECIPE FOR BRIOCHE, I couldn't believe the amount of butter in it. I have reduced the amount by a third in my recipe, and the brioche is still rich and delicious. Brioches can be baked in molds or in ordinary loaf pans. (See photograph, page 74.)

2	teaspoons active dry yeast
¼	cup lukewarm water
4	large eggs, at room temperature
	About 3⅓-3½ cups unbleached white flour
3	tablespoons sugar (use 2 tablespoons for a less sweet brioche)
1	teaspoon salt
½	cup (1 stick) unsalted butter, softened
1	egg, beaten, for glazing

Dissolve the yeast in the warm water in a large bowl. Let stand for 5 to 10 minutes, until creamy.

Beat in the eggs.

To knead by hand: Combine 3⅓ cups of the flour, the sugar and salt in a medium bowl. Gradually add to the yeast mixture, folding it in with a wooden spoon. Lightly flour a work surface and scrape out the dough. Knead, using a pastry scraper to help lift the dough, slap it down onto the work surface, pull it up and slap it down again. Flour your hands often, and continue this method of kneading for about 15 minutes; the dough will be sticky. When it begins to come away from your fingers easily, knead in the butter by placing the butter on the dough, pushing it in and squeezing the dough through your fingers. Lift and slap the dough down, and squeeze through your fingers again. Continue until all of the butter has been incorporated into the dough; the dough will be quite soft and a bit tacky.

To knead with an electric mixer: Combine 3⅓ cups of the flour, the sugar and salt in a medium bowl. Add to the yeast mixture. Beat together using the paddle. Change to the dough hook, and beat on low speed for 1 minute. Beat on medium speed for 8 to 10 minutes. Add the softened butter and beat for 2 minutes longer, or until incorporated. Add up to 2 tablespoons flour if the dough is very sticky; the dough will be soft and a bit tacky.

Rinse, dry and butter the bowl. Place the dough in it, turning to coat with the butter.

Cover with plastic wrap and a towel and set in a warm place to rise for about 1 hour, or until doubled.

Punch down, cover again and let rise another hour, or until doubled.

Punch down the dough and scrape it out onto the work surface. Divide the dough into 2 equal pieces or 8 equal pieces for small brioches.

To shape the traditional large topknotted brioche: Generously butter 2 brioche pans or small loaf pans. If using brioche pans, divide each piece of dough into 2 pieces, one twice as large as the other. Shape each into a tight ball. Place the larger ball in a pan and make a depression in the center with your thumb. Place the smaller ball on top of this depression and press down lightly. If using loaf pans, divide each piece into 2 equal-size balls and place side by side in the loaf pans.

To shape small brioches: Generously butter 8 small brioche molds or muffin tins. Shape each piece of dough into a tight ball. Make a loop with your thumb and forefinger and grab the dough about ⅓ of the way down (see illustrations, right). Squeeze the dough so that you form a "neck" and a small topknot. Press this topknot down into the center of the remaining ball so that it sits squarely on top; place in a brioche mold. Repeat with the remaining pieces.

Cover the pans with plastic wrap, place in the refrigerator and let rise for about 1 hour or more, until the dough has risen slightly.

About 30 minutes before baking, preheat the oven to 400 degrees F, with a rack in the middle. Place a baking sheet in the oven. (For smaller brioches, use 2 baking sheets, placing the racks in the lower and upper third of the oven.)

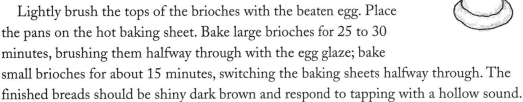

Lightly brush the tops of the brioches with the beaten egg. Place the pans on the hot baking sheet. Bake large brioches for 25 to 30 minutes, brushing them halfway through with the egg glaze; bake small brioches for about 15 minutes, switching the baking sheets halfway through. The finished breads should be shiny dark brown and respond to tapping with a hollow sound.

Remove from the molds and cool on racks.

Croissants

12 CROISSANTS

THE RICH, FLAKY LAYERS in a croissant result from the alternating layers of dough and butter. Croissants are relatively easy to make. You make a dough and let it rise. Then you roll it out, spread it with butter and fold it like a business letter. Then you roll this out, and turn the dough a quarter turn, let it rest in the refrigerator, fold again, and roll it out again. After three turns, the dough is ready to roll out, cut and shape.

It's important to keep the croissant dough cool when you are doing the turns. If the butter gets too warm, it will ooze out from between the layers. Work quickly, don't handle the dough too much and sprinkle it very lightly with flour to prevent sticking.

I learned to make croissants at the École de Gastronomie Française Ritz-Escoffier in Paris; this recipe is based on theirs, but I've reduced the amount of butter.

1	teaspoon active dry yeast
¾	cup water, at room temperature
2	tablespoons sugar
2	tablespoons heavy cream
2-2½	cups unbleached white flour
1	teaspoon salt
½	cup (1 stick) cold unsalted butter
1	egg, beaten, for glaze

Dissolve the yeast in the water in a large bowl. Let stand for 5 to 10 minutes, until creamy.

To knead by hand: Add the sugar and cream to the yeast mixture. Mix together 2 cups of the flour and the salt in a medium bowl. Fold into the liquid. As soon as the dough coheres, scrape it out onto a lightly floured board and knead for 10 to 15 minutes, adding up to ½ cup more flour as needed; the dough will be sticky.

To knead with an electric mixer: Add the sugar and the cream to the yeast mixture. Mix together 2 cups of the flour and the salt in a medium bowl. Add to the bowl, and mix together using the paddle. Scrape the dough off the paddle and change to the dough hook. Knead on low speed for 2 minutes. Knead on medium speed for 8 to 10 minutes, adding up to ½ cup more white flour if the dough is very sticky.

Rinse, dry and butter the bowl. Shape the dough into a ball and place it in the bowl. Cover with plastic wrap and a towel, and set in a warm place to rise for about 2 hours, or until doubled.

Punch down the dough. Cover and let rise in the refrigerator for about 1 hour, until doubled.

To turn the dough: Roll out the dough into a ⅜-inch-thick square that is slightly thicker in the center. Place the butter on the counter and slap it with a rolling pin to soften it. Place it in the center of the dough, and fold in the sides of the dough over the butter all the way around to enclose it completely. Roll the dough out to a long rectangle that is 3 times as long as its width.

First turn: Fold the dough in thirds like a business letter. Turn the dough a quarter turn, so that the edge of the top layer is now facing right. Place the dough in a plastic bag, and refrigerate for 10 minutes.

Second and third turns: With the folded edge of the dough still facing right, roll out the dough into a long rectangle as before. Fold it again like a business letter, and turn another quarter turn. Place in the plastic bag and refrigerate again for 10 minutes. Fold and turn the dough one more time, refrigerating for 10 minutes after the third turn.

To cut and shape the croissants: Line 2 baking sheets with parchment, or butter nonstick baking sheets. Roll out the dough to a rectangle about ⅛ inch thick. Cut the dough into bands about 8 inches wide, then cut each band crosswise into triangles, about 4 or 5 inches wide at the wide end. Roll up the triangles, beginning at the wide end, and curl in the ends slightly once the crescents are rolled up (see illustrations, right). As they are rolled, place the croissants on the baking sheets, leaving about 1 inch between them. Cover loosely with a towel and let rise in a warm place for about 1½ hours, or until nearly doubled.

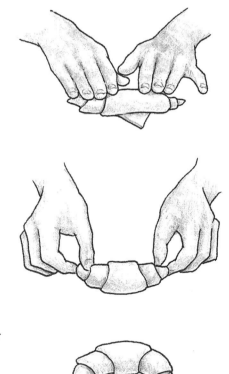

About 30 minutes before baking, preheat the oven to 400 degrees F, with a rack in the middle and another in the upper third.

Brush the croissants with the beaten egg. Bake for 18 minutes, switching the baking sheets halfway through, until brown.

Remove from the pans and cool on a rack.

Challah

2 VERY LARGE OR 3 MEDIUM-SIZE BRAIDED LOAVES

CHALLAH IS A RICH EGG BREAD. The loaves are braided and shiny with egg wash, beautiful to look at and heavenly to eat. Traditional challah is made with white flour only, but I like to add a little whole wheat flour for its nutty flavor and nutritional value. This dough is smooth and easy to work with. (See photograph, page 74.)

1	tablespoon active dry yeast
½	cup lukewarm water
1	cup lukewarm milk
3	large eggs
3	tablespoons mild-flavored honey
	About 3½-4½ cups unbleached white flour
¼	cup melted unsalted butter or sunflower, safflower or canola oil
2½	teaspoons salt
1½	cups whole wheat pastry flour or whole wheat flour
1	egg, beaten with 2 tablespoons water, for egg wash
2-3	tablespoons poppy seeds or sesame seeds (optional)

Dissolve the yeast in the warm water in a large bowl. Let stand for 5 to 10 minutes, until creamy.

Beat in the warm milk, eggs and honey. Whisk in 2½ cups of the white flour, 1 cup at a time, to make a sponge. Stir 100 times with a wooden spoon, changing directions every once in awhile, and scraping down the sides of the bowl, or beat with an electric mixer for 3 minutes. Cover the sponge with plastic wrap and set in a warm place for 1 hour, or until bubbly.

To knead by hand: Fold the melted butter or oil and salt into the sponge with a wooden spoon. Fold in the whole wheat flour. Begin adding the remaining white flour, 1 cup at a time, and as soon as you can, scrape the dough out onto a lightly floured work surface. Knead, adding white flour as needed, for 10 minutes, or until the dough is stiff, very elastic and somewhat silky.

To knead with an electric mixer: Pour the butter or oil over the sponge. Combine 1 cup of the remaining white flour, the salt and the whole wheat flour in a medium bowl. Add all at once to the sponge, and mix with the paddle until combined. Change to the dough hook, and mix on low speed for 2 minutes. Mix on medium speed for 8 to 10 minutes. If the dough seems very wet and sticky, sprinkle in up to 1 cup white flour. Scrape out the dough onto a lightly floured surface and knead for a minute or so by hand; the dough should be stiff, very elastic and somewhat silky.

Rinse, dry and lightly oil the bowl. Shape the dough into a ball. Place the dough in the bowl, turning to coat with the oil. Cover with plastic wrap and a towel, and set in a warm place to rise for about 1½ hours, or until doubled in bulk.

Oil 1 or 2 baking sheets. Punch down the dough and turn out onto a lightly floured work surface. To make 2 large loaves, divide the dough into 6 equal pieces. To make 3 medium loaves, divide it into 9 equal pieces. Shape each piece into a ball and keep covered lightly with plastic wrap.

Take 3 balls, shape each one into a rectangle, as for a thin baguette (see page 25), and then shape each into a thin, tight rope, 12 to 14 inches long. Place the 3 ropes parallel to one another. Gather one end of the 3 ropes and pinch together (see illustrations below). Braid and pinch the opposite ends together; fold the ends under.

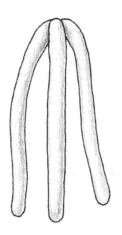  

Place the braided loaf on the sheet and brush it with oil. Repeat with the remaining dough, making 1 or 2 more loaves. As each loaf is finished, transfer it to the baking sheet and brush lightly with oil.

Brush the loaves with the egg wash. Sprinkle with poppy seeds or sesame seeds, if desired. Brush again with egg wash. Cover with a dry towel and set in a warm spot to rise for about 30 minutes, or until they have risen by about 50 percent.

About 30 minutes before baking, preheat the oven to 375 degrees F, with a rack in the middle and one in the upper third of the oven, if you are using 2 baking sheets.

Bake for about 35 to 45 minutes, brushing the loaves halfway through with the egg wash and switching the baking sheets, until the loaves are shiny and dark brown and sound hollow when tapped.

Remove from the pan(s) and cool on a rack.

Spicy Challah with Currants

2 VERY LARGE OR 3 MEDIUM-SIZE LOAVES

I USUALLY MAKE THIS SPECIAL, slightly sweet challah to use as gifts during the holiday season.

Proceed as directed, but increase the honey to ¼ cup, and add 1 teaspoon vanilla extract, ¼ teaspoon ground allspice, ½ teaspoon ground cardamom and 2 tablespoons finely grated orange zest with the eggs and honey. Before dividing into pieces for braiding, knead ⅔ cup currants into the dough.

Sally Lunn

1 LOAF

THIS SIMPLE, RICH TEA CAKE is much like brioche, but cakier. The name comes from a corruption of the French *soleil et lune*, "sun and moon," which was the name of a similar kind of yeasted cake in the eighteenth century. Other food writers insist that the bread is named for a woman called Sally Lunn who lived in Bath, England, and sold the cakes in the street, crying out their name. Sally Lunn cakes are sometimes baked in small muffin pans, sometimes in rings. I like this loaf version. This tea cake can be eaten warm or at room temperature.

1	teaspoon active dry yeast
2	tablespoons lukewarm water
1	tablespoon sugar
½	cup heavy cream, warm or at room temperature
2	large eggs, at room temperature
	Finely chopped zest of 1 lemon
	About 2-2¼ cups unbleached white flour
1	teaspoon salt
2	tablespoons milk, mixed with 1 tablespoon sugar, preferably superfine, for glaze

Dissolve the yeast in the warm water in a large bowl. Let stand for 5 to 10 minutes, until creamy. Beat in the sugar, cream, eggs and lemon zest.

To knead by hand: Mix together 2 cups of the flour and the salt in a medium bowl. Gradually fold into the yeast mixture with a wooden spoon. As soon as you can, scrape out the dough onto a floured work surface. Knead, adding flour to the dough as needed and flouring your hands, for 10 minutes; the dough will be very sticky and you will need a pastry scraper to manipulate it. Work briskly and slap the dough against the work surface rather than folding it and leaning on it.

To knead with an electric mixer: Combine 2 cups of the flour and the salt in a medium bowl. Add all at once to the yeast mixture, and mix together with the paddle. Change to the dough hook, and mix on low speed for 2 minutes. Mix on medium speed for 8 to 10 minutes. If the dough is so wet and sticky that it doesn't adhere to the dough hook, sprinkle in up to ¼ cup white flour. Scrape out the dough onto a lightly floured surface (the dough will be quite sticky), and knead a few times by hand.

Generously butter an 8-x-4-inch loaf pan and dust it with flour. Transfer the dough to the pan and pat out gently to fill the pan. Cover with a towel and let rise in a warm place for about 1½ hours, or until the dough just reaches the top edges of the pan.

About 30 minutes before baking, preheat the oven to 375 degrees F, with a rack in the middle.

Bake for 20 to 25 minutes, until the loaf is golden and pulls away from the sides of the pan.

While the loaf is baking, pour the milk-and-sugar mixture into a small saucepan. Heat to the boiling point. As soon as you take the cake from the oven, brush the top with the hot glaze.

Let the cake cool in the pan for 10 minutes, or until it pulls away from the sides easily. Remove from the pan and cool on a rack.

Welsh Spicy Fruit Bread
(*Bara Brith*)

1 LOAF

Called Bara Brith in Wales, *Barmbrach* in Ireland, this sweet and spicy fruit bread is perfect for afternoon tea. Thinly slice it and lightly toast it, if you wish. It also makes a delicious after-school snack for kids.

1	teaspoon active dry yeast
¼	cup lukewarm water
½	cup lukewarm milk
6	tablespoons (¾ stick) unsalted butter, melted and cooled
1	large egg
¼	cup raw brown sugar (turbinado) or packed dark brown sugar
1⅔	cups whole wheat flour or whole wheat pastry flour
1¼-1⅔	cups unbleached white flour
1	teaspoon salt
1-2	teaspoons Elizabeth David's Spice Blend (*recipe follows*)
½	cup dried currants
½	cup dark or golden raisins
¼	cup candied citrus peel (optional)

Dissolve the yeast in the warm water in a large bowl and stir in the warm milk. Let stand for 5 to 10 minutes, until creamy. Stir in the butter, egg and sugar.

Combine the whole wheat flour, 1¼ cups of the white flour, the salt and spice blend in a medium bowl. Gradually stir into the yeast mixture with a wooden spoon, and mix until you have a soft dough. Turn out onto a lightly floured board and knead for about 10 minutes, adding white flour as needed. The dough should be quite stiff, elastic and smooth. Cover with plastic wrap and a towel and set in a warm place to rise for 1 to 1½ hours, or until doubled.

Meanwhile combine the currants, raisins and candied citrus peel, if using.

Punch down the dough and knead in the fruit mixture. Add a little milk if the dough is too stiff. Shape into a ball and let rest for 5 minutes. Shape into a loaf (see page 24).

Generously butter a loaf pan. Place the dough in it, seam side up first, then seam side down, to coat with the butter. Pat out the dough so that it fills the pan evenly. Cover with a towel and set in a warm place to rise until the top of the loaf curves above the sides of the pan, about 1 hour.

About 30 minutes before baking, preheat the oven to 400 degrees F, with a rack in the middle.

Bake for 30 to 40 minutes, until the loaf is brown on the top and responds to tapping with a hollow sound. Cover the top with a piece of foil during the last 10 minutes if the bread becomes too brown.

Cool for 10 minutes in the pan. Turn out onto a rack to cool completely. Serve thinly sliced, with tea.

Elizabeth David's Spice Blend

1	large whole nutmeg, grated
1	tablespoon white or black peppercorns or allspice berries
1	cinnamon stick (6 inches long)
2	teaspoons (about 30) whole cloves
1½	teaspoons ground ginger

Combine all of the ingredients and grind to a powder in a spice mill. Store in a well-sealed jar.

English Currant Bread

1 LOAF

THIS SPICY, FRUITY TEA BREAD from the British Isles is made with white flour only and is packed with currants.

1½	teaspoons active dry yeast
2	tablespoons lukewarm water
½	cup lukewarm milk
2	tablespoons packed light brown sugar
¼	cup (½ stick) unsalted butter, softened
2	large eggs, beaten
	About 3-4 cups unbleached white flour
1½	teaspoons Elizabeth David's Spice Blend (*previous page*)
1	teaspoon salt
⅔	cup dried currants

For the glaze

2	tablespoons milk
1	tablespoon mild-flavored honey or sugar

Dissolve the yeast in the warm water in a medium bowl. Stir in the warm milk. Let stand for 5 to 10 minutes, until creamy. Stir in the sugar, the butter and the eggs.

To knead by hand: Place 3 cups of the flour in a large bowl and stir in the spice blend and the salt. Make a well in the center and pour in the yeast mixture; fold with a wooden spoon. Fold in the currants; the dough will be quite wet.

Place ½ cup of the white flour on a work surface and scrape the dough out of the bowl. Knead, flouring your hands and the work surface, for 5 to 10 minutes, adding flour as needed, until the dough is elastic.

To knead with an electric mixer: Combine 3½ cups of the flour, the spice blend and the salt in a medium bowl. Add all at once to the yeast mixture, along with the currants. Mix together with the paddle. Change to the dough hook, and mix on low speed for 2 minutes. Mix on medium speed for 8 to 10 minutes. If the dough seems very wet and sticky, sprinkle in up to ½ cup more white flour. Scrape out the dough onto a lightly floured surface and knead for a minute or so by hand.

Rinse, dry and lightly oil the bowl. Shape the dough into a ball and place the dough in the bowl, turning to coat with the oil. Cover the bowl with plastic wrap and a towel and set in a warm place to rise for 1½ hours, or until doubled in bulk.

Generously butter a loaf pan. Punch down the dough and knead for a minute or two on a lightly floured surface. Shape into a loaf (see page 24) and place in the pan. Cover loosely with a towel and let rise for 30 to 45 minutes, or until the top of the loaf curves above the sides of the pan.

Meanwhile, preheat the oven to 400 degrees F, with a rack in the middle.

Bake for 30 to 40 minutes, or until the loaf is brown and responds to tapping with a hollow sound.

Meanwhile, mix together the milk and honey or sugar and heat, stirring, to dissolve. As soon as you remove the bread from the oven, brush with the glaze. Remove from the pan and cool on a rack.

Swedish Limpa

1 LARGE ROUND LOAF OR 2 SMALL LOAVES

SWEDISH LIMPA BREADS ALWAYS CONTAIN RYE FLOUR and spices. They make marvelous breakfast and tea breads. This sweet, subtly spiced version is adapted from James Beard's recipe. Like all rye-based doughs, this one is sticky and unwieldy; you'll have to have patience. The finished bread is dense, with a fine texture. It toasts beautifully.

1	tablespoon active dry yeast
¾	cup lukewarm water
1½	cups dark beer (one 12-ounce bottle), heated to lukewarm
⅓	cup honey
¾	teaspoon ground cardamom
1	teaspoon crushed anise seeds
2	tablespoons grated orange zest
2	cups rye flour
	About 3-4 cups unbleached white flour
2	tablespoons cooled melted unsalted butter or sunflower, safflower or canola oil, plus additional for brushing the bread
2	teaspoons salt
1	egg, beaten with 2 tablespoons water, for egg wash (optional)

Dissolve the yeast in the warm water in a large bowl. Let stand for 5 to 10 minutes, until creamy.

Stir in the beer, honey, cardamom, anise seeds and orange zest with a wooden spoon, and mix together well.

Mix together the rye flour and 1 cup of the white flour in a medium bowl. Stir into the yeast mixture with a wooden spoon. Stir 100 times, changing directions every once in awhile and scraping down the sides of the bowl, or beat for 3 minutes with an electric mixer. Cover with plastic wrap and a towel and set in a warm place for 1 hour, until bubbly.

Stir down the sponge and fold in the melted butter or oil.

To knead by hand: Combine 2 cups of the white flour and the salt in a medium bowl. Fold the flour mixture into the sponge. When the dough coheres, place ½ cup of the white flour on a work surface and turn out the dough (it will be sticky). Knead for 10 to 15 minutes, adding just enough extra flour to make the dough workable, about ½ cup.

To knead with an electric mixer: Combine 2½ cups of the white flour and the salt in a medium bowl. Add all at once to the sponge and mix together with the paddle. Change to the dough hook, and mix on low speed for 2 minutes. Mix on medium speed for 8 to 10 minutes. If the dough seems very wet and sticky, sprinkle in up to ½ cup more white flour. Scrape out the dough onto a lightly floured surface and knead for a minute or so by hand.

Rinse, dry and lightly oil the bowl. Shape the dough into a ball, and place it in the bowl, turning to coat with the oil. Cover with plastic wrap and a towel and set in a warm place to rise for 1½ hours, or until doubled in bulk.

Punch down the dough and shape into 1 large ball or 2 smaller balls (see page 24). Oil a baking sheet and place the dough on it; brush the dough with oil or melted butter. Cover loosely with wax paper or plastic wrap, and refrigerate for 2 to 3 hours, or until nearly doubled.

Remove from the refrigerator and let sit for 30 minutes, while you preheat the oven to 375 degrees F, with a rack in the middle.

Bake a large loaf for 1 hour, or 2 small loaves for 40 to 45 minutes, or until the bread is golden brown and responds to tapping with a hollow sound.

Remove from the pan and cool on a rack.

Fruit-Filled Bread

1 LARGE LOAF

THIS BIG, RICH BREAD bursts with a sweet, spicy dried-fruit filling. The finished bread is pleasantly heavy because of all the fruit. Serve it for a Sunday brunch. It also makes a nice gift. (See photograph, page 39.)

For the filling

1	cup orange juice
1⅓	cups chopped dried figs, prunes, apricots, dates or raisins or a combination
3	tablespoons mild-flavored honey
1	tablespoon grated orange zest (optional)
1	teaspoon vanilla extract
1	teaspoon ground cinnamon
¼	teaspoon freshly grated nutmeg
½	cup chopped walnuts (optional)
2	tablespoons unsalted butter

For the dough

2½	teaspoons active dry yeast
¼	cup lukewarm water
½	cup orange juice
½	cup lukewarm milk
2-3	tablespoons mild-flavored honey
2	large eggs, beaten
3	tablespoons melted unsalted butter or canola oil
1½	cups whole wheat pastry flour
	About 2-3 cups unbleached white flour
1½	teaspoons salt

1	egg, mixed with 2 tablespoons water and 1 teaspoon sugar, for egg wash

To make the filling: Pour the orange juice over the dried fruit, and let soak for at least 3 hours, or overnight.

Drain the juice into a small nonreactive saucepan. Add water if necessary; you should have ¼ cup liquid. Add the plumped fruit to the saucepan, along with the honey, zest (if using), vanilla and spices.

Bring the mixture to a simmer over medium heat and simmer, stirring occasionally, until thick. Remove from the heat and stir in the nuts, if using, and the butter; set aside while you make the dough.

To make the dough: Dissolve the yeast in the warm water in a large bowl. Let stand for 5 to 10 minutes, until creamy.

Stir in the orange juice, warm milk, honey, eggs and butter or oil.

To knead by hand: Mix together the whole wheat pastry flour, 2 cups of the white flour and the salt in a medium bowl. Fold into the yeast mixture, 1 cup at a time, with a wooden spoon. As soon as the dough coheres, scrape it out onto a lightly floured work surface. Knead, adding white flour as needed, for 10 minutes.

To knead with an electric mixer: Combine the whole wheat pastry flour, 2 cups of the white flour and the salt in a medium bowl. Add all at once to the yeast mixture, and mix together with the paddle. Change to the dough hook, and mix on low speed for 2 minutes. Mix on medium speed for 8 to 10 minutes. If the dough seems very wet and sticky, sprinkle in up to 1 cup more white flour. Scrape out the dough onto a lightly floured surface and knead for a minute or so by hand; the dough will be soft and slightly sticky.

Rinse, dry and lightly oil the bowl. Shape the dough into a ball and place in the bowl, turning to coat with the oil. Cover with plastic wrap and a towel and set in a warm place to rise for 1½ hours, or until doubled in bulk.

Punch down the dough and turn out onto a lightly floured work surface. Shape into a ball; roll out into a long, wide rectangle, about 12 x 14 inches. Spread the dried fruit lengthwise down the center of the rectangle. You can shape the dough in one of two ways:

Fold up one of the short ends of the rectangle over the fruit, then the other. Then fold in one long side, then the other and pinch together the edges. With a razor blade or a sharp knife, slash across the top of the dough at 1½-inch intervals (see illustrations below).

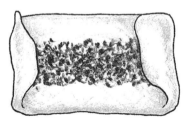
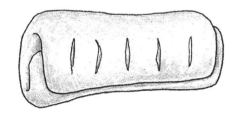

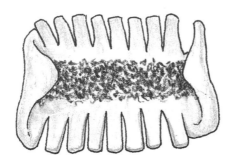

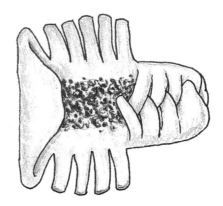

Or, for a lattice effect, fold up the short ends of the rectangle over the fruit and cut the long sides of the rectangle into 1½-inch strips. Fold the strips over the fruit, overlapping them, pulling and twisting the dough to cover the fruit (see illustrations, above and right).

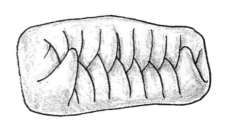

Butter a baking sheet. Carefully transfer the dough to the baking sheet and brush with the egg wash. Let rise in a warm place for 20 minutes, while you preheat the oven to 350 degrees F, with a rack in the middle.

Bake for 1 hour, brushing halfway through with the egg wash.

Remove from the pan and cool on a rack.

Dark Malted Bread with Dried Fruit

1 LOAF

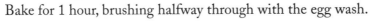

DARK AND SPICY, this makes a good tea or breakfast bread and toasts nicely.

1½	teaspoons active dry yeast
1	cup lukewarm water
½	cup warm Guinness stout
2	tablespoons malt extract (page 15)
1	tablespoon molasses
2½	cups whole wheat flour or whole wheat pastry flour
1	teaspoon Elizabeth David's Spice Blend (page 161, optional)
1½	teaspoons salt
2	tablespoons sunflower, safflower or canola oil
	About 1-1½ cups unbleached white flour
½	cup dried currants
½	cup golden or dark raisins
1	egg, beaten with 2 tablespoons water, for egg wash

Dissolve the yeast in the warm water in a large bowl. Let stand for 5 to 10 minutes, until creamy. Stir in the Guinness, malt extract and molasses.

To knead by hand: Mix together 1¼ cups of the whole wheat flour, the spice blend, if using, and the salt in a medium bowl. Gradually stir this mixture into the yeast mixture, 1 cup at a time, with a wooden spoon. Fold in the oil, and begin adding the remaining 1¼ cups whole wheat flour, along with 1 cup of the white flour, 1 cup at a time. As soon as you can, scrape the dough out of the bowl onto a floured work surface.

Begin kneading, using a pastry scraper to facilitate folding, and adding flour to the board and your hands as needed.

Knead for about 15 minutes; the dough will be very sticky at first, but will stiffen after about 5 minutes. At the end of the kneading, the dough will be stiff, dense and elastic.

To knead with an electric mixer: Mix together the whole wheat flour, the spice blend, if using, the salt and 1 cup of the white flour in a medium bowl. Add all at once to the yeast mixture, add the oil and mix together using the paddle. Scrape off the dough and change to the dough hook. Knead on low speed for 2 minutes. Mix on medium speed for 8 to 10 minutes, adding up to ½ cup more white flour if the dough is very sticky; it should be stiff, dense and elastic. Scrape the dough out of the bowl onto a floured work surface. Knead for about a minute.

Rinse, dry and lightly oil the bowl. Shape the dough into a ball and place it in the bowl, turning to coat with the oil. Cover tightly with plastic wrap and a towel and let rise in a warm place for 1½ to 2 hours, or until doubled.

Punch down the dough and turn out onto a lightly floured surface. Add the currants and raisins, and knead them into the dough until evenly distributed. Shape the dough into a ball and let rest for 5 to 10 minutes.

Oil or butter an 8-x-4-inch loaf pan. Shape the dough into a loaf (see page 24), and place the loaf in the pan, seam side up first, then seam side down, to coat. Brush with the egg wash. Cover with a damp towel and set in a warm place to rise for about 45 minutes, until the top of the loaf curves above the sides of the pan.

About 30 minutes before baking, preheat the oven to 375 degrees F, with a rack in the middle.

Bake for 50 to 55 minutes, or until the loaf is nutty brown and responds to tapping with a hollow sound.

Remove from the pan and cool on a rack.

Cornish Saffron Cake with Fruit

1 LOAF

THIS SAFFRON-HUED TEA BREAD is filled with dried fruit and spices. The saffron gives it a beautiful color. It makes a nice holiday bread.

¾   cup milk
½   teaspoon saffron threads
1   teaspoon active dry yeast
¼   cup lukewarm water
    About 2½-3½ cups unbleached white flour, plus 1 additional tablespoon for
        dried fruit
¼   cup sugar
1   teaspoon salt
¼   teaspoon freshly grated nutmeg
¼   teaspoon ground cinnamon
¼   teaspoon ground allspice
⅛   teaspoon ground cloves
½   cup (1 stick) unsalted butter, softened, or heavy cream
⅓   cup golden raisins
⅓   cup dried currants
2   tablespoons milk, mixed with 1 tablespoon sugar, for glaze

Bring ½ cup of the milk to a boil. Crumble the saffron into a small bowl and pour the boiling milk over it; let cool to lukewarm.

Dissolve the yeast in the warm water in a small bowl. Warm the remaining ¼ cup milk to lukewarm and add to the yeast mixture. Let stand for 5 to 10 minutes, until creamy.

To knead by hand: Combine 2½ cups of the flour, the sugar, salt and spices in a large bowl. Make a well in the center and add the yeast mixture, the butter or cream and the saffron mixture. Stir together with a wooden spoon to make a dough, and turn out onto a lightly floured board. Knead until firm and elastic, about 10 minutes, adding white flour as needed.

To knead with an electric mixer: Combine 2½ cups of the flour, the sugar, salt and spices in the bowl of your mixer. Add the yeast mixture, the butter or cream and the saffron mixture. Mix together using the paddle. Scrape the dough off the paddle and change to the dough hook, and knead on low speed for 2 minutes. Mix on medium speed for 8 to 10 minutes, adding up to 1 cup white flour if the dough is very sticky. Scrape the dough out of the bowl onto a floured work surface and finish kneading for a minute or so by hand.

Rinse, dry and lightly oil the bowl. Shape the dough into a ball. Place the dough in the bowl, turning to coat with the the oil. Cover with plastic wrap and a towel, and let rise in a warm place for 2 hours or more, until doubled in volume.

Punch down the dough. Toss the raisins and currants with 1 tablespoon of the white flour and knead into the dough until evenly distributed. Shape the dough into a loaf (see page 24).

Generously butter a loaf pan. Place the dough in it; gently shape it to fit the pan. Cover lightly with a towel and let rise in a warm place for 45 to 60 minutes, or until the top of the loaf almost curves above the sides of the pan.

About 30 minutes before baking, preheat the oven to 375 degrees F, with a rack in the middle.

Bake for 40 to 45 minutes, until the loaf is golden and responds to tapping with a hollow sound.

Meanwhile, heat the milk and sugar together, stirring to dissolve the sugar. Immediately brush the mixture over the hot loaf. Let cool in the pan for 15 minutes. Turn out and serve warm.

Chelsea Raisin Buns

12 TO 16 BUNS

THESE SWEET ROLLS ARE FILLED WITH RAISINS and topped with a glaze. I'm not sure which is more famous, Chelsea Buns or the Chelsea Bun House that gave them their reputation and their name. The Bun House, built either at the end of the seventeenth century or early in the eighteenth, was located in London near Sloane Square on what is now the Pimlico Road. A combination pastry shop, bakery and teahouse, The Bun House was also famous for its hot cross buns.

This dough is rich, smooth and easy to work with.

For the sponge

2	teaspoons active dry yeast
¼	cup lukewarm water
½	cup lukewarm milk
1	tablespoon sugar
½	cup unbleached white flour

For the dough

	About 2½-3½ cups unbleached white flour (or use half whole wheat pastry flour and half unbleached white flour)
¼	cup packed light brown sugar
1	teaspoon salt
1	teaspoon ground cinnamon
6	tablespoons (¾ stick) unsalted butter, softened
2	large eggs, at room temperature, beaten
	Grated zest of 1 lemon or orange (optional)

For the filling and topping

¼	cup (½ stick) unsalted butter, melted
⅓	cup packed light brown sugar
½	cup dried currants or raisins
1	teaspoon ground cinnamon or Elizabeth David's Spice Blend (page 161)
2	tablespoons sugar, preferably superfine, for topping

For the glaze

2	tablespoons sugar
2	tablespoons milk

To make the sponge: Dissolve the yeast in the warm water in a medium bowl. Stir in the warm milk and the sugar. Let stand for 5 to 10 minutes, until creamy.

Whisk in the white flour and mix well. Cover with plastic wrap and set in a warm place for 30 minutes, until bubbly.

To knead by hand: Combine 2½ cups of the flour, the sugar, salt and cinnamon in a large bowl. Rub the butter into the flour mixture by taking up handfuls and rubbing briskly between the palms of your hands. Add the beaten eggs and lemon or orange zest, if desired. Make a well in the center and stir in the sponge with a wooden spoon. Turn out the dough onto the work surface, and knead, adding white flour as needed, until the dough is stiff and elastic, about 10 minutes.

To knead with an electric mixer: Combine 2½ cups of the flour, the sugar, salt and cinnamon in a mixing bowl. Add the butter, eggs, lemon or orange zest and the sponge mixture. Mix together with the paddle. Change to the dough hook, and mix on low speed for 2 minutes. Mix on medium speed for 8 to 10 minutes, adding flour as needed, until the dough is stiff and elastic.

Scrape out of the bowl and knead for about a minute by hand. Shape into a ball.

Rinse, dry and lightly oil the bowl. Place the dough in it, turning to coat with the oil. Cover with plastic wrap and a towel, and let rise in a warm place for about 1 hour, or until doubled.

To fill and top the buns: Sprinkle the dough with flour and punch down. Turn out of the bowl and knead for a couple of minutes.

Divide the dough into 2 equal portions. Roll out each portion into a rectangle, about ½ inch thick. Brush each rectangle with an equal amount of the butter, and sprinkle each with half the brown sugar, currants or raisins and the cinnamon or spice blend.

Fold each rectangle into thirds, like a business letter. Roll out again into 2 rectangles, each about 8 x 10 inches. Roll up tightly, lengthwise like a jellyroll. Cut slices, 1 to 2 inches thick. Place the slices on a buttered baking sheet, spacing them about 1 inch apart. Cover lightly with a towel and place in a warm place to rise for 45 minutes, or until nearly doubled.

Meanwhile, 30 minutes before baking, preheat the oven to 400 degrees F, with a rack in the middle. When the buns are ready, sprinkle the tops with the superfine sugar. Bake for 15 to 20 minutes, until browned and risen.

Meanwhile, make the glaze: Heat the sugar and milk, stirring to dissolve the sugar. As soon as you remove the buns from the oven, brush with the glaze.

Remove from the baking sheet and cool on racks.

Hot Cross Buns

2 DOZEN BUNS

THESE HOT CROSS BUNS ARE SLIGHTLY SWEET and spicy. Made with half whole wheat flour, half white, the dough is light and pliable and easy to work with after an initial stickiness. They are marvelous warm, with tea.

1	tablespoon active dry yeast
2	tablespoons lukewarm water
1	cup lukewarm milk
¼	cup mild-flavored honey
¼	cup (½ stick) unsalted butter, melted and cooled
2	large eggs, beaten
1½	cups whole wheat pastry flour
	About 2½-3 cups unbleached white flour
2	teaspoons Elizabeth David's Spice Blend (page 161)
1	teaspoon salt
⅔	cup dried currants
1	egg white, beaten
2	tablespoons lemon juice
1	tablespoon mild-flavored honey or sugar

Dissolve the yeast in the warm water in a medium bowl or the bowl of your electric mixer. Stir the warm milk into the yeast mixture. Let stand for 5 to 10 minutes, until creamy.

Stir in the ¼ cup honey, the melted butter and the eggs.

To knead by hand: Combine the whole wheat pastry flour, 1 cup of the white flour, the spice blend and the salt in a large bowl. Make a well in the center and pour in the yeast mixture; fold with a wooden spoon. Fold in the currants; the dough will be quite wet.

Place ½ cup of the white flour on a work surface and scrape the dough out of the bowl. Knead, flouring your hands and the work surface, for 10 minutes, adding more flour as necessary, until the dough is elastic.

To knead with an electric mixer: Combine the whole wheat flour, 2 cups of the white flour, spice blend, the salt and the currants. Add all at once to the yeast mixture, and mix together with the paddle. Change to the dough hook, and mix on low speed for 2 minutes. Mix on medium speed for 8 to 10 minutes. If the dough seems very wet and sticky, sprinkle in up to 1 cup white flour. Scrape out the dough onto a lightly floured surface and knead for a minute or so by hand.

Rinse, dry and lightly oil the bowl. Shape the dough into a ball and place it in the bowl, turning to coat with the oil. Cover the bowl with plastic wrap and a towel and set in a warm place to rise for about 1½ hours, or until doubled in bulk.

Punch down the dough and knead for 1 to 2 minutes on a lightly floured surface. Divide the dough in half; divide each half into 12 equal pieces. Shape these pieces into tight round balls (see page 25).

Oil 2 baking sheets. Place the balls of dough on the baking sheets about 1 inch apart and press them down gently with the bottom of a jar or glass or with moistened fingers. Cover and let rise in a warm place for 45 to 60 minutes, or until nearly doubled.

About 30 minutes before baking, preheat the oven to 375 degrees F, with a rack in the middle and another in the upper third.

Gently brush the tops of the buns with the beaten egg white. With a razor blade or sharp knife, cut an X across the top of each bun.

Bake for 20 minutes, or until lightly browned, switching the baking sheets halfway through.

While the buns are baking, mix together the lemon juice and honey or sugar. As soon as you remove the buns from the oven, brush them with the mixture.

Remove from the baking sheets and cool on racks.

Pecan Rolls

2 DOZEN ROLLS

Make these breakfast rolls for a holiday brunch. The whole wheat flour in the dough contributes to their nutty flavor. The dough is soft and fairly easy to work with.

For the dough

1	cup raisins
	Boiling water
1	tablespoon active dry yeast
¾	cup lukewarm milk
½	cup lukewarm orange juice
⅓	cup mild-flavored honey
¼	cup sunflower, safflower or canola oil or melted, cooled unsalted butter
2	large eggs, at room temperature, beaten
1⅔	cups whole wheat flour
2	teaspoons salt
½	teaspoon ground mace or nutmeg
	About 4-5 cups unbleached white flour

For the filling

¼	cup (½ stick) unsalted butter
2	tablespoons honey
	About 1 teaspoon ground cinnamon
1½	cups chopped pecans

For the topping

2	tablespoons unsalted butter, melted
2	tablespoons honey
½	teaspoon ground cinnamon
1	egg, beaten with 2 tablespoons water, for egg wash

Soak the raisins in boiling water to cover for 15 minutes, or until plumped.

Drain over a bowl, and set raisins aside. Reserve ½ cup of the soaking water; let cool to lukewarm.

Dissolve the yeast in the cooled soaking water in a large bowl. Stir in the warm milk, warm orange juice and the honey. Let stand for 5 to 10 minutes, until creamy.

To knead by hand: Stir the oil or melted butter into the yeast mixture and add the eggs. Mix together the whole wheat flour, salt and the mace or nutmeg in a medium bowl. Fold into the yeast mixture, 1 cup at a time, with a wooden spoon. Begin folding in the white flour, and when the dough comes away from the sides of the bowl, turn it out onto a floured work surface; it will be very sticky.

Knead for 5 minutes, using a pastry scraper to help turn the dough and adding white flour as needed to the work surface. Add the raisins and knead them into the dough. Continue kneading for 5 to 10 minutes more, adding white flour as needed.

To knead with an electric mixer: Add the oil or butter to the yeast mixture, along with the eggs. Mix together the whole wheat flour and 4 cups white flour with the salt and the mace or nutmeg in a medium bowl. Add to the yeast mixture all at once, and mix together with the paddle. Change to the dough hook, and knead on low speed for 2 minutes. Mix on medium speed for 8 to 10 minutes. Add up to 1 cup more white flour if the dough is very moist. Add the raisins and knead them into the dough. Turn out onto a lightly floured work surface and knead a few times by hand.

Rinse, dry and lightly oil the bowl. Shape the dough into a ball, and place it in the bowl, turning to coat with the oil. Cover with plastic wrap and a towel and let rise in a warm place for 1½ to 2 hours, or until doubled in bulk.

Punch down the dough, knead a few times and cut in half. Roll out each half into a 12-x-14-inch rectangle, about ¼ inch thick.

To make the filling: Melt the butter and the honey together over low heat. Brush the rectangles of dough with the butter-honey mixture and sprinkle generously with the cinnamon. Evenly spread half of the pecans over each rectangle. Roll up each rectangle tightly, like a jellyroll.

Butter 2 baking sheets. Cut each cylinder into 12 rolls, each 1½ to 2 inches thick. Place the rolls, cut sides down, about 1 inch apart on the baking sheets. Cover lightly with plastic wrap and a towel, and set in a warm place to rise for about 1 hour, until nearly doubled.

About 30 minutes before baking, preheat the oven to 400 degrees F, with a rack in the middle and another in the upper third.

To make the topping: Melt together the butter and honey. Stir in the cinnamon. Brush the rolls gently with the mixture; brush with the egg wash.

Bake for 20 to 25 minutes, until golden brown, brushing halfway through with the egg wash and switching the baking sheets.

Remove the rolls from the baking sheets with a spatula and cool on a rack.

Pizzas, Calzones and Focacce

Partly Whole Wheat Pizza Dough

ONE 12-TO-15-INCH CRUST

THIS DELICIOUS, CRUNCHY CRUST has a slightly sour flavor that develops during the dough's long (4-hour) rising time. Alternatively, you can double the quantity of yeast and allow the dough to rise for 2 hours.

Bake the pizza at the highest possible heat to get a crisp texture.

The dough can be doubled or tripled and frozen for up to 6 months. Frozen dough thaws in about 2 hours.

For the dough

1	scant teaspoon active dry yeast
⅔	cup lukewarm water
1	tablespoon olive oil
1	cup whole wheat pastry flour
½	teaspoon salt
	About 1-1¼ cups unbleached white flour

For the garlic-oil topping

3	tablespoons olive oil
2	large garlic cloves, minced

Dissolve the yeast in the warm water in a large bowl. Let stand for 5 to 10 minutes, until creamy.

To knead by hand: Add the olive oil to the yeast mixture and mix well. Combine the whole wheat pastry flour and the salt in a medium bowl. Stir into the yeast mixture with a wooden spoon. Begin adding the white flour, and as soon as the dough coheres, scrape it out of the bowl and knead on a lightly floured surface for 10 to 15 minutes. The dough will be sticky; keep flouring your hands and add only enough flour to prevent the dough from sticking to the work surface.

To knead with an electric mixer: Add the olive oil to the yeast mixture and mix well. Combine the whole wheat pastry flour, salt and 1 cup of the white flour in a medium bowl. Add to the yeast mixture all at once, and mix together using the paddle. Change to the dough hook, and knead on low speed for 2 minutes. Mix on medium speed for 8 to 10 minutes. Add up to ¼ cup more white flour if the dough seems very sticky.

Shape the dough into a ball on a floured work surface. Rinse, dry and lightly oil the bowl. Place the dough in it, turning to coat with the oil. Cover with plastic wrap and a towel and let rise for 4 hours or up to 8 hours, or until doubled in bulk. If the dough doubles before this, punch it down and let rise again for the remaining time; it needs the full time to develop its flavor.

Oil your hands and the top of the dough. Punch down the dough and turn out onto a lightly floured work surface. Shape into a ball and let rest under a kitchen towel for 30 minutes.

Oil a 12-to-15-inch pizza pan or baking sheet. Roll out or stretch out the dough with your hands, keeping them oiled so the dough doesn't stick, to a thickness of ⅛ inch, with a thick edge. Pinch the edges all the way around to make an attractive border. The dough can sit, covered with a towel, for up to 1 hour before being topped and baked.

About 30 minutes before baking, preheat the oven to 500 degrees F, with a rack in the middle.

Combine the olive oil and garlic in a small bowl. Brush the crust with the mixture so the dough will be crisp. Cover with the topping of your choice (see pages 183 to 187). Bake until the edges of the dough are browned, 15 to 20 minutes. If you're using cheese, add it halfway through the baking, or it will burn.

Quick Whole Wheat Pizza Dough

ONE 10-INCH CRUST

I LEARNED TO MAKE this easy no-yeast pizza crust in Provence; it can be assembled very quickly.

1⅔	cups whole wheat pastry flour
1	teaspoon baking powder
½	teaspoon salt
½	teaspoon baking soda
⅔	cup water
2	tablespoons olive oil
	About ¼-½ cup unbleached white flour

Mix together the whole wheat pastry flour, baking powder, salt and baking soda in a large bowl or in a food processor fitted with the metal blade. Add the water and blend in. Add the oil. Add as much of the white flour as needed if the dough is sticky; it should be somewhat stiff.

Oil a 10-inch pizza pan, pie pan or quiche pan. Roll out the dough ¼ inch thick and line the pan. Since the dough is stiff, keep pounding it down with the rolling pin and rolling it out until you get a flat round. Don't worry if the dough tears; you can patch it together later. Pinch a border around the edge and refrigerate until ready to use. (*The pizza crust can also be frozen at this point. Wrap in foil. Defrost before continuing.*)

About 30 minutes before baking, preheat the oven to 450 degrees F, with a rack in the middle.

Spread the desired topping (see pages 183 to 187) over the crust. Bake for 15 to 20 minutes, or until the crust is brown and crisp.

Pizza with Wild Mushroom Topping

ONE 12-TO-15-INCH PIZZA

A TOPPING OF FRAGRANT MUSHROOMS, combined with sage and lots of garlic, makes a marvelous, light pizza.

1	ounce (1 cup) dried porcini mushrooms
	Boiling water
2	tablespoons olive oil
4	large garlic cloves, minced
1-2	teaspoons soy sauce
3	tablespoons dry white wine
1	tablespoon chopped fresh sage leaves
2	tablespoons chopped fresh parsley
	Salt and freshly ground pepper
	Partly Whole Wheat Pizza Dough (page 180) or Quick Whole Wheat Pizza Dough (page 182)
	Garlic oil (page 180)
1-2	ounces (¼-½ cup) freshly grated Parmesan cheese

Preheat the oven to 500 degrees F, with a rack in the middle.

Soak the mushrooms in boiling water to cover for 30 minutes.

Squeeze the liquid out of the mushrooms over a bowl, and strain the soaking liquid through a strainer lined with paper towels or cheesecloth. Retain the liquid (you should have about ½ cup). Rinse the mushrooms thoroughly; squeeze dry.

Heat the oil in a small nonreactive saucepan over medium heat. Add the mushrooms and garlic and sauté for about 5 minutes, until the garlic begins to color. Add the soy sauce and wine and sauté for about 5 minutes, or until the liquid evaporates.

Add the mushroom-soaking liquid and the sage, raise the heat to medium-high and cook, stirring often, until the liquid reduces to a glaze, about 5 to 10 minutes. Stir in the parsley; add salt and freshly ground pepper to taste. Remove from the heat.

Brush the prepared pizza crust with the garlic oil. Bake for 7 minutes, or until lightly browned.

Remove from the oven, spread the mushroom mixture over the crust in an even layer, and sprinkle with the Parmesan. Return to the oven and bake for 8 to 10 minutes, until golden brown and fragrant.

Remove from the heat and serve.

Fresh Tomato and Fresh Goat Cheese Topping

ONE 12-TO-15-INCH PIZZA

THIS PUNGENT TOPPING can be assembled in minutes.

Partly Whole Wheat Pizza Dough (page 180) or Quick Whole Wheat
    Pizza Dough (page 182)
Garlic oil (page 180)
¾   pound ripe tomatoes (canned or fresh), peeled, seeded and chopped
    (1⅓ cups chopped)
1   red bell pepper, seeded and sliced
3   ounces fresh goat cheese, thinly sliced
2   tablespoons capers, rinsed
    Freshly ground pepper, to taste

About 30 minutes before baking, preheat the oven to 500 degrees F, with a rack in the middle.

Brush the prepared pizza crust with the garlic oil. Sprinkle on the tomatoes, bell pepper, goat cheese and capers. Season with pepper.

Bake for 15 minutes, or until the pizza is browned and crisp.

Pizza with Sweet Peppers

ONE 12-TO-15-INCH PIZZA

THE PEPPERS FOR THIS VERY PRETTY, EASY PIZZA can be sautéed hours in advance and reheated gently just before baking. (See photograph, page 37.)

1   tablespoon olive oil

1   pound (2 large) red bell peppers, seeded and thinly sliced

1   pound (2 large) yellow bell peppers, seeded and thinly sliced

    Salt, to taste

2   garlic cloves, minced

1   tablespoon fresh thyme, or 1 teaspoon dried

    Freshly ground pepper, to taste

    Partly Whole Wheat Pizza Dough (page 180) or Quick Whole Wheat
       Pizza Dough (page 182)

    Garlic oil (page 180; optional)

Preheat the oven to 500 degrees F, with a rack in the middle.

Heat the oil in a heavy-bottomed or nonstick skillet over medium heat. Sauté the peppers with a little salt until they begin to soften, about 5 minutes. Add the garlic and cook, stirring, for another 5 minutes, or until the peppers are softened but still have some texture. Stir in the thyme and season with salt and pepper.

Brush the prepared pizza crust with the garlic oil, if using. Spread with the sautéed pepper mixture.

Bake for 15 to 20 minutes, until the crust is browned.

Tomato-Onion Topping

ONE 12-TO-15-INCH PIZZA

T HE TOPPING FOR THIS PIZZA is a gutsy tomato sauce smothered with plenty of onions. Green peppers, cheese, anchovies or mushrooms can be substituted for the onions.

For the tomato sauce

- 1 tablespoon olive oil
- 2-3 garlic cloves, minced
- 2 pounds (8 medium) tomatoes (fresh or canned), seeded and chopped (3 cups chopped)
- 1 tablespoon tomato paste (optional)
  Salt, to taste
- 1 teaspoon dried oregano
- ½ teaspoon dried thyme, or 1 teaspoon fresh
  Pinch of cinnamon
  Freshly ground pepper, to taste

For the onion topping

- 1 tablespoon olive oil
- 2-3 onions, sliced into rings
  Salt and freshly ground pepper, to taste

  Partly Whole Wheat Pizza Dough (page 180) or Quick Whole Wheat
  Pizza Dough (page 182)
  Garlic oil (page 180; optional)

Preheat the oven to 500 degrees F, with a rack in the middle.

Meanwhile, make the tomato sauce: Heat the oil in a heavy-bottomed nonreactive skillet over medium heat. Sauté the garlic until it begins to color, about 1 minute. Add the tomatoes and tomato paste, if using, and bring to a simmer. Add salt to taste and cook, uncovered, over medium-low heat for about 30 minutes, stirring from time to time.

Add the oregano and thyme and cook for 10 minutes. Add the cinnamon and freshly ground pepper. Taste and correct the seasonings, adding salt, garlic or herbs, if you wish. Set aside.

To make the onion topping: Heat the oil in a skillet over medium heat. Sauté the onions, stirring often, until they just begin to brown, about 10 minutes. Remove from the heat. Season with salt and pepper.

Brush the prepared pizza crust with the garlic oil, if desired. Spread with the tomato sauce and top with the onions.

Bake for 15 to 20 minutes, until the crust is nicely browned.

Variations

Other toppings

2	green bell peppers, seeded and sliced
¼	pound mozzarella cheese, thinly sliced
4	ounces olives, pitted and halved (⅔ cup)
16	anchovy fillets
1-2	6½-ounce jars artichoke hearts, drained and sliced
2	ounces (½ cup) freshly grated Parmesan cheese
2	tablespoons capers, rinsed

Calzones

6 CALZONES

CALZONES ARE ITALIAN STUFFED TURNOVERS. A pizza dough is rolled into an oval shape, topped with a filling, folded over and sealed at the edges. They can be filled with any number of ingredient combinations.

2	teaspoons active dry yeast
1⅓	cups lukewarm water
2	tablespoons olive oil
2	cups whole wheat pastry flour or whole wheat flour
1	teaspoon salt
	About 2-2½ cups unbleached white flour
	Filling of choice (pages 189 to 191)
1	egg, beaten with 2 tablespoons water

For the garlic oil

¼	cup olive oil
2	garlic cloves, minced

Follow the instructions for Partly Whole Wheat Pizza Dough (page 180) from the beginning through the first rise.

When the dough has risen, punch it down, divide it into 6 equal pieces and shape into balls. Place on a lightly floured surface, cover with a towel and let sit in a warm place for 30 minutes, until the dough rises slightly.

Meanwhile, preheat the oven to 450 degrees F, with a rack in the middle.

Roll or press out each ball into an oval, ⅛ to ¼ inch thick. If the dough is very sticky, dust lightly with flour or oil your fingertips. Spread the filling over half the oval, leaving a ½-inch margin all around. Brush the edges of the oval with the beaten egg; fold in half. Firmly pinch the edges together.

To make the garlic oil: Mix together the oil and garlic. Brush the calzones with the mixture.

Cut 1 or 2 slits in the top of each calzone with a sharp knife to allow steam to escape during baking.

Oil a baking sheet; place the calzones on the baking sheet. Bake for 20 to 25 minutes, until brown.

Brush again with the garlic oil and serve hot.

Tomato-Mozzarella Filling

FOR 6 CALZONES

1   tablespoon olive oil
2   large garlic cloves, minced
2   pounds tomatoes (fresh or canned), peeled, seeded and chopped (3 cups chopped)
Salt and freshly ground pepper
Pinch of sugar
2   tablespoons chopped fresh basil or ½ teaspoon dried thyme or oregano
½   pound mozzarella, shredded
2   ounces (½ cup) freshly grated Parmesan cheese

Heat the oil in a heavy nonreactive skillet over medium-low heat. Add the garlic and sauté until the garlic begins to color. Add the tomatoes and increase the heat to medium-high. Season with salt and pepper and sugar, and sauté over medium-high heat until the tomatoes are cooked down and fragrant, about 15 minutes. Add the basil, thyme or oregano, and adjust the seasonings; set aside.

Spread the tomato sauce over the rolled-out calzones, leaving a ½-inch margin all around. Top with mozzarella and Parmesan. Seal and bake as directed.

Fresh Goat Cheese and Olive Filling

FOR 6 CALZONES

¾   pound fresh goat cheese
4   ounces imported black olives, pitted and coarsely chopped (about ⅔ cup)
2   garlic cloves, minced
1-2 teaspoons fresh thyme, or ½-1 teaspoon dried
1   teaspoon chopped fresh rosemary, or ½ teaspoon crumbled dried
Freshly ground pepper

Mash the goat cheese with a wooden spoon in a medium bowl. Stir in all of the remaining ingredients.

Spread over the rolled-out calzones, leaving a ½-inch margin all around. Seal and bake as directed.

Fresh Goat Cheese and Herb Filling

FOR 6 CALZONES

- ½   pound fresh goat cheese
- 2   tablespoons low-fat plain yogurt
- ¼   pound mozzarella, diced
- 2   tablespoons chopped fresh chives
- 1   teaspoon fresh thyme leaves, or ½ teaspoon dried
- 2   teaspoons chopped fresh rosemary, or 1 teaspoon crumbled dried
- 2   garlic cloves, minced or put through a press
  Freshly ground pepper

Mash together the goat cheese and yogurt in a medium bowl. Stir in the mozzarella, herbs, garlic and pepper.

Spread over the rolled-out calzones, leaving a ½-inch margin all around. Seal and bake as directed on page 188.

White Bean and Sage Filling

FOR 6 CALZONES

ALTHOUGH CANNED BEANS are more convenient here, they are not as good as dried beans you have cooked yourself because canned beans tend to have a viscous texture.

- ½   pound (1 heaped cup) dried white beans, cooked, or 1½ fifteen-ounce cans white beans, drained (2 cups cooked)
- 2   tomatoes, peeled, seeded and chopped (optional)
- 2   ounces (½ cup) freshly grated Parmesan cheese
- ¼   cup chopped fresh parsley
- 2   tablespoons chopped fresh sage
- 1   teaspoon fresh thyme leaves, or ½ teaspoon dried
- 1-2 garlic cloves, minced
  Salt and freshly ground pepper

Mix together all of the ingredients in a medium bowl.

Spread over the rolled-out calzones, leaving a ½-inch margin all around. Seal and bake as directed on page 188.

Potato and Pesto Filling

FOR 6 CALZONES

1½   pounds (6 medium) waxy potatoes, unpeeled, scrubbed and diced
½   ounce (about ½ cup) dried porcini mushrooms
     Boiling water
½   cup pesto (see Pesto Bread, page 142)
2   garlic cloves, minced or put through a press
2   ounces (½ cup) freshly grated Parmesan cheese
2   tablespoons olive oil
     Salt and freshly ground pepper, to taste

Steam the potatoes until tender; drain.

Meanwhile, soak the mushrooms in boiling water to cover for 15 to 30 minutes. Drain and rinse thoroughly.

Toss together the potatoes, mushrooms, pesto, garlic, Parmesan, olive oil and salt and pepper.

Spread this mixture over the rolled-out calzones, leaving a ½-inch margin all around. Seal and bake as directed on page 188.

Focaccia

THREE 9- OR 10-INCH ROUND FOCACCE, OR
TWO 15½-X-10½-INCH-RECTANGULAR FOCACCE

Focaccia is a rustic round or rectangular leavened bread, usually ¾ to 1 inch thick, with a dimpled top and a variety of seasonings. Sometimes, it is merely sprinkled with coarse salt and olive oil, or it can be flavored with herbs like sage or rosemary or studded with olives, anchovies or garlic. It is very easy to make. I often serve focaccia, cut into small squares, with cocktails. The dough is light and easy to work with. It requires a long rising time. (See photograph, page 77.)

2½	teaspoons active dry yeast
2½	cups lukewarm water
¼	cup olive oil
	About 5½-7 cups unbleached white flour
2½	teaspoons salt
	Olive oil, for brushing the breads

Dissolve the yeast in the warm water in a large bowl. Let stand for 5 to 10 minutes, until creamy. Stir in the oil.

To knead by hand: Combine the flour and salt in a medium bowl. Fold the flour mixture into the yeast mixture with a wooden spoon, 1 cup at a time. As soon as the dough comes together, turn out onto a lightly floured surface and knead, adding flour as necessary, for 10 minutes, or until the dough is smooth and elastic.

To knead with an electric mixer: Combine 5½ cups of the flour and the salt. Add all at once to the yeast mixture, and mix together using the paddle. Change to the dough hook, and knead for 2 minutes on low speed. Mix for 8 to 10 minutes on medium speed. Add up to 1½ cups more flour as necessary if the dough seems very sticky.

Rinse, dry and lightly oil the bowl. Shape the dough into a ball and place it in the bowl, turning to coat with the oil. Cover with plastic wrap or a damp towel and let rise in a warm place for about 1½ hours, or until doubled.

Turn the dough out onto a lightly floured surface and knead for 1 minute. Cut into 3 pieces for round focacce or 2 pieces for rectangular ones. Oil pizza pans or jellyroll pans and roll or press out the dough to fit the pans. Place in the pans, cover with damp towels and let rise in a warm place for 30 minutes; the breads will puff slightly.

Using your fingertips, dimple the surface of the dough all over. Cover again and let rise for 1½ to 2 hours, or until nearly doubled.

About 30 minutes before baking, preheat the oven to 400 degrees F, with a rack in the middle and another in the upper third.

Brush the dough lightly with olive oil. Bake for 20 to 25 minutes, spraying with water 3 times during the first 10 minutes of baking, or until the tops are golden brown.

Invert the breads on a rack, so that the bottoms don't get soggy.

Serve warm or at room temperature, preferably the same day you bake them. Do not refrigerate.

Whole Wheat Focaccia with Herbs

THREE 9- OR 10-INCH ROUND FOCACCE, OR
TWO 15½-X-10½-INCH RECTANGULAR FOCACCE

MADE WITH A COMBINATION OF WHOLE WHEAT and unbleached white flours, this focaccia has even more flavor than the traditional all-white version.

2½	teaspoons active dry yeast
2½	cups lukewarm water
3	tablespoons olive oil
3	tablespoons chopped fresh sage or rosemary
3	cups whole wheat flour
1	scant tablespoon salt
	About 2½-3 cups unbleached white flour
	Olive oil, for brushing the breads

Dissolve the yeast in the warm water in a large bowl. Let stand for 5 to 10 minutes, until creamy.

Stir in the olive oil and sage or rosemary.

To knead by hand: Combine the whole wheat flour and salt in a medium bowl. Fold into the yeast mixture, 1 cup at a time, with a wooden spoon. Fold in the white flour, 1 cup at a time. As soon as the dough comes together, turn it out onto a lightly floured surface and knead, adding flour as needed, for 10 minutes, or until the dough is smooth and elastic.

To knead with an electric mixer: Combine the whole wheat flour, salt and 2½ cups of the white flour in a medium bowl. Add all at once to the yeast mixture, and mix together using the paddle. Change to the dough hook, and knead for 2 minutes on low speed. Mix for 8 to 10 minutes on medium speed. Add up to ½ cup more white flour if the dough seems very sticky; it should be somewhat tacky.

Rinse, dry and lightly oil the bowl. Shape the dough into a ball and place it in the bowl, turning to coat with the oil. Cover with plastic wrap and a damp towel and let rise in a warm place for about 1½ hours, or until doubled.

Turn out the dough onto a lightly floured surface and knead for 1 minute. Cut into 3 pieces for round focacce or 2 pieces for rectangular ones. Oil pizza pans or jellyroll pans and roll or press out the dough to fit the pans. Place in the pans, cover with damp towels and let rise for 30 minutes; the breads will rise slightly.

Using your fingertips, dimple the surface of the dough all over. Cover again and let rise for 1½ to 2 hours, or until nearly doubled.

About 30 minutes before baking, preheat the oven to 400 degrees F, with a rack in the middle and another in the upper third.

Brush the dough lightly with olive oil. Bake for 20 to 25 minutes, spraying with water 3 times during the first 10 minutes of baking, or until the tops are golden brown.

Invert the breads on a rack, so that the bottoms don't get soggy.

Serve warm or at room temperature, preferably the same day you bake them. Do not refrigerate.

Variations

Focaccia with Coarse Salt: Omit the herbs, if desired. Sprinkle 2 to 3 teaspoons coarse salt, to taste, over each focaccia before brushing with olive oil and baking.

Focaccia with Sweet Red Peppers: Omit the herbs, if desired. Roast 2 large sweet red bell peppers over a gas burner or under the broiler until blackened on all sides. Remove from the heat and place in a plastic or paper bag until cool enough to handle. Remove the charred skins, cut in half and remove the seeds and membranes. Rinse and pat dry. Chop the peppers into small dice and set aside.

Mix the dough, and when you are ready to knead, add the chopped roasted peppers and knead into the dough. Proceed with the recipe.

Focaccia with Olives: Omit the herbs, if desired. Just before baking, stud the dimples with ½ pound (about 1⅓ cups) pitted imported black olives.

Focaccia with Sun-Dried Tomatoes: Drain 6 ounces (about 1 cup) chopped sun-dried tomatoes that have been marinated in oil and add them to the dough after you've added the flour and kneaded for a few minutes. Knead the tomatoes into the dough (the dough will take on a pale orange color). The olive oil in which the tomatoes were marinated can be used in the dough instead of regular olive oil.

Focaccia with Gorgonzola and Parmesan: Mix together ½ pound (about 1½ cups) crumbled Gorgonzola, 2 ounces (½ cup) freshly grated Parmesan, 1 to 2 garlic cloves, minced, and ¼ cup milk in a food processor or mixing bowl and beat to form a smooth mixture. After you have shaped the focaccia, dimple the bread and spread this mixture over the top. Let rise for about 1½ hours. Bake as above, until the cheese is bubbly and beginning to brown.

Focaccia with Anchovies: Omit the herbs, if desired. Chop 8 to 10 anchovy fillets and mix with ¼ cup olive oil. Brush some of the olive oil mixture over each focaccia before baking.

Breadsticks, Crackers and Flatbreads

Whole Wheat-Sesame Breadsticks

2 DOZEN

THESE ARE VERY DIFFERENT from commercial breadsticks that are loaded with fat and have very little character. They are very simple to make, and the dough is easy to handle. They require only one rise, and shaping them takes no time at all. They're a great item to have on hand, and they always impress guests. (See photograph on the cover.)

2	teaspoons active dry yeast
1½	cups lukewarm water
1	tablespoon malt extract (page 15) or 1 teaspoon honey
2	tablespoons olive oil, plus additional for brushing the dough
½	heaped cup sesame seeds
1½	teaspoons salt
¾	cup unbleached white flour
	About 2½-3 cups whole wheat flour
1	egg white, lightly beaten, for glaze

Dissolve the yeast in the warm water in a large bowl. Stir in the malt extract or honey and let stand for 5 to 10 minutes, until creamy.

Stir in the olive oil, ¼ cup of the sesame seeds and the salt with a wooden spoon. Stir in the white flour. Fold in the whole wheat flour, 1 cup at a time. After the second cup, you should be able to scrape out the dough onto a lightly floured work surface. Knead, adding additional whole wheat flour as needed, for about 10 minutes, or until the dough is stiff and elastic.

Lightly flour a large cutting board. Using your hands or a rolling pin, press out the dough into a 14-x-4-inch rectangle on the board. Lightly oil the top of the dough. Cover with plastic wrap and a towel, and set in a warm place to rise for about 1 hour, or until nearly doubled.

Preheat the oven to 400 degrees F, with a rack in the middle and another in the upper third.

Oil 3 baking sheets. Cut the dough crosswise into 4 equal pieces. Brush each piece with the beaten egg white, and sprinkle each with about 1 heaping tablespoon of the remaining sesame seeds. Cut each piece crosswise into 6 short strips (they'll look like fat fingers).

Roll each strip between your hands and the board until it is as long as the width of your baking sheet. Twist each into a pretty shape and place 1 inch apart on the baking sheets.

Bake for 25 minutes, switching the top and bottom baking pans, and turning the breadsticks halfway through the baking, until they are golden brown (they will probably be darker on one side). Turn off the oven and leave the breadsticks inside for 15 minutes. Repeat with the remaining baking sheet.

Remove from the baking sheets and cool on racks. The breadsticks will keep for several days (wrap them all together in foil) and can be frozen.

Variations

Parmesan Breadsticks: Omit the sesame seeds. Add ½ cup grated Parmesan toward the end of the kneading and work it into the dough. Bake at 450 degrees F for 12 to 15 minutes, until golden.

Thyme Breadsticks: Omit the sesame seeds. Add 1 tablespoon fresh thyme leaves or 1½ teaspoons dried, along with the salt and flour. Proceed as directed.

Spinach and Garlic Breadsticks: Omit the sesame seeds. Use 1¾ cups unbleached white flour and 2 cups whole wheat flour. Add 1 minced garlic clove to the yeast mixture when you add the salt. Proceed as directed, but at the end of kneading, knead in 1¼ cups fresh spinach that has been washed, dried thoroughly and very finely chopped.

Sesame Bread Rings

THIS IS MY VERSION OF A BREAD sold by street vendors in Cairo and Athens, where they string these hard, nutty bracelets of sesame-encrusted bread on thin ropes and sell them throughout the day. I have enriched the recipe by using some whole wheat flour.

1	teaspoon active dry yeast
¼	cup lukewarm water
	Pinch of sugar
½	cup lukewarm milk
1	tablespoon olive oil
½	cup whole wheat flour
¼	cup finely ground semolina
½	teaspoon salt
	About ¾-1 cup unbleached white flour
1	large egg, beaten
½	cup sesame seeds

Dissolve the yeast in the warm water in a large bowl. Stir in the sugar, and let stand for 5 to 10 minutes, until creamy. Stir in the warm milk and oil.

Combine the whole wheat flour, semolina and salt in a medium bowl. Stir into the yeast mixture. Add ¾ cup of the white flour, fold it in, and knead for a few minutes in or out of the bowl, until the dough comes together in a soft ball.

Rinse, dry and lightly oil the bowl. Place the dough in it, turning to coat with the oil. Cover with plastic wrap and a towel and let rest for 15 minutes; it will relax and become pliable.

Turn out the dough onto a lightly floured board and knead vigorously for 10 minutes, adding more white flour if needed; the dough will be stiff, elastic and smooth. Shape into a ball and place in an oiled bowl, turning to coat with the oil. Cover with plastic wrap and a towel and set in a warm place to rise for about 2 hours, or until nearly doubled in size.

Punch down the dough and turn out onto a lightly floured work surface. Cut the dough into 8 to 12 pieces and roll out each piece into a thin rope, about 10 to 12 inches long by 1 to 1½ inches wide.

Oil 2 baking sheets. Place the sesame seeds on a large plate. Brush the ropes of dough with the beaten egg and roll them in the sesame seeds. Join the pieces of dough at the ends, so that they form a bracelet-like circle. Brush again with the egg.

Place the rings on the baking sheets, leaving about 1½ inches between them. Lightly cover with parchment paper or a towel. Set in a warm place to rise for 30 minutes, or until nearly doubled.

Meanwhile, preheat the oven to 425 degrees F, with a rack in the middle and another in the upper third.

Bake the rings for 10 minutes. Reduce the heat to 325 degrees and bake for 10 to 20 minutes, switching the position of the baking sheets halfway through, or until the rings are golden brown and respond to tapping with a hollow sound.

Remove from the baking sheets and cool on racks.

Sesame Crackers

3 TO 4 DOZEN

THESE DELICIOUS, CRUNCHY, nutty-tasting crackers go well with cheese and with foods like hummus or tapenade. They are very easy to make.

1¼   cups whole wheat flour
½   cup sesame seeds
½   teaspoon salt
¼   cup sunflower, safflower or canola oil
1   tablespoon sesame tahini (optional)
    About ¼-⅓ cup water

Preheat the oven to 350 degrees F, with a rack in the middle and another in the upper third. Oil 2 baking sheets.

Mix together the flour, sesame seeds and salt in a mixing bowl or food processor fitted with the metal blade. Add the oil and sesame tahini, if using, and cut in or process until somewhat combined.

Add ¼ cup of the water and work the dough until it has the consistency of coarse pie crust. If it is too dry, add a little more water.

Gather up the dough into a ball and roll out about ⅛ inch thick on a well-floured work surface, or between pieces of wax paper.

Cut into squares or cut with a cookie cutter. Place the squares or rounds close together but not touching on the baking sheets. Bake for 20 to 25 minutes, until browned, switching the positions of the baking sheets halfway through the baking. Don't let the crackers get too brown, or they will taste bitter.

Remove from the baking sheets and cool on racks.

Sardinian Flatbread
(*Carta Musica*)

10 LARGE FLATBREADS

THIS PAPER-THIN, CRISP SARDINIAN FLATBREAD was a rare treat for me until I learned how easy it is to make at home. The bread lasts for weeks and is great to have on hand for snacks and cocktails. This recipe is based on one in Carlo Middione's book, *The Food of Southern Italy*.

1⅔	cups unbleached white flour
¾	cup finely ground semolina
¾	teaspoon salt
1-1½	cups warm water

Mix together the flour, semolina and salt in a large bowl. Gradually add 1 cup of the water and stir in with a wooden spoon. Add more water if necessary to form a smooth, pliable dough that isn't sticky or elastic.

Gather the dough into a ball (dust with flour if it is sticky), and divide into 10 equal-size pieces. Form each piece into a small ball. Place on a lightly dusted board or baking sheet, cover with plastic wrap and a towel, and set aside for 20 minutes.

Meanwhile, preheat the oven to 400 degrees F, with 2 ungreased baking sheets or a baking stone on the lowest rack of the oven.

On a lightly floured work surface, roll out each ball of dough to a very thin (less than 1⁄16-inch) disk, dusting the top of the dough and the work surface as necessary to avoid sticking.

Transfer to the hot baking sheet or baking stone and bake for 2½ to 3 minutes, or until the top is beginning to blister.

Turn over the bread and bake for 2½ to 3 minutes. Watch carefully, since once the dough begins to burn, it will burn very quickly. The flatbreads should be paper-thin and crisp, with brown bubbles.

Remove from the oven, and cool on a rack. Bake the remaining breads.

Store in sealed plastic bags in a cool, dry place. The breads will keep for about 2 weeks.

Buckwheat-Sesame Crackers

3 TO 4 DOZEN

Buckwheat flour gives these crackers a distinctive earthy flavor that combines nicely with the nutty flavor of sesame seeds.

1¼	cups whole wheat flour
½	cup buckwheat flour
2	heaping tablespoons sesame seeds
½	teaspoon salt
¼	cup sunflower, safflower or canola oil
	About ⅓ cup water

Preheat the oven to 350 degrees F, with a rack in the middle and another in the upper third. Oil 2 baking sheets.

Mix together the flours, sesame seeds and salt in a mixing bowl or food processor fitted with the metal blade. Add the oil and cut in or process until somewhat combined.

Add ¼ cup of the water and work the dough until it has the consistency of coarse pie crust. If it is too dry, add a little more water.

Gather up the dough and roll out about ⅛ inch thick on a well-floured work surface or between pieces of wax paper.

Cut into squares or cut with a cookie cutter. Place the squares or rounds close together, but not touching, on the baking sheets. Bake for 20 to 25 minutes, until browned, switching the positions of the baking sheets halfway through the baking. Don't let the crackers get too brown, or they will taste bitter.

Remove from the baking sheets and cool on racks.

Whole Wheat Pita Bread

8 TO 12 LOAVES, DEPENDING ON THE SIZE DESIRED

THESE ARE NOTHING LIKE THE CARDBOARD-LIKE PITAS we often find in restaurants and supermarkets; they are moist, pliable and very tasty. There are two tricks to making pita. First, the oven must be very hot so that the bread puffs up. Second, the bread should not be left in the oven too long, or it will begin to crisp and won't be flexible.

2	tablespoons active dry yeast
¼	teaspoon sugar
2	cups lukewarm water
2	tablespoons olive oil or canola oil
2½	cups whole wheat flour
1	scant tablespoon salt
2-2½	cups unbleached white flour

Dissolve the yeast and sugar in ½ cup of the warm water in a large bowl. Let stand for 5 to 10 minutes, until creamy.

Add the remaining 1½ cups warm water and mix well. Whisk in the oil.

To knead by hand: Mix together the whole wheat flour and salt in a medium bowl. Stir into the yeast mixture, 1 cup at a time, with a wooden spoon. Fold in 1 cup of the white flour. Place 1 cup white flour on a work surface and scrape out the dough on it. Knead for 10 to 15 minutes, adding flour as needed, until the dough is smooth and elastic.

To knead with an electric mixer: Combine the whole wheat flour, salt and 2 cups of the white flour in a medium bowl. Add all at once to the yeast mixture, and mix together with the paddle. Change to the dough hook, and mix on low speed for 2 minutes. Mix on medium speed for 8 to 10 minutes. If the dough seems very wet, sprinkle in up to ½ cup of the remaining white flour. Scrape out the dough onto a lightly floured surface and knead for 1 to 2 minutes by hand; the dough will be medium-soft and smooth.

Shape the dough into a ball. Rinse, dry and lightly oil the bowl. Place the dough in it, turning to coat with the oil. Cover with plastic wrap and a towel and allow to rise in a warm place for 1½ to 2 hours, or until doubled in bulk.

Punch down the dough and turn it out onto a lightly floured work surface. Knead for 1 to 2 minutes. Let rest for 10 minutes.

Divide the dough into 8 to 12 equal pieces. Shape each piece into a ball, and place the balls on a floured work surface. Cover with a towel and let rise in a warm place for 30 minutes; the dough will rise slightly.

Using a well-floured rolling pin, flatten each ball and roll out into an 8-inch circle about ⅛ inch thick. Dust 2 ungreased baking sheets with cornmeal. Place 2 dough circles on each sheet. (Leave the remaining ones on the work surface.) Cover all of the breads with a towel and let rise again for 30 minutes; the dough will rise just slightly.

Meanwhile, preheat the oven to 500 degrees F, with a rack in the middle.

Place 1 baking sheet on the oven rack and bake for 5 minutes, without opening the oven door. Check your loaves, and if they are beginning to brown, remove from the oven. If they still smell yeasty, bake for another 2 to 5 minutes.

Remove from the baking sheets, and cool on racks.

Bake the remaining pitas in this way.

Yeasted Indian Flatbread
(*Naans*)

8 LARGE NAANS

Naans are flat, yeasted breads that traditionally are baked in a Tandoori oven but still yield delicious results when baked under a broiler. This version is made with part whole wheat flour, part white flour.

Naans can be plain or topped with a sweet or savory mixture.

2	teaspoons active dry yeast
¼	cup lukewarm water
1	cup lukewarm milk
¼	cup low-fat plain yogurt or buttermilk
1	teaspoon mild-flavored honey
3	tablespoons sunflower, safflower or canola oil or melted unsalted butter
1	cup unbleached white flour
1	teaspoon salt
	About 2-2½ cups whole wheat flour

Dissolve the yeast in the warm water in a large bowl. Stir in the warm milk, yogurt or buttermilk, honey and oil or melted butter.

To knead by hand: Combine the white flour and the salt in a medium bowl. Fold into the yeast mixture with a wooden spoon. Fold in the whole wheat flour, 1 cup at a time. As soon as the dough coheres, turn it out onto a generously floured work surface and knead, adding whole wheat flour as needed, for 10 minutes, or until the dough is elastic.

To knead with an electric mixer: Add the white flour, salt and 2 cups of the whole wheat flour to the yeast mixture. Mix together with the paddle until combined. Change to the dough hook, and mix on low speed for 2 minutes. Mix on medium speed for 8 to 10 minutes, adding up to ½ cup more whole wheat flour as needed. Scrape the dough out onto a work surface and knead for 1 to 2 minutes; the dough will be stiff and smooth.

Rinse, dry and lightly oil the bowl. Place the dough in the bowl, turning to coat with the oil. Cover with plastic wrap and a damp towel and let rise in a warm place for 1½ to 2 hours, or until doubled in bulk.

About 30 minutes before baking, preheat the oven to 500 degrees F, with a rack in the middle.

Punch down the dough. Turn out onto a lightly floured work surface and knead a few times. Divide into 8 equal pieces. Shape each piece into a ball. Roll each ball out into a ¼-inch-thick round or oval shape. Place on unoiled baking sheets, 2 to a sheet; cover with a damp towel and let rise for 20 minutes; they will rise only slightly.

Bake the *naans*, 1 baking sheet at a time, for 5 minutes. Turn on the broiler and place them under the broiler for 10 to 20 seconds, just until brown spots form on the tops. Remove from the oven and serve hot.

The *naans* can be reheated in the oven, wrapped in foil, and will keep for several days in the refrigerator. You can also roll out the *naans* and keep the dough refrigerated, covered with plastic, for up to 1 day.

Naans with Sweet Pine Nut and Raisin Topping

8 LARGE NAANS

THESE NAANS ARE TOPPED with a sweet, anise-flavored paste made from raisins and pine nuts. They are great for breakfast, snacks, lunch or dinner.

	Yeasted Indian Flatbread dough (*previous page*)
1⅓	cups raisins
	Boiling water
½	cup pine nuts
1¼	teaspoons crushed anise seeds
¼	cup low-fat plain yogurt

While the dough is rising, make the topping: Place the raisins in a bowl and pour on boiling water to cover. Let soak for 15 minutes, until plump.

Drain the raisins and pat dry with paper towels. Mash to a paste in a mortar. Add the pine nuts and anise seeds and mash together. The pine nuts should retain some texture; some can remain whole. Work in the yogurt.

Roll out the dough and bake as directed.

Turn over, and spread each with some of the raisin and pine nut topping. Place under the broiler and broil for 30 to 60 seconds, making sure the *naans* are not too close to the broiler, or the topping will burn. It should just begin to brown. Serve warm.

Naans with Spicy Chickpea Topping

8 LARGE NAANS

THESE NAANS have a hearty, spicy topping.

Yeasted Indian Flatbread dough (page 206)
1   15-ounce can chickpeas, drained, or 1 cup dried chickpeas, cooked and
        drained (2 cups cooked)
½   cup low-fat plain yogurt
1   teaspoon crushed cumin seeds
⅛   teaspoon cayenne pepper, or to taste
    Salt and freshly ground pepper to taste

While the dough is rising, make the topping: Coarsely mash the chickpeas in a mortar. Add the yogurt, cumin seeds and cayenne. Season to taste with salt and pepper and more cayenne; it should be somewhat piquant and should have a coarse, paste-like consistency.

Roll out the dough and bake as directed on page 207.

Turn over, and spread each with some of the chickpea topping. Place under the broiler and broil for 30 to 60 seconds, making sure the *naans* are not too close to the broiler, or the topping will burn. It should just begin to brown. Serve warm.

Savory and Sweet Quick Breads

Whole Wheat Irish Soda Bread

1 ROUND LOAF

IT'S AMAZING HOW EASY it is to make a good loaf of bread with no yeast at all. This Irish soda bread has a very dense crumb. The dough should be quite wet and should be handled gingerly, with moistened hands. Soda bread does not keep well; store it in the refrigerator in a plastic bag.

2½	cups whole wheat flour
1	cup unbleached white flour
1½	teaspoons salt
1	teaspoon baking soda
¾	teaspoon baking powder
1½-2	cups buttermilk or low-fat plain yogurt

Preheat the oven to 375 degrees F, with a rack in the middle. Butter a baking sheet.

Mix together the flours, salt, baking soda and baking powder in a large bowl. Blend thoroughly so that the soda and baking powder are distributed evenly throughout.

Add 1½ cups of the buttermilk or yogurt and stir together to make a soft but firm dough. Add more if necessary; the dough should be quite wet.

Moisten your hands, and knead the dough gently on a floured work surface for about 3 minutes, until the dough is uniform. Shape into a round loaf. Place the loaf on the baking sheet, and cut a ½-inch-deep X across the top with a razor blade or sharp knife.

Bake for 35 to 45 minutes, or until the loaf is nicely browned and responds to tapping with a hollow sound.

Remove from the baking sheet, and cool on a rack. Slice very thin.

Variation

White Irish Soda Bread: Substitute unbleached white flour for the whole wheat flour, using 3 cups in all, and proceed as directed.

Barley Meal Soda Bread

1 ROUND LOAF

THIS SODA BREAD is made with a combination of barley flour and wheat flour. Barley flour has a pleasant, slightly sour flavor. The bread is full-flavored and hearty with a close crumb.

1⅔	cups barley flour
1⅔	cups unbleached white flour
1½	teaspoons salt
1	teaspoon baking powder
1	teaspoon baking soda
¼	cup (½ stick) unsalted butter
1	cup plus 2 tablespoons buttermilk

Preheat the oven to 375 degrees F, with a rack in the middle. Butter or oil a baking sheet.

Combine the barley flour, white flour, salt, baking powder and baking soda in a large bowl or a food processor. Cut in the butter, using 2 knives, a pastry cutter or the processor. Stir the buttermilk into the flour mixture; mix together well.

Shape the dough into a round loaf. Place on the baking sheet, and slash a ½-inch-deep X in the top of the loaf.

Bake for 45 to 60 minutes, or until the loaf is golden brown and responds to tapping with a hollow sound.

Remove from the baking sheet, and cool on a rack.

Boston Brown Bread

2 LARGE OR SEVERAL SMALL LOAVES

THIS IS ONE OF MY FAVORITE AMERICAN BREADS. It's practically black in color, with a moist, chewy, wholesome texture. The bread is steamed like a Christmas pudding and has great staying power if kept in the refrigerator in a well-sealed bag. I love it at breakfast or teatime, spread with a little ricotta cheese or fromage blanc. You can steam it in coffee cans, juice cans, vegetable cans or pudding molds. It steams for hours, so plan on doing this while you're around the house.

1	cup whole wheat flour
1	cup rye flour
1	cup stone-ground yellow cornmeal
2	teaspoons baking soda
1	teaspoon salt
½	cup blackstrap molasses
2	cups buttermilk or a combination of low-fat plain yogurt and milk
1	cup raisins

Sift together the whole wheat flour, rye flour, cornmeal, baking soda and salt. Stir in the molasses and buttermilk or yogurt-milk mixture; blend well. Stir in the raisins.

Generously butter 2 one-pound coffee or juice cans, or several small cans or pudding molds. Fill each three-fourths full of the batter. Butter pieces of foil and cover the open end, sealing well with the lid or with tape, if necessary.

Stand the cans or molds in a large pot (deep enough so that the pot can be covered when the cans stand on end in it). Pour in hot water to reach 2 inches up the sides of the cans or molds. Bring the water to a boil over high heat. Cover the pot, reduce the heat to a simmer and steam for 3 hours, checking every so often to make sure the water hasn't boiled away. Add water, as needed, during the steaming process.

Remove the cans from the pot. Unmold the breads and cool on a rack. If the bread seems too moist, bake in a 375-degree oven for 10 minutes.

Texas Cornbread

1 ROUND OR SQUARE LOAF; SERVES 8 TO 10

THIS IS MY FAVORITE CORNBREAD RECIPE. It's moist and rich, with a grainy texture and sweet corn flavor. It goes very well with soups and stews. I brought it with me to Europe from Texas and make it often. It's very quick to prepare.

1	cup stone-ground cornmeal
½	cup whole wheat flour
1	tablespoon baking powder
½	teaspoon baking soda
¾	teaspoon salt
1	cup low-fat plain yogurt or buttermilk
½	cup milk
1	tablespoon mild-flavored honey
2	large eggs
3	tablespoons unsalted butter

Preheat the oven to 450 degrees F, with a rack in the middle.

Sift together the cornmeal, flour, baking powder, baking soda and salt in a large bowl. Beat together the yogurt or buttermilk, milk, honey and eggs in another bowl.

Place the butter in a 9-x-9-inch heatproof baking pan or a 9-inch cast-iron skillet. Place in the oven for 3 or 4 minutes, or until the butter melts.

Remove the pan from the oven, and brush the butter over the sides and bottom. Pour off the excess melted butter into the yogurt and egg mixture. Stir together. Quickly fold the liquid ingredients into the dry ingredients with just a few strokes of a wooden spoon. Don't worry about lumps; you don't want to overwork the batter.

Pour the batter into the pan or skillet. Bake at once for 30 to 35 minutes, or until the top is golden brown and a toothpick inserted into the center comes out clean.

Cool in the pan on a rack or serve hot.

Savory Oatmeal Pan Bread

1 ROUND BREAD; SERVES 6

Based on a recipe by Jacques Pépin, this easy, quick bread tastes like a stuffing. It is savory and filling and makes a nice accompaniment to soups and salads. It's the kind of bread you can whip up at a moment's notice.

1	cup flaked or rolled oats
½	cup unbleached white flour or whole wheat pastry flour
2	teaspoons baking powder
½	teaspoon salt
¼	teaspoon freshly ground pepper
½	cup milk
1	large egg
½	cup chopped fresh parsley
½	small onion, grated
2½	tablespoons olive, sunflower or safflower oil

Preheat the oven to 400 degrees F, with a rack in the middle.

Mix together all of the ingredients except the oil in a large bowl or food processor fitted with the steel blade.

Pour 2 tablespoons of the oil into an 8-inch heatproof pie pan or a heavy 7- or 8-inch ovenproof skillet. Place it in the oven and preheat for about 5 minutes.

Spread the batter in the hot pan and brush the remaining ½ tablespoon oil over the top. Bake for 20 minutes.

Flip the bread over, either like a crêpe, using a wide spatula, or by sliding it onto a plate and reversing it back into the pan. Bake for 5 to 8 minutes more, or until it is brown and a toothpick inserted in the middle comes out clean.

Remove from the oven, and let cool for a couple of minutes on a rack. Cut into wedges, and serve warm (reheat in a warm oven if it has cooled).

French Spice Bread
(*Pain d'Épices*)

1 LOAF

THIS FRENCH SPICE BREAD is rich, sweet with honey and spices and very easy to make. The garam masala, which is my own addition to a traditional recipe, gives the bread a peppery flavor. This is another bread I often make to give away at Christmas. The spices ripen over time, and the bread tastes best a few days after it is made. It goes wonderfully with tea.

Garam masala is an Indian spice mixture. You can find it in stores that specialize in Indian food products.

½	cup (1 stick) unsalted butter, at room temperature
½	cup strong-flavored honey, such as buckwheat honey
¾	cup milk
1	large egg, beaten
1	cup whole wheat pastry flour
1	cup unbleached white flour
1	teaspoon baking soda
1½	tablespoons ground anise
½	teaspoon garam masala or ¼ teaspoon freshly ground pepper
½	teaspoon freshly grated nutmeg
¼	teaspoon ground allspice
¼	teaspoon ground ginger
¼	teaspoon ground cloves
¼	teaspoon salt

Preheat the oven to 375 degrees F, with a rack in the middle. Butter a loaf pan and line with buttered wax paper.

Cream together the butter and honey in a large bowl with an electric mixer. Beat in the milk and egg.

Sift together the flours, baking soda, spices and salt in a medium bowl. Stir the dry ingredients into the liquid ingredients and mix together well.

Turn the batter into the prepared pan. Bake for 50 to 60 minutes, or until a toothpick inserted in the middle comes out clean.

Let cool in the pan for 10 to 15 minutes. Turn out onto a rack, and carefully peel off the wax paper. Let the bread cool completely. Wrap tightly in foil, and let sit at room temperature for several days to develop the flavor before eating. This bread will keep for 2 weeks.

Gingerbread

1 ROUND OR RECTANGULAR LOAF

GINGERBREAD CAN BE CLOYINGLY SWEET, but this one has a perfect balance of sweet and spice. The bread is moist and delicious. Thin slices go nicely with tea, and thicker portions, topped with whipped cream or yogurt, make a good dessert. It keeps well for up to 10 days in the refrigerator.

3	large eggs
½	cup blackstrap molasses
½	cup raw brown sugar (turbinado) or packed light brown sugar
6	tablespoons (¾ stick) unsalted butter, melted
1	teaspoon grated lemon zest (optional)
1	cup whole wheat pastry flour
1	cup unbleached white flour
2½	teaspoons ground ginger
1	teaspoon ground cinnamon
½	teaspoon ground allspice
¼	teaspoon freshly grated nutmeg
1	teaspoon baking soda
¼	teaspoon salt
½	cup low-fat plain yogurt or buttermilk
	Whipped cream or yogurt, for topping (optional)

Preheat the oven to 350 degrees F, with a rack in the middle. Butter and lightly flour a loaf pan or an 8-inch cake pan.

Beat the eggs in a large bowl until light and frothy. Add the molasses and sugar and beat on medium speed for 1 to 2 minutes. Beat in the butter and beat for 1 to 2 minutes. Stir in the lemon zest, if using.

Sift together the flours, spices, baking soda and salt in a medium bowl. Gradually add 1 cup of the dry ingredients to the liquid ingredients, beating slowly. Add the yogurt or buttermilk, and then the remaining flour mixture; mix just until blended. Pour into the pan.

Bake for about 45 minutes for a cake pan, 1 hour for a loaf pan, or until the gingerbread shrinks away from the sides of the pan and a toothpick inserted in the center comes out clean.

Cool for 10 minutes in the pan. Invert onto a rack to cool further. Serve with whipped cream or yogurt, if desired.

Quick Irish Tea Bread

1 LOAF

T HIS IS A BAKING-POWDER-RAISED TEA BREAD, very tasty, with lots of fruit and spice. (See photograph, page 75.)

1⅔	cups mixed dark raisins, golden raisins and currants
2	cups boiling black tea
1	large egg, beaten
1	tablespoon orange or ginger marmalade
½	cup packed dark brown sugar
2	cups unbleached white flour
2	teaspoons baking powder
1½	teaspoons Elizabeth David's Spice Blend (page 161)
½	teaspoon baking soda
½	teaspoon salt

Place the mixed fruit in a medium bowl and pour on the hot tea; let sit for at least 1 hour, or overnight.

Drain the tea through a strainer into a measuring cup. You should have 1½ cups; add water if necessary. Set aside the raisins.

Preheat the oven to 375 degrees F, with a rack in the middle. Generously butter a loaf pan or an 8-inch square pan.

Beat together the egg, marmalade and brown sugar in a large bowl. Beat in the tea.

Sift together the flour, baking powder, spice blend, baking soda and salt in a medium bowl. Stir the dry ingredients into the liquid ingredients and mix together well; don't over-beat. The batter will be runny. Stir in the raisins. Scrape the batter into the pan.

Bake for 1 to 1½ hours, or until a toothpick inserted in the middle comes out clean.

Let cool in the pan for 10 minutes. Turn out onto a rack to cool completely. Serve cut into thin slices.

Banana Bread

1 LOAF

WHEN YOUR BANANAS start to turn black, don't throw them out! Make this bread instead. Most of the sweetness in this bread comes from the spices and the bananas themselves. The bread freezes well and is delicious for breakfast or tea.

1	cup whole wheat flour
1	cup unbleached white flour
¼	cup raw brown sugar (turbinado) or packed light brown sugar
1	teaspoon baking soda
1	teaspoon ground cinnamon
½	teaspoon freshly grated nutmeg
½	teaspoon salt
¼	cup mild-flavored honey
¼	cup melted unsalted butter, sunflower or canola oil
¼	cup low-fat plain yogurt
1	pound ripe bananas, mashed (about 1 cup)
2	large eggs
1	teaspoon vanilla extract
1	cup chopped walnuts

Preheat the oven to 375 degrees F, with a rack in the middle. Butter a loaf pan.

Sift together the flours, sugar, baking soda, spices and salt in a medium bowl.

Beat together the honey, butter or oil, yogurt, bananas, eggs and vanilla in a large bowl. Quickly stir the dry ingredients into the liquid ingredients and mix well; don't overbeat. Fold in the walnuts. Scrape the batter into the pan.

Bake for 50 to 60 minutes, or until the bread is firm and a toothpick inserted in the middle comes out clean.

Let cool in the pan for 10 to 15 minutes. Turn out onto a rack to cool completely.

Zucchini and Apricot Bread

1 LOAF

THIS MOIST, SPICY BREAD is nice with tea or for dessert. It's only moderately sweet; if you want it sweeter, add 2 to 4 tablespoons more sugar. The zucchini is hardly discernible but gives the bread its moist texture.

½	cup sunflower, safflower or canola oil
4	large eggs
½	cup raw brown sugar (turbinado) or packed light brown sugar
¼	cup milk
2	teaspoons vanilla extract
½	pound zucchini, scrubbed and grated (about 2 cups)
1	tablespoon grated orange zest
1	cup whole wheat pastry flour
1	cup unbleached white flour
2	teaspoons baking powder
1	teaspoon baking soda
2	teaspoons ground cinnamon
1	teaspoon ground cloves
1	teaspoon freshly grated nutmeg
½	teaspoon ground allspice
½	teaspoon salt
¾	cup chopped walnuts or pecans
½	cup chopped dried apricots

Preheat the oven to 350 degrees F, with a rack in the middle. Butter a loaf pan.

In a large bowl, beat together the oil, eggs, sugar, milk and vanilla; stir in the zucchini and orange zest.

Sift together the flours, baking powder, baking soda, spices and salt into a medium bowl. Stir the dry ingredients into the liquid ingredients; mix just until combined. Fold in the nuts and apricots. Pour into the pan.

Bake for about 1 hour and 15 minutes, or until a toothpick inserted in the middle comes out clean.

Cool for 10 minutes in the pan. Turn out onto a rack to cool completely. Wrap in foil and let sit overnight to develop the flavors.

Sweet Carrot Bread with Raisins

1 LOAF

Made with grated carrots and golden raisins, this bread is less cloying than most carrot cakes.

⅔	cup golden raisins
	Boiling water
½	cup sunflower, safflower or canola oil
4	large eggs
½	cup raw brown sugar (turbinado) or packed light brown sugar
2	teaspoons vanilla extract
1	tablespoon grated lemon zest
1	cup whole wheat pastry flour
1	cup unbleached white flour
2	teaspoons baking powder
1	teaspoon baking soda
2	teaspoons ground cinnamon
1	teaspoon ground cloves
1	teaspoon freshly grated nutmeg
½	teaspoon ground allspice
½	teaspoon salt
½	pound carrots, peeled and grated (about 2 cups)

Preheat the oven to 350 degrees F, with a rack in the middle. Butter a loaf pan.

Place the raisins in a small bowl and cover with boiling water. Let sit for 3 to 5 minutes. Drain the raisins and pat dry; set aside.

Beat together the oil, eggs, sugar and vanilla in a large bowl. Stir in the lemon zest.

Sift together the flours, baking powder, baking soda, spices and salt in a medium bowl. Stir the dry ingredients into the liquid ingredients and mix just until well blended. Fold in the raisins and carrots. Pour into the pan.

Bake for about 1 hour and 15 minutes, or until a toothpick inserted in the middle comes out clean.

Cool for 10 minutes in the pan. Turn out onto a rack to cool completely. Wrap in foil and let sit overnight to develop the flavors.

Biscuits, Scones, Muffins and Popovers

Thyme Biscuits

1 DOZEN

THESE ARE SAVORY AND LIGHT, go well with cheese and with soups and are also terrific with herb-flavored jellies.

1	cup unbleached white flour
1	cup whole wheat flour or whole wheat pastry flour
1	teaspoon sugar
¾	teaspoon salt
2	teaspoons baking powder
½	teaspoon baking soda
1	tablespoon finely minced fresh thyme, or 1½ teaspoons dried
5	tablespoons cold unsalted butter, cut into bits
¾	cup buttermilk or low-fat plain yogurt

Preheat the oven to 400 degrees F, with a rack in the middle. Butter a baking sheet.

Sift together the flours, sugar, salt, baking powder and baking soda into a large bowl or a food processor fitted with the steel blade. Stir in the thyme. Cut in the butter until the mixture has the consistency of coarse cornmeal.

Stir the buttermilk or yogurt into the mixture. Gather up the dough and gently knead it, pressing it with lightly floured hands so that it just comes together; it will be slightly sticky. The less you work the dough, the lighter your biscuits will be.

Roll out about ¾ inch thick. Cut into squares, triangles or rounds. Place the biscuits on the baking sheet, spacing them about 1 inch apart.

Bake for 12 to 15 minutes, or until the biscuits begin to brown. Serve warm.

Whole Wheat Scones

1 DOZEN

I LIKE WHOLE WHEAT SCONES better than those made with white flour because of their grainy texture and rich taste. These are light as can be, irresistible with afternoon tea or for breakfast. They will remain moist for several days. The trick to making good scones is handling the dough as little as possible.

2	cups whole wheat pastry flour or 1 cup whole wheat pastry flour and 1 cup unbleached white flour
1	tablespoon sugar
2	teaspoons baking powder
½	teaspoon baking soda
¼	teaspoon salt
6	tablespoons (¾ stick) cold unsalted butter, cut into bits
⅔	cup low-fat plain yogurt or buttermilk
1	tablespoon mild-flavored honey
½	cup dried currants

Preheat the oven to 400 degrees F, with a rack in the middle. Butter a baking sheet.

Sift together the flour, sugar, baking powder, baking soda and salt into a large bowl or a food processor fitted with the steel blade. Cut in the butter until the mixture has the consistency of coarse cornmeal.

Mix together the yogurt or buttermilk and honey in a small bowl. Stir into the flour mixture, along with the currants. Mix together to form a soft dough.

Turn out the dough onto a lightly floured work surface and gently knead about 10 times, just until the ingredients are combined. Press or roll the dough into a rectangle about ¾ inch thick. Cut into 12 triangular pieces or use a round biscuit cutter. Place the scones about 1 inch apart on the baking sheets.

Bake for 12 to 15 minutes, until the scones begin to brown on top. Remove from the pan and cool on a rack, or serve warm.

Buttermilk Drop Scones

18 TO 24 SCONES

THESE WHITE, SLIGHTLY CAKEY scones are very nice with tea. (See photograph, page 76.)

2	cups unbleached white flour
3	tablespoons sugar
1	tablespoon baking powder
½	teaspoon baking soda
¾	teaspoon salt
½	teaspoon ground cinnamon
½	cup (1 stick) cold unsalted butter, cut into bits
½	cup golden raisins or dried currants
¾	cup buttermilk
2	large eggs

Preheat the oven to 400 degrees F, with a rack in the middle and another in the upper third. Butter 2 baking sheets.

Sift together the flour, sugar, baking powder, baking soda, salt and cinnamon into a large bowl or a food processor fitted with the steel blade. Cut in the butter until the mixture has the consistency of coarse cornmeal. Add the raisins or currants.

Beat together the buttermilk and eggs in a medium bowl. Stir the liquid ingredients into the dry ingredients. Stir together to form a smooth dough; don't overbeat.

Drop by heaping tablespoonfuls onto the baking sheets, leaving about 2 inches between each scone. Moisten your fingers and gently press the tops for a flatter scone.

Bake for 15 to 20 minutes, switching the baking sheets halfway through, until the scones are golden. Remove from the baking sheets and serve warm.

Cream Scones

1 DOZEN

THESE SCONES ARE RICH, sweet and flaky. You can make them with or without the currants.

1¾	cups unbleached white flour
2	tablespoons sugar
2	teaspoons baking powder
½	teaspoon baking soda
¼	teaspoon salt
6	tablespoons (¾ stick) cold unsalted butter, cut into bits
½	cup dried currants (optional)
½	cup heavy cream

Preheat the oven to 400 degrees F, with a rack in the middle. Butter a baking sheet.

Sift together the flour, sugar, baking powder, baking soda and salt into a large bowl or a food processor fitted with the steel blade. Cut in the butter until the mixture has the consistency of coarse cornmeal. Add the currants, if using. Stir in the cream and mix to form a soft dough.

Gather up the dough and turn out onto a lightly floured work surface. Gently knead about 10 times, just until the ingredients are combined.

Press or roll the dough into a rectangle about ¾ inch thick. Cut into 12 triangular pieces, or use a round biscuit cutter. Place on the baking sheets, about 1 inch apart.

Bake for 12 to 15 minutes, or until the scones begin to brown on the top. Remove from the pan and cool on a rack, or serve warm.

Stilton Scones

1 DOZEN

THESE RICH AND SAVORY SCONES make a nice accompaniment to soups and salads. (See photograph, page 76.)

¾	cup unbleached white flour
¾	cup whole wheat flour or whole wheat pastry flour (or use all unbleached white flour)
2	teaspoons baking powder
½	teaspoon baking soda
½	teaspoon salt
¼	cup (½ stick) cold unsalted butter, cut into bits
4	ounces Stilton, crumbled (¾ cup)
1	large egg
2	tablespoons milk

Preheat the oven to 400 degrees F, with a rack in the middle. Butter a baking sheet.

Sift together the flours, baking powder, baking soda and salt into a large bowl or a food processor fitted with the metal blade. Cut in the butter until the mixture has the consistency of coarse cornmeal; cut in the Stilton.

Beat together the egg and milk. Stir into the flour mixture. Gather up the dough and gently knead with lightly floured hands, pressing so that it just comes together; the dough will be slightly sticky. The less you work it, the lighter your scones will be.

Roll out the dough about ¾ inch thick. Cut into squares, triangles or rounds. Place on the baking sheet, about 1 inch apart.

Bake for 12 to 15 minutes, or until the scones begin to brown. Serve warm.

Fig and Orange Drop Scones

12 TO 15 SCONES

THESE SCONES HAVE A MARVELOUS CRUNCHY TEXTURE and the sweet-tart flavor of figs and orange. The dough is quite moist. (See photograph, page 76.)

⅔	cup dried figs
1	cup orange juice
1⅔	cups whole wheat pastry flour
1	tablespoon packed brown sugar
2	teaspoons baking powder
½	teaspoon baking soda
¼	teaspoon salt
6	tablespoons (¾ stick) cold unsalted butter, cut into bits
¼	cup low-fat plain yogurt
1	tablespoon mild-flavored honey

Place the figs in a small bowl, pour on the orange juice and let stand overnight. Alternatively, you can bring the orange juice to a simmer in a nonreactive saucepan, pour it over the figs and let stand for 1 to 2 hours, until the figs are soft and infused with the juice.

Drain the figs, reserving ¼ cup of the orange juice. Chop the figs finely in a food processor or with a sharp knife; set aside.

Preheat the oven to 400 degrees F, with a rack in the middle and another in the upper third. Butter 2 baking sheets.

Sift together the flour, sugar, baking powder, baking soda and salt in a large bowl or a food processor fitted with the steel blade. Cut in the butter until the mixture has the consistency of coarse cornmeal.

Mix together the yogurt, honey and the reserved orange juice in a small bowl. Stir the liquid ingredients into the flour mixture; stir in the figs.

Drop the batter by heaping tablespoonfuls onto the baking sheets, about 1 inch apart.

Bake for 12 to 15 minutes, switching the position of the baking sheets halfway through, until the scones begin to brown on top.

Remove from the pans and cool on a rack, or serve warm.

Savory Rye Muffins

10 TO 12 MUFFINS

A FIRM, GRAINY TEXTURE and savory flavor make these muffins go well with soups, salads and cheese.

4	tablespoons sunflower, safflower or canola oil or melted unsalted butter
¼	cup finely chopped onion
⅓	cup stone-ground cornmeal
⅔	cup unbleached white flour
⅔	cup rye flour
2	teaspoons baking powder
½	teaspoon salt
½	teaspoon dried thyme
½	teaspoon dried sage
1	cup milk, low-fat plain yogurt or a combination
2	large eggs
2	teaspoons mild-flavored honey

Preheat the oven to 400 degrees F, with a rack in the middle. Oil or butter 12 muffin cups.

Heat 1 tablespoon of the oil or butter in a skillet over medium heat. Sauté the onion until translucent, 3 to 5 minutes; remove from the heat.

In a large bowl, sift together the cornmeal, flours, baking powder and salt. Stir in the thyme and sage.

Beat together the milk or yogurt, eggs, honey and the remaining 3 tablespoons oil or butter in a medium bowl. Quickly fold the liquid ingredients into the flour mixture; fold in the sautéed onion.

Spoon the mixture into muffin cups, filling each two-thirds full. Bake for 20 minutes, or until lightly browned on top.

Let cool for 10 minutes in the muffin cups. Remove from the cups and cool on a rack.

Overnight Bran Muffins

20 TO 24 MUFFINS

Y OU DON'T HAVE TO LET THIS BATTER SIT OVERNIGHT, but it makes breakfast very easy. The batter will last for a week in the refrigerator, so you can prepare a large quantity on Sunday night and have the makings for fresh muffins every day of the week. The muffins are moist and sweet. If you don't like molasses, reduce the quantity to 1 tablespoon or substitute honey.

1	cup dark or golden raisins, chopped dried figs or chopped dried apricots
1¾	cups boiling water
2	cups bran
2	large eggs
½	cup sunflower oil or melted unsalted butter
½	cup mild-flavored honey
¼	cup regular or blackstrap molasses
1½	cups buttermilk or milk soured with 1 tablespoon lemon juice
1⅔	cups whole wheat flour
1	cup unbleached white flour
2½	teaspoons baking soda
½	teaspoon salt

Place the raisins or chopped dried fruit in a small bowl and pour on the boiling water. Let stand for 5 minutes.

Stir the bran into the fruit mixture and let stand for 10 minutes more.

Meanwhile, preheat the oven to 400 degrees F, with a rack in the middle. Oil 24 muffin cups.

Beat together the eggs, oil or melted butter, the honey and the molasses in a large bowl. Stir in the buttermilk or sour milk. Stir the raisins and bran, with their liquid, into the milk-egg mixture; combine well.

In another large bowl, sift together the flours, baking soda and salt. Quickly fold the liquid ingredients into the dry ingredients. Bake immediately, or cover with plastic wrap or foil and refrigerate overnight.

Stir the batter and spoon into the muffin cups, filling each two-thirds full.

Bake for 20 to 30 minutes, or until the muffins are puffed, brown and cooked through.

Remove from the oven and let cool for 15 minutes (or more) in the cups. Remove from the cups and cool on a rack.

Cheese Muffins with Sweet Red Pepper

10 MUFFINS

T HESE SAVORY MUFFINS have lots of flavor baked into them. Serve them with a salad for a quick lunch or with soup or stew for dinner. (See photograph, page 79.)

¾	cup whole wheat flour
¾	cup unbleached white flour
½	teaspoon salt
2½	teaspoons baking powder
1	cup milk
2	large eggs
¼	cup sunflower, safflower or canola oil
1	cup grated Cheddar cheese
1	red bell pepper, seeded and diced

Preheat the oven to 375 degrees F, with a rack in the middle. Oil or butter 10 muffin cups.

Sift together the flours, salt and baking powder in a large bowl.

Beat together the milk, eggs and oil in a medium bowl. Stir in the cheese. Quickly fold the liquid ingredients into the dry ingredients. Fold in the bell pepper.

Spoon into the muffin cups, filling each two-thirds full.

Bake for 20 minutes, or until lightly browned. Let cool for a few minutes in the cups. Remove from the cups and cool on a rack.

Sweet or Savory Cornmeal Muffins

10 TO 12 MUFFINS

VARY THESE MUFFINS by serving them plain or with corn kernels, dried sage and/or chili peppers.

1	cup stone-ground cornmeal
1	cup whole wheat flour
1	tablespoon baking powder
½	teaspoon baking soda
½	teaspoon salt
1-2	teaspoons rubbed sage (optional)
1	cup low-fat plain yogurt or buttermilk
½	cup milk
2	tablespoons mild-flavored honey
2	large eggs
3	tablespoons melted unsalted butter
1	small (8¾-ounce) can corn kernels, drained (1 cup; optional)
1-2	hot chili peppers, seeded and chopped (optional)

Preheat the oven to 425 degrees F, with a rack in the middle. Oil 12 muffin cups.

Sift together the cornmeal, flour, baking powder, baking soda and salt into a large bowl. Stir in the sage, if using.

Beat together the yogurt or buttermilk, milk, honey, eggs and melted butter in a medium bowl.

Quickly fold the liquid ingredients into the dry ingredients. Fold in the corn kernels and/or chili peppers, if using.

Preheat the muffin cups for 5 minutes in the oven. Spoon in the batter, filling each cup two-thirds full.

Bake for 20 minutes, or until lightly browned on top. Let cool for 10 minutes in the cups. Remove from the cups and cool on a rack.

Lemon Muffins

10 TO 12 MUFFINS

THESE ARE CAKEY AND RICH. They go well with afternoon tea and can be halved to serve as a base for strawberry shortcake with berries and their juices spooned over the top. (See photograph, page 79.)

1¾	cups all-purpose flour
½	cup sugar
1	teaspoon baking powder
½	teaspoon baking soda
2	tablespoons finely chopped lemon zest
2	large eggs
¾	cup low-fat plain yogurt or buttermilk
¼	cup freshly squeezed lemon juice
¼	cup (½ stick) unsalted butter, melted

Preheat the oven to 400 degrees F, with a rack in the middle. Oil or butter 12 muffin cups.

Sift together the flour, sugar, baking powder and baking soda into a large bowl. Stir in the lemon zest.

Beat together the eggs, yogurt or buttermilk, lemon juice and butter in a medium bowl.

Quickly stir the liquid ingredients into the dry ingredients. Do not beat; it's all right if there are a few lumps.

Spoon the mixture into muffin cups, filling each two-thirds full.

Bake for about 20 minutes, or until lightly browned on top. Let cool for 10 minutes in the tins. Turn out and cool on a rack.

Oat and Apple Muffins

10 TO 12 MUFFINS

THESE ARE SWEET, moist, spicy and delicious.

1	cup milk
1	cup rolled or flaked oats
¾	cup whole wheat flour
⅓	cup raw brown sugar (turbinado) or packed light brown sugar
2½	teaspoons baking powder
1	teaspoon ground cinnamon
½	teaspoon freshly grated nutmeg
¼	teaspoon salt
2	large eggs
¼	cup (½ stick) melted unsalted butter or sunflower, safflower or canola oil
1	medium-size tart apple, peeled, cored and diced

Preheat the oven to 400 degrees F, with a rack in the middle. Oil 12 muffin cups.

Combine the milk and oats in a small bowl. Let sit for 10 minutes, or until the oats soften slightly.

Sift together the flour, sugar, baking powder, cinnamon, nutmeg and salt into a large bowl.

Beat together the eggs and melted butter or oil in a medium bowl; stir in the milk-oat mixture. Quickly fold the liquid ingredients into the dry ingredients. Fold in the chopped apple.

Spoon into muffin cups, filling each two-thirds full.

Bake for 20 to 25 minutes, or until lightly browned. Let cool for 10 minutes in the cups. Remove from the cups and cool on a rack.

Orange-Date Muffins

10 TO 12 MUFFINS

TANGY AND SWEET, these muffins are delicious with tea. (See photograph, page 79.)

1¼	cups unbleached white flour
½	cup whole wheat pastry flour
2½	teaspoons baking powder
½	teaspoon ground cinnamon
¼	teaspoon salt
	Grated zest of 1 orange
½	cup fresh orange juice (from 2 medium oranges)
¼	cup milk
¼	cup mild-flavored honey
¼	cup (½ stick) melted unsalted butter or sunflower, safflower or canola oil
2	large eggs
½	cup chopped dates

Preheat the oven to 400 degrees F, with a rack in the middle. Oil 12 muffin cups.

Sift together the flours, baking powder, cinnamon and salt into a large bowl.

Whisk together the zest, orange juice, milk, honey, melted butter or oil and eggs in a medium bowl.

Quickly fold the liquid ingredients into the dry ingredients; fold in the chopped dates.

Spoon into the muffin cups, filling each two-thirds full.

Bake for 15 to 20 minutes, or until lightly browned. Cool in the muffin cups for 10 minutes. Remove from the cups and cool on a rack.

Maple Pecan Muffins

10 TO 12 MUFFINS

MAPLE SYRUP AND PECANS always make a good marriage.

¾	cup unbleached white flour
¾	cup whole wheat flour
1½	teaspoons baking powder
¼	teaspoon salt
⅔	cup milk
⅓	cup maple syrup
¼	cup (½ stick) melted unsalted butter or sunflower, safflower or canola oil
2	large eggs
½	cup chopped pecans
12	unbroken pecan halves

Preheat the oven to 375 degrees F, with a rack in the middle. Oil or butter 12 muffin cups.

Sift together the flours, baking powder and salt into a large bowl.

Beat together the milk, maple syrup, melted butter or oil and eggs in a medium bowl. Quickly fold the liquid ingredients into the dry ingredients; fold in the chopped pecans.

Spoon into the muffin cups, filling each two-thirds full. Top each muffin with an unbroken pecan half.

Bake for 20 minutes, or until lightly browned on top. Let cool in the cups for a few minutes. Remove from the cups and cool on a rack.

Popovers

10 TO 12 POPOVERS

POPOVERS ARE WONDERFUL with savory dishes and are even better spread with butter and jam. A mixture of flour, water and eggs, they are baked in muffin cups or pudding dishes and puff up much like cream puffs. Butter the pans generously so they don't stick; they fall as quickly as they rise.

1   cup milk
3   large eggs
1   teaspoon sugar (optional)
2   tablespoons melted unsalted butter
1   cup unbleached white flour
¼   teaspoon salt

Preheat the oven to 400 degrees F, with a rack in the middle. Generously butter 12 muffin cups or custard cups.

In a blender or food processor, combine the milk, eggs, optional sugar, butter, flour and salt. Blend until smooth, stopping the machine every once in awhile to stir down the flour from the sides of the container.

Pour the batter into the cups, filling each about half full.

Bake for 35 to 40 minutes, until the popovers are puffed, browned and firm to the touch. Avoid opening the oven until the end of the baking time. Serve hot.

Griddle Breads, Pancakes and Crêpes

English Muffins

10 MUFFINS

I GREW UP ON PACKAGED ENGLISH MUFFINS, and even long after I'd begun making bread, I always thought English muffins were one of those mysterious things one couldn't easily make at home. When I was researching this book, I learned how easy they are and how satisfying freshly made English muffins can be.

The trick to making them successfully is to have a very moist dough, a dough that is too difficult to knead by hand. You cook them on a griddle and finish them off in a medium oven. (See photograph, page 36.)

1½	teaspoons active dry yeast
½	cup lukewarm water
½	teaspoon sugar
1	cup lukewarm milk
2	tablespoons olive oil or cooled melted unsalted butter
	About 1½-1⅔ cups unbleached white flour
1½	cups whole wheat flour
1¾	teaspoons salt

Dissolve the yeast in the warm water in a large bowl; stir in the sugar. Let stand for 5 to 10 minutes, until creamy.

Stir in the warm milk and oil or melted butter.

Mix together 1½ cups of the white flour, the whole wheat flour and the salt in a medium bowl. Add to the yeast mixture, and stir together, using a wooden spoon or the paddle attachment of an electric mixer. Change to the dough hook, if using a mixer, and knead, or knead in the bowl, using the spoon to help turn the dough, for 10 minutes. Add more white flour as needed, until the dough is uniform and elastic. The dough should be quite moist and sticky.

Cover the bowl with plastic wrap and a towel and set in a warm place to rise for about 1½ hours, or until nearly doubled.

Generously dust a work surface with flour. Divide the dough into 10 equal portions, and transfer them to the work surface. Sprinkle each portion with flour and gently shape into a 4-inch round or square. They will be very sticky, so work quickly. Dust with flour. Cover loosely with a towel and let rise for 35 to 45 minutes, until doubled.

Warm a griddle over very low heat for 10 minutes, until a drop of water sizzles and evaporates. Preheat the oven to 325 degrees F, with a rack in the middle.

Quickly and carefully, slide a spatula under 1 piece of dough and transfer it to the griddle. Cook for 5 minutes on one side.

Turn and cook for 5 minutes on the other side.

Turn again and cook for another 3 to 5 minutes, or until the surfaces are bordered with a light, baked film.

Turn again and cook for 3 to 5 minutes on the other side.

Remove from the griddle and place on an unoiled baking sheet. Bake for 5 minutes, or until the muffins are brown on the top and bottom and light in the middle.

Continue cooking 1 or more muffins at a time, depending on the size of the griddle, until you use up all of the dough.

Cool the muffins on a rack. Split in half and toast under the broiler or in a toaster. Serve with butter and jam.

Crumpets

ABOUT 20 CRUMPETS, EACH ABOUT 3 INCHES IN DIAMETER

ACCORDING TO ENGLISH FOOD WRITER ELIZABETH DAVID, the probable origin of the word "crumpet" is the Welsh *crempog*, which means pancake or fritter.

These yeasted pancakes, with their funny surface full of holes (meant, I am told, to be filled with the butter you should spread on your hot crumpets) are easy to make. They are baked on a hot griddle in crumpet rings, which you can improvise with tunafish cans. Take both ends off the cans, wash the cans thoroughly and keep them on hand for crumpets.

1	teaspoon active dry yeast
1	cup plus 2 tablespoons lukewarm water
1	cup plus 2 tablespoons lukewarm milk
1	teaspoon sugar
2	tablespoons sunflower, safflower or canola oil
3⅓	cups unbleached white flour
1½	teaspoons salt
½	teaspoon baking soda, dissolved in ½ cup lukewarm water

Dissolve the yeast in the warm water in a large bowl. Let stand for 5 to 10 minutes, until creamy.

Stir in the warm milk, sugar and oil.

Mix together the flour and salt. Stir into the yeast mixture, and beat vigorously until smooth and somewhat elastic, about 5 minutes.

Cover the bowl with plastic wrap and a towel and let rise in a warm place for about 1½ hours, or until bubbly.

Stir the baking soda and warm-water mixture into the batter and combine well. Cover again and let rise in a warm place for 30 minutes.

Meanwhile, preheat the oven to 250 degrees F. Brush a griddle and crumpet rings lightly with butter, and heat over medium heat until hot. Ladle the batter into the rings, filling them ½ inch high. Cook until the top surfaces form a thin skin and holes have broken through, 7 to 10 minutes. If holes don't break through, the batter is too thick; thin the batter with a little warm milk or water.

Carefully remove the rings and flip the crumpets over. Cook for about 3 minutes on the other side; the crumpets should be floppy.

Keep warm in a towel in the oven while cooking the remaining crumpets. Serve hot or toasted, with butter and jam or cheese.

Crumpets keep well, stored in a plastic bag. Reheat in the oven or toast before serving.

Yeasted Griddle Cakes

1 DOZEN LARGE OR 2 DOZEN SMALL PANCAKES

Yeasted griddle cakes are more substantial than the breakfast flapjacks we grew up on. They have a savory flavor and a pleasing, spongy texture. I like them equally well with butter and sweet toppings or with savory toppings like smoked fish and yogurt. They can be served as breakfast or dinner fare.

1	teaspoon active dry yeast
½	cup lukewarm water
½	cup lukewarm milk
2	large eggs
2	teaspoons melted unsalted butter, plus additional for cooking
1½	cups unbleached white flour
1	teaspoon salt

Dissolve the yeast in the warm water in a large bowl. Add the warm milk. Let stand for 5 to 10 minutes, until creamy.

Beat in the eggs and butter.

Combine the flour and salt in a medium bowl. Beat into the yeast mixture until you have a smooth, thick batter. Cover with plastic wrap and set in a warm place for about 1½ hours, or until bubbly.

Preheat the oven to 250 degrees F.

Heat a griddle or a heavy skillet over medium-low heat and brush with butter; the butter should sizzle. Ladle in full or half ladlefuls of the batter, depending on the size you want the pancakes to be. Cook on one side until holes break through and you can turn the pancake easily. Turn and cook the other side for about 1 minute, until browned. Total cooking time is 3 to 4 minutes.

Wrap the cooked cakes in a towel and keep warm in the oven until all of the pancakes are cooked.

The pancakes can be refrigerated for up to 3 days or frozen for up to 3 months. To store, layer them between pieces of wax paper or parchment and seal in a plastic bag or wrap in foil. Reheat them in a warm (250-degree) oven.

Welsh Yeasted Oatmeal Pancakes

24 MEDIUM PANCAKES OR 12 TO 14 LARGE PANCAKES

THESE TASTY, SPONGY PANCAKES are based on an Elizabeth David recipe. The batter will keep for several days in the refrigerator and can be brought back to life by stirring vigorously and leaving at room temperature until bubbly.

1	cup oatmeal
2½	cups water
1	teaspoon active dry yeast
2	tablespoons lukewarm water
¼	cup buttermilk
2	large eggs
1½	cups unbleached white flour
1	teaspoon salt

Combine the oatmeal and the 2½ cups water in a medium bowl. Set aside to soak for 12 hours or overnight.

Drain, reserving 1 cup of the soaking water and set aside.

Dissolve the yeast in the 2 tablespoons lukewarm water in a large bowl. Let stand for 5 to 10 minutes, until creamy. Stir in the buttermilk. Beat in the eggs, flour, salt and the drained oatmeal. Stir in the reserved 1 cup oatmeal-soaking water to make a thick batter.

Cover with plastic wrap and let rise in a warm place for 1½ to 2 hours, or until bubbly.

Preheat the oven to 250 degrees F.

Heat a lightly greased griddle or a heavy skillet over medium-low heat until hot. Ladle in the batter, 2 to 3 tablespoons at a time, and let it spread. Medium pancakes should be about 4 inches in diameter and fairly thin; ladle in more batter if you prefer larger pancakes. Cook until holes break through and the pancakes are firm enough to turn, about 1½ to 2 minutes. Turn and cook on the other side for about 30 seconds.

Keep warm in the oven as you cook the rest of the batter.

Yeasted Blinis

15 LARGE OR 24 SMALL BLINIS

BLINIS ARE EARTHY-TASTING, yeasted buckwheat pancakes. These, based on an Elizabeth David recipe, are hefty and thick and quite easy to make. They have a moist texture and a rich buckwheat flavor. They are marvelous with smoked salmon and fromage blanc or sour cream.

1	teaspoon active dry yeast
2	tablespoons lukewarm water
1	cup plus 2 tablespoons lukewarm milk
¾	cup plus 2 tablespoons buckwheat flour
¾	cup plus 2 tablespoons unbleached white flour
¾	teaspoon salt
½	cup buttermilk or low-fat plain yogurt
2	large eggs, separated

Dissolve the yeast in the warm water in a large bowl. Stir in the warm milk. Let stand for 5 to 10 minutes, until creamy.

Combine the flours and salt in a medium bowl. Stir into the yeast mixture. Stir in the buttermilk or yogurt. Beat in the egg yolks.

Cover with plastic wrap and a towel and let rise in a warm place for 1 hour or longer, until spongy and bubbly.

Beat the egg whites to soft peaks. Fold them into the batter. Cover and let rise for 1 hour or more; the batter will continue to bubble.

Lightly grease a heavy cast-iron griddle or skillet and heat over medium-low heat until hot. Ladle on 1 large or a few small ladlefuls of batter. Cook for 1 minute or so, until holes break through. Turn and brown on the other side for about 30 seconds. Transfer to a plate.

If you are not serving the blinis immediately, wrap them in a towel or foil and reheat for 30 minutes in a 325-degree oven. Blinis and crêpes can be refrigerated for up to 2 days and frozen for up to 3 months.

To freeze, stack between pieces of wax paper or parchment and wrap tightly in foil. Seal in a plastic bag. To thaw, remove from the plastic bag, and place in a 350-degree oven, still wrapped in foil, for 1 hour.

Cornmeal Blinis

15 LARGE OR 24 SMALL BLINIS

THESE BLINIS CAN BE SERVED WITH SWEET TOPPINGS like maple syrup but also go beautifully with salsas and smoked fish.

1	teaspoon active dry yeast
2	tablespoons lukewarm water
¼	teaspoon sugar
1	cup plus 2 tablespoons lukewarm low-fat milk
⅔	cup stone-ground yellow cornmeal
¾	cup plus 2 tablespoons unbleached white flour
¾	teaspoon salt
½	cup buttermilk or nonfat plain yogurt
2	large eggs, separated

Dissolve the yeast in the warm water in a large bowl. Stir in the sugar and warm milk. Let stand for 5 to 10 minutes, until creamy.

Combine the cornmeal, flour and salt in a medium bowl. Gradually stir into the yeast mixture; mix together well. Stir in the buttermilk or yogurt. Beat in the egg yolks.

Cover with plastic wrap and let sit in a warm place for about 1 hour, or until the batter is quite bubbly and spongy.

Beat the egg whites to soft peaks. Gently fold into the batter. Cover again and let rise for 1 hour more; the batter should be spongy and light.

Lightly grease a heavy griddle, skillet or a heavy-bottomed nonstick skillet or crêpe pan and heat over medium heat until hot. Ladle on 1 large or a few small ladlefuls of batter. Cook for about 1 minute, until bubbles break through and you can turn the blinis without breaking them. Turn the blinis and brown on the other side for about 30 seconds. Transfer to a plate.

Continue to cook the blinis in this fashion, overlapping them on the plate as you transfer them from the pan. (If they are stacked one on top of the other, they will become too soggy.)

If you are not serving them immediately, wrap the plate in a towel or foil and reheat for 30 minutes in a 325-degree oven.

To freeze and thaw, see page 243. Reheat for 1½ hours in a 325-degree oven.

Crêpes

20 TO 30 CRÊPES

WHETHER YOU MAKE THESE with whole wheat or white flour or a combination of the two, they are as tasty as can be. You can wrap them around any number of fillings— a great way to transform leftovers into a new dish. Crêpes are very easy to make and store. You can keep them in the refrigerator for a couple of days, or freeze them.

To make crêpes, you need a well-seasoned 6- or 7-inch crêpe pan that you should use only for crêpes. Wipe it clean—never wash it. If you don't have one of these, a nonstick omelet pan will work, but not quite as well.

3	large eggs
⅔	cup milk
⅔	cup water
3	tablespoons melted unsalted butter, plus additional for cooking
¼	teaspoon salt
1	cup flour (either sifted whole wheat pastry flour, half whole wheat pastry flour and half unbleached white flour or all unbleached white flour)

Put the eggs, milk, water, melted butter and salt in a blender or a food processor fitted with the steel blade. Turn it on and slowly add the flour. Whirl at high speed for 1 minute.

Alternatively, if you don't have a blender or food processor, sift together the flour and salt in a medium bowl. Beat the eggs in a large bowl and stir in the flour mixture. Gradually add the milk, water and the butter, beating vigorously with a whisk. Strain through a sieve.

Refrigerate the batter for 1 to 2 hours. (This allows the flour particles to swell and soften, so the crêpes will be light.)

Have the batter ready in a bowl, with a whisk on hand for stirring, as the flour tends to settle. Also have at the ready a ladle and a plate on which to put the finished crêpes.

Place the crêpe pan over medium-high heat and brush the bottom with butter. When the pan just begins to smoke, remove from the heat and ladle on about 3 tablespoons of batter. Immediately tilt the pan or swirl to distribute the batter evenly. Return the pan to the heat and cook for about 1 minute. Loosen the edges gently with a spatula or a butter knife, and if the crêpe comes up from the pan easily, turn and cook for about 30 seconds on the other side. If the crêpe sticks, wait another 30 seconds, then turn. (Don't panic if the first few stick; the pan will eventually become well seasoned and they will come away easily.) Turn the crêpe from the pan onto a plate, with the side you cooked first down. When you fill the crêpes, place the filling on the least-cooked side.

Brush the pan again with butter and continue cooking the remainder of the batter. After the first 3 or 4 crêpes, you won't have to brush the pan each time, but only after every 3 or 4 crêpes.

To store in the refrigerator and reheat or to freeze, see page 243.

Variation

Dessert Crêpes: Replace ¼ cup of the water with ¼ cup Grand Marnier or orange juice and top up with enough water to make ⅔ cup. Proceed as directed.

Barley Flour Crêpes

2 DOZEN CRÊPES

THESE YEASTED CRÊPES make marvelous wrappers for cheese, eggs, smoked fish or ham. Or serve them for breakfast, with jam and honey.

1	teaspoon active dry yeast
2	tablespoons lukewarm water
1½	cups lukewarm milk
4	large eggs
⅔	cup unbleached white flour
⅔	cup barley flour
½	teaspoon salt

Dissolve the yeast in the warm water. Add the warm milk. Let stand for 5 to 10 minutes, until creamy.

Beat in the eggs.

Mix together the flours and salt in a medium bowl. Whisk the flour mixture into the yeast mixture and mix well.

Cover and let rise in a warm place for 1 to 1½ hours, or longer, until spongy and bubbly.

Lightly grease a 7-inch crêpe pan or an omelet pan. Heat over medium-low heat until hot. Ladle in 2 to 3 tablespoons batter and tilt or swirl the pan to distribute the batter evenly. Cook until small holes appear and the pancakes can be turned with a spatula. Turn and cook for 15 to 30 seconds on the other side. Transfer to a plate.

To store in the refrigerator and reheat or to freeze, see page 243.

Buckwheat Crêpes

ABOUT 20 CRÊPES

Buckwheat crêpes are my favorite French "fast food." They are made in little stands and in small restaurants called *crêperies* in Paris and all over Brittany, where they originate, and are topped with a number of nutritious ingredients—cheese, eggs, spinach, smoked salmon, tomatoes, ham and more.

These crêpes rank among the world's greatest street food, made right in front of you on large round griddles. The vendor pours some of the batter, which has been mixed up in a huge bowl, onto the middle of the griddle, then spreads it over the surface with a flat spatula. The batter is so thin that it needs to be cooked on only one side.

If you have ordered an "*oeuf/fromage*," the crêpe maker will fry the egg right on top of the crêpe, sprinkle on the cheese, fold the crêpe in half and then in half again and wrap it like a cone in a piece of wax paper. The vendor hands it to you, hot and buttery. *Voila!* a nutritious and mouth-watering quick lunch.

I make my own buckwheat crêpes in a well-seasoned crêpe pan. They freeze well and are good to have on hand.

1	cup milk
⅓	cup water
3	large eggs
½	teaspoon salt
⅔	cup buckwheat flour
½	cup unbleached white flour
3	tablespoons melted unsalted butter, plus additional for cooking

Place the milk, water, eggs and salt in a blender or food processor fitted with the steel blade. With the motor running, add the flours, then the melted butter and blend at high speed for 1 minute.

Cover and refrigerate for 1 to 2 hours before making the crêpes.

Place a 6-to-7-inch crêpe pan or a cast-iron or nonstick skillet over medium heat and brush the bottom with butter. When the pan just begins to smoke, remove from the heat and pour in or ladle in about 3 tablespoons of batter per crêpe. Immediately tilt or swirl the pan to distribute the batter evenly; return to the heat.

Cook the crêpe for about 1 minute, gently loosening the edges by running a butter knife or thin spatula around the edge. If the crêpe comes up from the pan easily and is nicely browned, turn and cook the other side for 30 seconds. If it sticks, wait 30 seconds and then turn. Turn the crêpe onto a plate. Continue cooking all the crêpes in this way until all of the batter is used.

To store in the refrigerator and reheat or to freeze, see page 243.

Variation

Buckwheat Crêpe with Egg and Cheese: For each serving, fry 1 egg, sunny-side up, and place on top of the warm crêpe. Sprinkle with 2 to 3 tablespoons grated Gruyère cheese, fold over, if desired, and serve.

Yesterday's Bread

Bruschette with Tomato Topping

SERVES 4

BRUSCHETTE ARE GRILLED SLICES OF CRUSTY BREAD rubbed with garlic and brushed with olive oil. These are very easy to prepare and make a nice late supper or luncheon dish.

For the topping

  1   tablespoon olive oil
  3   garlic cloves, minced
  1½ pounds very ripe tomatoes, peeled, seeded and coarsely chopped (2¼ cups)
  2   tablespoons chopped fresh basil
      Salt and freshly ground pepper

For the bruschette

  8-12 slices of coarse bread, sliced 1 inch thick
  2   garlic cloves, halved lengthwise
  2-3   tablespoons olive oil

To make the topping: Heat the oil in a nonreactive saucepan or skillet over low heat. Sauté the garlic for 1 minute, or until softened. Add the tomatoes, raise the heat to medium-high and cook for 15 minutes, stirring and crushing the tomatoes with the back of a wooden spoon, until the tomatoes cook down and are fragrant.

Stir in the basil and salt and pepper to taste. Cook for 1 minute. Remove from the heat and adjust the seasonings.

To make the bruschette: Grill or broil the bread, about 3 inches from the heat, just until beginning to brown at the edges, 1 to 2 minutes per side. (The bread should remain soft inside.)

Remove from the heat and rub while still hot with a cut clove of garlic. Brush with the olive oil, spread with the tomato topping, and serve.

Garlic Crostini

CROSTINI ARE SIMILAR TO BRUSCHETTE (previous page) but thinner and a little more delicate. They're toasted in the oven and can be cooled and held for several hours, so they are very convenient for entertaining. They can be served with any number of toppings or added to soups and salads like croutons.

The ingredients are the same as for bruschette, but cut the bread only ½ inch thick.

Preheat the oven to 350 degrees F. Toast the bread until it begins to color, 10 to 20 minutes; it should be crisp all the way through. Remove from the heat, rub with garlic and brush with olive oil. Use immediately or cover lightly with foil or transfer to a paper bag. If adding to salads, cut into small squares.

Thick Tuscan Bean and Vegetable Soup

SERVES 6

THIS IS A THICK, HEARTY BEAN SOUP, with lots of dark leafy greens. The soup is thickened by pureeing some of the beans.

½	pound (1 heaped cup) dried white beans, picked over, washed and soaked overnight or for several hours in cold water to cover
9-10	cups water
1	bay leaf
	Salt
1-2	tablespoons olive oil
2	medium yellow onions, chopped
4	large garlic cloves, minced
3	medium carrots, peeled and diced
2	celery ribs, diced
3	pounds Swiss chard, stems removed, leaves cleaned and chopped
1	pound kale, stems removed, leaves cleaned and chopped
½	Savoy cabbage, cored and finely shredded
1	pound (4 medium) potatoes, diced
1	pound (4 medium) tomatoes, chopped, or one 28-ounce can Italian plum tomatoes, drained and chopped
1	tablespoon tomato paste
1	dried hot red chili pepper
1	teaspoon dried thyme
	Freshly ground pepper
12	slices sourdough or country bread
1	large garlic clove, halved

Drain the beans. Combine with 4 cups of the water in a soup pot or large saucepan and bring to a boil. Add the bay leaf, reduce the heat, cover and simmer for 1 to 2 hours, until tender.

Add salt to taste to the cooking liquid. Drain the beans, reserving the cooking liquid. Puree half of the beans in some of the reserved cooking liquid in a blender or food processor; set aside.

Heat the olive oil in a large, heavy-bottomed nonreactive pot over low heat. Add the onions and sauté for about 5 minutes, until the onions begin to soften.

Add half of the garlic, the carrots and celery. Sauté for 10 minutes, until the vegetables are tender and fragrant.

Add all of the remaining vegetables, the whole cooked beans, tomato paste, chili pepper, thyme, 5 cups water and the remaining cooking liquid from the beans.

Season with salt and bring to a simmer. Cover and simmer for 1 hour.

If the vegetables aren't covered, add another cup of water. Stir in the pureed beans and the remaining garlic and mix well. Taste and add salt, freshly ground pepper, more thyme or garlic, if you wish.

Toast the bread and rub each piece with garlic.

Place 2 pieces of bread in each soup bowl. Ladle in the hot soup and serve.

Bread and Tomato Soup
(*Pappa al Pomodoro*)

SERVES 4 TO 6

THIS SOUP IS FRAGRANT with basil and tomatoes. It's nearly thick enough to serve on a plate—more stew than soup.

2   tablespoons olive oil
1   small onion, chopped
4   garlic cloves, coarsely chopped
1½ pounds (6 medium) ripe tomatoes, quartered, or one-and-a-half
      28-ounce cans, drained
3   tablespoons tomato paste
      Pinch of cayenne pepper or hot pepper flakes
1   pound whole wheat or white bread, preferably a coarse country variety, a few
      days old, if possible, cut into cubes (about 7 cups)
2   tablespoons coarsely chopped or torn fresh basil
4   cups water
      Salt
      Freshly ground pepper

Heat the oil in a large, heavy-bottomed nonreactive soup pot over low heat. Sauté the onion for 10 to 15 minutes, until soft and just beginning to color. Add the garlic and cook, stirring, for 1 minute, or until the garlic begins to color.

Add the tomatoes, tomato paste and cayenne or pepper flakes. Simmer for 20 minutes, stirring occasionally, until the tomatoes are cooked down and are fragrant.

Add the bread cubes, basil, water and salt. Simmer for 10 to 15 minutes, stirring and mashing the bread with a wooden spoon from time to time, being careful that the bread doesn't scorch on the bottom of the pot.

Add lots of pepper, taste and season with salt. Cover and remove from the heat. Serve warm, at room temperature or chilled, on plates or in bowls.

Italian Bread Salad
(*Panzanella*)

SERVES 6

THIS IS ONE of the most delicious ways to use up stale bread.

Note: If you are using bread that isn't stale and hard, moisten it with water and squeeze; omit the soaking step.

1	pound stale country or French bread, cubed (about 7 cups)
	Cold water
1	small red onion, halved
1	pound (4 medium) ripe tomatoes, chopped
2	tablespoons chopped fresh basil
2	tablespoons chopped fresh parsley
4-5	tablespoons red wine vinegar
1	large garlic clove, minced
	Salt and freshly ground pepper
⅓	cup olive oil

Place the bread in a bowl and cover with cold water. Place the onion halves on top of the bread. Set aside to soak for 20 minutes.

Drain; squeeze all of the water out of the bread. Don't worry if the bread crumbles (whole wheat bread usually does).

Very thinly slice the onion. Toss with the bread, tomatoes, basil and parsley.

Mix together the vinegar, garlic and salt and pepper to taste. Whisk in the oil. Pour over the bread mixture and toss. Cover and refrigerate for at least 2 hours before serving.

Chicken and Pita Casserole
(*Fattet* with Chicken)

SERVES 6 TO 8

Fatta are Middle Eastern casserole dishes made with crisp pita breads that are broken into small pieces, soaked in tasty stock and topped with delicious foods, ranging from rice and chicken (as in this one) to chickpeas, eggplant and mushrooms.

For this recipe, choose yogurt made without thickeners like vegetable gums or gelatin.

For the chicken stock

1	medium (3-pound) chicken, skinned and cut up
8	cups water
1	onion, quartered
4	garlic cloves, crushed
1	bay leaf
	Salt
	Juice of 3 lemons
	Seeds from 2 cardamom pods, ground to a powder in a spice mill
	Freshly ground pepper

For the rice and fattet

1	quart low-fat plain yogurt
1	tablespoon olive oil
1	large onion, chopped
1	scant cup basmati rice, washed
1	teaspoon ground cinnamon
1	teaspoon ground allspice
	Salt and freshly ground pepper
3	pita breads
4	garlic cloves, pounded to a paste in a mortar or put through a press

To make the chicken stock: Place the chicken, water to cover, the onion, garlic, bay leaf and salt to taste in a large nonreactive pot; bring to a boil.

Skim off any foam and add the lemon juice, cardamom and pepper. Simmer gently for 1 hour, or until the chicken is very tender and almost falls off the bones.

Remove the chicken from the stock and strain the stock. Refrigerate for several hours or overnight.

Skim off the layer of fat that forms on top of the stock; set aside 1½ cups for soaking the pita and reserve the rest for cooking the rice. Bone the chicken and tear into pieces; set aside.

To make the rice and fattet: Place the yogurt in a cheesecloth-lined sieve and let drain for about 1 hour, until thick.

Meanwhile, heat the oil in a heavy-bottomed saucepan over medium heat. Sauté the onion until tender and beginning to color. Add the rice, cinnamon, allspice and salt and pepper to taste. Cover with enough of the reserved chicken stock to reach 1 inch above the rice; add water if necessary. Bring to a simmer. Cover the pan and cook over low heat for 15 to 20 minutes, or until the rice is tender and the liquid has been absorbed.

Meanwhile, preheat the oven to 350 degrees F.

Split the pita bread into 2 thin halves. Toast in the oven until brown and crisp, 5 to 10 minutes.

Oil a baking dish or casserole and crumble the pitas into it. Spread the rice mixture over the bread; top with the chicken pieces. Bring the reserved 1½ cups of chicken stock to a simmer. Pour on enough to moisten the pita bread.

Beat the garlic into the thickened yogurt. Spread over the chicken, and serve.

You can reheat this dish in a 350-degree oven if you want to serve it hot.

Syrian Salad with Crisp Pitas
(*Fattoush*)

SERVES 6

THIS SYRIAN SALAD is made with vegetables and crisp pieces of pita bread.

2	pita breads (stale is fine)
	Juice of 2 lemons
2	garlic cloves, minced
	Salt and freshly ground pepper
¼	cup olive oil
¼	cup low-fat plain yogurt
1	pound (4 medium) firm, ripe tomatoes, chopped
1	green bell pepper, chopped (optional)
1	large or 2 small cucumbers, chopped, or 1 small head Romaine lettuce, washed and cut into 1-inch pieces
1	bunch scallions, chopped, or 1 medium-size red onion, chopped
1	bunch parsley, finely chopped (about ½ cup)
3	tablespoons chopped fresh cilantro
2	tablespoons chopped fresh mint

Split the pitas into 2 thin halves. Place on a baking sheet and toast until crisp and brown. Break into small pieces and place in a salad bowl.

Mix together the lemon juice, garlic, salt and pepper, the olive oil and yogurt; toss with the bread. Add the vegetables and herbs; toss again. Adjust the seasonings and serve.

Cheese and Bread Pudding

SERVES 6

A SAVORY, COMFORTING CASSEROLE DISH, this is easy to throw together.

1	tablespoon unsalted butter
¼	pound (about 8 medium) mushrooms, cleaned and sliced
1	garlic clove, minced
2	tablespoons dry white wine
1	tablespoon chopped fresh parsley
	Salt and freshly ground pepper
½	pound sharp Cheddar cheese, grated (2 cups)
4-6	slices whole wheat bread
2	cups low-fat milk
4	large eggs
½	teaspoon dried thyme
½	teaspoon dry mustard

Preheat the oven to 350 degrees F. Butter a 2-quart soufflé dish or gratin dish.

Heat the butter in a large nonreactive skillet over medium heat. Sauté the mushrooms and the garlic until the mushrooms begin to soften and release their liquid. Add the wine and cook until it is absorbed. Add the parsley and season with salt and pepper to taste.

Toss the cooked mushrooms with the cheese. Place the slices of bread in a single layer on the bottom of the casserole dish. Top with a layer of mushrooms and cheese. Make 1 or 2 more layers, depending on the shape of your dish. Beat together the milk, eggs, thyme and mustard. Add a pinch of salt and some pepper to the milk mixture. Pour over the cheese and bread.

Bake for 40 to 45 minutes, or until puffed and browned. Serve at once.

Pain Perdu
(French Toast)

SERVES 6

THIS IS AN INGENIOUS French way of using up stale brioche. Of course, you can use other breads as well, but eggy, light breads are best. Challah (page 156) also makes a very good choice.

1   cup plus 2 tablespoons milk

4   large eggs

1   tablespoon mild-flavored honey or sugar (optional)

     Pinch of salt

     Pinch of freshly grated nutmeg

     Pinch of ground cinnamon (optional)

     About 2-3 tablespoons unsalted butter for frying

12   thick slices of slightly stale bread

     Powdered sugar, honey, jam or maple syrup, for topping

If you aren't serving the French toast as you cook the slices, preheat the oven to 250 degrees F.

Beat together the milk, eggs and honey or sugar, if using. Stir in the salt, nutmeg and cinnamon, if using.

Heat 2 tablespoons of the butter in a large, heavy skillet over medium-low heat. Dip the bread into the batter and turn it over so that the batter soaks in from both sides. It should be saturated, but not so soggy that it falls apart. Place the bread in the skillet and fry slowly until golden brown, 5 to 7 minutes.

Turn and fry the other side until golden brown. Place on a baking sheet in the oven or wrap in a towel if you aren't serving at once. Continue frying the remaining slices of bread.

Dust with powdered sugar, or serve with honey, jam or maple syrup.

Bread Pudding with Peaches

SERVES 8

THIS EXQUISITE BREAD PUDDING with dried fruit and peaches macerated in eau-de-vie is an adaptation of a recipe by Richard Olney. I love the combination of flan-like custard, crispy fried bread and fruit. You can serve this hot from the oven or at room temperature.

1	cup (6 ounces) mixed currants and raisins
	Eau-de-vie or kirsch, to cover the dried fruit
¼	cup (½ stick) unsalted butter
5	ounces leftover bread, hard crusts removed, torn into pieces or cubed (2 cups)
3-4	large ripe peaches, peeled, stoned and sliced, or substitute a 1-pound can, drained
4	large eggs
⅓	cup mild-flavored honey
1½	cups milk
1	tablespoon packed brown sugar
	Cream or sabayon sauce (*recipe follows*) for topping

Several hours before you wish to make the pudding, place the currants or raisins in a bowl and pour on enough eau-de-vie or kirsch to cover.

Preheat the oven to 350 degrees F. Butter a 12-to-15-inch gratin dish or shallow baking pan.

Melt the butter over low heat in a large nonreactive skillet. Add the bread cubes and sauté until the bread is slightly crisp on the outside, about 5 minutes.

Turn the bread into the prepared baking dish and spread out into an even layer. Drain the currants and raisins. Sprinkle the fruits over the bread. Arrange the peaches over the top.

In a medium bowl, beat together the eggs and honey; whisk in the milk. Pour the mixture over the bread and fruit.

Bake for 45 to 60 minutes, or until the custard is set and the top begins to brown. About 15 minutes before the end of the baking, sprinkle the brown sugar over the top.

Serve hot or at room temperature, topped with cream or sabayon sauce.

Sabayon Sauce with Gewürztraminer

MAKES 1 CUP; SERVES 8

THIS FABULOUS SAUCE, from Richard Olney, is incredibly delicious on bread and fruit pudding. The sauce is easy to prepare; make it just before serving.

- 4 large egg yolks
- 2 heaping tablespoons sugar, preferably superfine
- ½ cup Gewürztraminer

Place a trivet or a small heatproof gratin dish inside a large saucepan or pot that is big enough to accommodate a smaller, heavy saucepan or bowl. Pour in enough water to reach one-third of the way up the sides of the smaller saucepan or bowl.

Heat the water in the larger saucepan until simmering.

Meanwhile, off the heat, in the smaller saucepan or bowl, beat together the egg yolks and sugar until the egg yolks are light yellow and thick. Add the wine and whisk together.

Place the smaller saucepan in the hot water on the trivet. Do not allow the hot water to come to a boil, but maintain it at just below a boil, while you whisk the sauce continuously in the smaller saucepan. If the water boils, immediately lift the smaller saucepan out and keep whisking while you turn down the heat. Whisk constantly until the sauce is thick and doubled in volume, about 5 minutes.

Remove from the heat and whisk for a couple of minutes longer. Serve immediately.

Bread Pudding with Raisins and Apples

SERVES 6 TO 8

A BREAD PUDDING made without much butter, this is spicy, sweet and filling.

4	thick slices bread (about 10 ounces)
3	tablespoons unsalted butter, softened
2-3	apples, peeled, cored and sliced
½	cup raisins
4	large eggs
⅓	cup mild-flavored honey or packed brown sugar
2½	cups milk
1	teaspoon vanilla extract
½	teaspoon grated nutmeg
3	tablespoons chopped pecans
	Cream, for topping (optional)

Preheat the oven to 350 degrees F. Butter a shallow 2-quart baking dish or gratin dish.

Butter both sides of the bread. Cut or tear into pieces. Toss the bread with the apples and place in the prepared baking dish. Sprinkle on the raisins.

In a medium bowl, beat together the eggs and honey or brown sugar. Beat in the milk, vanilla and nutmeg; pour over the bread. Add more milk if the bread isn't covered. Sprinkle the pecans and any leftover butter, cut into pieces, over the top.

Bake for 45 to 60 minutes, or until set.

Serve warm, topped, if you wish, with cream or with sabayon sauce (previous page).

Troubleshooting

MOST OF THE PROBLEMS that arise in breadmaking are the result of a few common mistakes. It may take a couple of tries to achieve a loaf you're really proud of, or you may have beginner's luck and run into a few problems later, but once you know the way dough should feel, your bread will turn out every time.

Here are some things that can go wrong and possible explanations for them:

The dough didn't rise, or the bread is like a rock:

1. The yeast could have been old. Make sure you have not kept it beyond the date recommended on the package, and always dissolve it in warm water and wait for it to cloud before continuing with the recipe.

2. You may have killed the yeast by dissolving it in water that was too hot. Or the dough may have become too hot (sometimes a bowl can overheat if you put it in too warm a spot).

3. You might have added too much salt, which can prevent the yeast from working.

4. You may have added too much flour, the most common reason for dough not rising and loaves being heavy and flat. Even the densest doughs should be pliable. When you add too much flour, the dough will not fold easily and it won't have any bounce but will feel dry and hard.

5. You may not have kneaded the dough for long enough (see page 22).

6. Sometimes the loaf is undersized or cracks around the side because it was not allowed to rise long enough before baking.

The finished loaf is squat: Make sure the shaped dough at least half fills the pan and that it rises for enough time.

The bread sags and is soggy: The dough may have needed more flour and may not have been sufficiently kneaded.

The bread is slightly soggy: It didn't bake long enough.

The loaf falls in the oven, and the slices have a gooey, uneven texture: The dough rose too long before baking.

The loaves are light on the bottom and hard on top: The loaves should be removed from the pans and allowed to brown in the oven for an additional 5 minutes before cooling.

The bread has a deep indentation on the bottom: Either the oven was too hot (as in the case of free-form loaves), causing the dough to rise in the oven too quickly, or you have crammed too much dough into the loaf pan, or both.

Your free-form loaf spread too much as it was rising or as it baked: The dough was too soft. You can control the spreading either by

264

adding a little more flour, or by making sure to reshape the loaf gently just before baking.

The crust separates from the top of the bread when you slice it: The loaf was not rolled tightly enough, or the dough was too stiff, containing too much flour. Separation can also happen if the dough dries out and crusts over during the final rise or if it has overrisen.

The crumb has holes in it and a very chewy texture: A porous texture is often desirable, especially in French bread and country breads, but it is not as good for sandwich loaves that will be sliced. Holes result from lots of kneading and a long, slow rise. If you don't want this texture, be careful not to overknead.

The crumb has holes in it and a crumbly, coarse texture: Sometimes this comes from improper shaping of the loaf. Other times the holes are caused by unabsorbed oil from the bowl or too much dusting with flour. It can also come from overrising, forgetting the salt or not heating the oven properly.

The bread has doughy, hard lumps in it: The bread was not kneaded properly, and too much flour may have been added. Remember to add flour gradually to dough. Or you may have incorporated the doughy scraps that dried onto the work surface or bowl when you were kneading the dough.

The bread is too crumbly: Crumbling often results from too much flour and insufficient kneading or from too many grains, such as wheat germ, bran or oatmeal. It can also be a result of overrising or overkneading.

The bread tastes bland: Did you forget the salt? Did you allow the bread enough rising time? If bread has not had enough time to rise, its flavor won't ripen.

The bread tastes yeasty: You used too much yeast, or you let the bread rise too long. As a rule, bread is best and lasts longest when made with a small amount of yeast and given a long rising time.

The bread stales or molds quickly: How did you store it? Avoid plastic bags and humid breadboxes. Overyeasted and overbaked bread goes stale quickly. Bread that is too heavy and floury also stales very quickly. (It is normal, however, for baguettes and white loaves to dry out rapidly.)

Equivalent Weights and Measures

Whole Wheat Flour and White Flour

2 ounces	scant ½ cup
4 ounces	heaped ¾ cup
5 ounces	1 cup
½ pound	1⅔ cups
¾ pound	2½ cups
1 pound	3⅓ cups

White and Brown Sugar

4 ounces	½ cup (heaped for white sugar)
½ pound	1 cup (heaped for white sugar)

Bibliography

Anderson, Jean. *The Food of Portugal*. Robert Hale, London, 1986.

Beard, James. *Beard on Bread*. Alfred A. Knopf, New York, 1974.

Brown, Edward Espe. *The Tassajara Bread Book*. Shambala Press, Berkeley, 1970.

California Culinary Academy. *Breads*. Ortho Books, San Francisco, 1985.

Clayton, Bernard Jr. *The Breads of France*. Bobbs Merrill, Indianapolis and New York, 1978.

David, Elizabeth. *English Bread and Yeast Cookery*. Viking Penguin, New York, 1980.

Fitzgibbon, Theodora. *A Taste of England in Food and in Pictures*. Pan Books, London, 1986.

Field, Carol. *The Italian Baker*. Harper & Row, New York, 1985.

Grigson, Jane. *English Food*. Penguin Books, Harmondsworth, Middlesex (England), 1977.

Luard, Elisabeth. *The Old World Kitchen: The Rich Tradition of European Peasant Cookery*. Bantam Books, New York and London, 1987.

Luard, Elisabeth. *The Princess and the Pheasant and Other Recipes*. Bantam Press, London, 1987.

McNeill, F. Marian. *The Scots Kitchen*. Blackie and Son Ltd., Edinburgh, 1929. Panther Books, London, 1974.

Olney, Richard. *Ten Vineyard Lunches*. Ebury Press, London, 1988.

Robertson, Laurel; Flinders, Carol; Godfrey, Bronwen. *The Laurel's Kitchen Bread Book*. Random House, New York, 1984.

Shulman, Martha Rose. *The Vegetarian Feast*. HarperCollins, New York, 1979, 1995.

Shulman, Martha Rose. *Herbs and Honey Cookery*. Thorsons Publishers Ltd., Wellingborough, Northamptonshire (England), 1984.

Shulman, Martha Rose. *Fast Vegetarian Feasts*. Doubleday, New York, 1985.

Shulman, Martha Rose. *Spicy Vegetarian Feasts*. Thorsons Publishers Ltd., Wellingborough, Northamptonshire (England), 1985.

Shulman, Martha Rose. *Mediterranean Light*. Bantam Books, New York, 1989.

Shulman, Martha Rose. *Martha Rose Shulman's Feasts & Fêtes*. Chapters Publishing Ltd., Shelburne, Vermont, 1992.

Viera, Edite. *The Taste of Portugal*. Robert Hale, London, 1988.

Wells, Patricia. *The Food Lover's Guide to France*. Workman, New York, 1987.

Index